SCHAUM'S
outlines

***Statistics in
Psychology***

Statistics in Psychology

Larry J. Stephens, PhD

Professor of Mathematics
University of Nebraska at Omaha

Schaum's Outline Series

New York   Chicago   San Fr⸳
Lisbon   London   Madrid   M⸳
Milan   New Delⱶ
Seoul   Singapore   S⸳

The McGraw-Hill Companies

LARRY J. STEPHENS is professor of Mathematics at the University of Nebraska at Omaha, where he has taught since 1974. He has also taught at the University of Arizona, Gonzaga University, and Oklahoma State University. He has worked for NASA, Lawrence Berkeley National Laboratory, and Los Alamos National Laboratory. He has consulted widely and spent ten years as a consultant for the engineering group at 3M in Valley, Nebraska. Starting in 2008, he now conducts a monthly statistical seminar for Omaha Public Power District employees in the pricing and forecasting services department at OPPD. He has over thirty-five years experience teaching statistical methodology, engineering statistics, and mathematical statistics. He has over fifty publications in professional journals and has published books in the Schaum's outline series as well as books in the Utterly Confused and Demystified line published by McGraw-Hill.

Schaum's Outline of
STATISTICS IN PSYCHOLOGY

2 3 4 5 6 7 8 9 10   DIG/DIG   15 14 13 12

ISBN 978-0-07-154599-0
MHID   0-07-154599-9

MINITAB® is a registered trademark of Minitab Inc.

Sponsoring Editor: Anya Kozorez
Production Supervisor: Tama L. Harris
Editing Supervisor: Maureen B. Walker
Interior Designer: Jane Tenenbaum
Project Manager: Techset Composition Ltd.
Composition: Techset Composition Ltd.

Library of Congress Cataloging-in-Publication Data is on file with the Library of Congress.

To the memory of my Mother and Father,
Rosie and Johnie Stephens and
to my wife Lana Christine Stephens.

L.J.S.

Preface

Psychology departments are among the primary users and teachers of statistics in the academic world. Not only do psychology professors make wide use of statistics, but psychology departments' statistics course serve as a service course to many disciplines in the academic world. As a result, many departments within colleges and universities require their students to take their beginning statistics course from the psychology department, realizing that the psychology faculty are well acquainted with the many applications of statistics. Students who choose careers in nursing, sociology, journalism, criminal justice, and numerous other areas are often required to take a Statistics in Psychology course.

One of the shortcomings of most textbooks for the introductory-level statistics in psychology course is failure to integrate computer software usage into the text. This author feels that statistical computer software should be integrated into all statistics courses; however, the student should not use the software to the point of exclusion of understanding the statistical principles. The proper blend of statistics and statistical software use is easily achieved. This author has blended the two for over thirty years and therefore knows that it can be done successfully. This book makes use of the statistical software EXCEL, MINITAB, STATISTIX, and SPSS. I feel that these four software packages cover the spectrum of the hundreds of statistical software packages that are currently available.

Because statistical software plays such an important role in the book, I thank the following people and companies for the right to use their statistical software output in the book.

MINITAB: Ms. Laura Brown, Coordinator of the Author Assistance Program, Minitab Inc. I am a member of the author assistance program that Minitab sponsors. "Portions of the input and output contained in this publication/book are printed with the permission of Minitab Inc. All material remains the exclusive property and copyright of Minitab Inc. All rights reserved." The web address for Minitab is www.minitab.com.

SPSS: Ms. Jill Rietema, Account Manager, Publications, SPSS. I quote from the Web site: "SPSS Inc. is a leading worldwide provider of predictive analytics software and solutions. Founded in 1968, today SPSS has more than 250,000 customers worldwide, served by more than 1,200 employees in 60 countries." The web address for SPSS is www.spss.com.

STATISTIX: Dr. Gerard Nimis, President, Analytical Software. I quote from the Web site: "If you have data to analyze, but you're a researcher, not a statistician, Statistix is designed for you. You'll be up and running in minutes without programming or using a manual. This easy to learn and simple to use software saves you valuable time and money. Statistix combines all the basic and advanced statistics and powerful data manipulation tools you need in a single, inexpensive package." The Web address for STATISTIX is www.statistix.com.

EXCEL: Microsoft Excel has been around since 1985. It is available to almost all college students. It is widely used in this book.

As an author, one of the questions to be decided was "What should be covered in the book?" I decided to follow the topics in my Statistical Methodology course, which I have taught for most of my career, and includes the following topics: descriptive techniques, probability, sampling distributions and the central limit theorem, and an introduction to inferential techniques as applied to psychological research problems. Based on experience, it was decided to go no further than two sample inferences (both independent and dependent samples), which will bring the student to analysis of variance, regression and correlation, and non-parametric techniques. It has been my experience that trying to teach students too much in a first statistical methods course, is counterproductive. If you can get them to understand testing hypotheses, with all the concepts that go along with it, you will have done well.

I have consulted many of the psychology websites and have incorporated many recent research developments into composing the problems for the book. The standard normal and student t tables were developed using EXCEL and are found in Table 6.1 (standard normal table) and Table 9.1 (student t table) rather than at the end of the book in an appendix, as is the case with most textbooks. I find that using EXCEL to build the tables takes much of the mystery out of using the tables.

I wish to thank the following people who have contributed indirectly to the book: My wife, Lana, who discussed with me this and every book that I write. She has a good statistics background and has been a user of statistics over the years in her nursing career. I wish to thank my long-time friend and computer consultant, Stanley Wileman, for his invaluable advice. Thanks goes to my McGraw-Hill editor, Anya Kozorez, and her staff. Thanks goes to Nick Barber, Books Manager, Techset Composition Limited, Salisbury, England and Richard Allan, Copy editor, Publishers Domain for their help and wonderful work.

Any comments or questions about the book may be sent to my e-mail address at lstephens@ unomaha.edu.

LARRY J. STEPHENS

Contents

Introduction to Statistics in Psychology

Introduction

This book is a mixture of both psychology and statistics with the emphasis on statistics. The reader will find it a modern approach to both topics. From the psychology standpoint, most of the examples are taken from the field with many coming from everyday sources such as *USA Today*, which often contains articles reporting the results of psychological studies. From the statistics standpoint, statistical software packages are widely used. Although not a true statistical program, EXCEL is heavily utilized because it contains several statistical routines and is important because it is available to almost everyone. One of the most important statistical packages in psychology is the Statistical Package for the Social Sciences (SPSS). Another package widely used in academia as well as industry, and utilized in this book, is MINITAB.

Two approaches to testing hypotheses will be presented: The *classical approach* where critical points in the tails of distributions are found and the computed value of a test statistic compared with the critical value to see if the test statistic exceeds that value. The *p-value approach*, where the *p*-value reflects the significance of the results, is the second approach and is always provided by the statistical software. This book uses results produced by software rather than going through the excruciating mathematical details to arrive at the results, as many other statistics in psychology textbooks do. The book will also utilize statistical software for finding critical points and *p*-values, rather than relying on tables that give only a partial glimpse of the distributions. Note that EXCEL, MINITAB, and SPSS are available for use at most colleges and universities. Both are available for free 30-day trial at Minitab.com and Spss.com. Also, the student will also be introduced to another software package STATISTIX.

Population and Sample

In a 2007 *USA Today* article entitled "Men, Women Are Equal—Talkers," a study from the psychology department at the University of Texas-Austin appearing in *Science* magazine was cited. It reported both men and women say 16,000 words a day on the average. The *population* here is all men and women. In the United States and Mexico, 396 students ages 18 to 29 were selected, of which 210 were women and 186 men. This group was the *sample*. The *variable* measured in the study is the number of words spoken per day by each subject. In general, a *population* is the complete set of interest to the researcher, and the *sample* is the set that the researcher is working with and intended to be representative of the population. The *variable* is a characteristic, defined on every member of the population, in which the researcher is interested.

> **EXAMPLE 1** The population is the set of all individuals taking care of their elderly parents (80 years or older). A sample of 800 individuals who are caring for their elderly parents is selected from across the country. The variable measured is the score these individuals achieve on a stress test. It is of interest to investigate the stress level of caregivers of elderly parents.

EXAMPLE 2 The reaction times of adults who take a medication are of interest. The medication is given to 80 adults composing a sample. The variable measured is the reaction time of people taking the medication. The population is the complete set of people who take the medication.

Descriptive and Inferential Statistics

Consider the study involving the number of words spoken per day. The variable, number of words spoken per day, was determined for each member of the sample of 396 participants in the study. As a result, a data file of 396 numbers resulted. The *descriptive statistics* for the study are the numbers that summarize the 396 sample values. The value that occurs most frequently is computed, the number that divides the data in half is calculated, and the number that gives a measure of the dispersion or variability of the data is computed. In addition, *descriptive statistics* includes graphs that show how the data are distributed. Do the data distribute symmetrically or is there a tail to the right or to the left? Men and women may be compared by computing *descriptive statistics* separately for the two groups.

EXAMPLE 3 A sample of men is found to speak 14,500 words per day on the average, and a sample of women is found to speak 16,250 words per day on the average. Do these descriptive statistics indicate that the population of women speak more words on the average than does the population of men? Certainly for this sample the women speak more words on the average than do the men. The question is "can we infer that the population of women speak more words than does the population of men?" We need to be able to compute probabilities concerning the differences in these descriptive statistics in order to answer the question.

Scales of Measurement

There are four *levels* or *scales of measurement* into which data can be classified. The *nominal scale* applies to data that are used for category identification. The *nominal level of measurement* is characterized by data that consist of names, labels, or categories only. *Nominal scale data* cannot be arranged in an ordering scheme. The arithmetic operations of addition, subtraction, multiplication, and division are not performed for nominal data.

EXAMPLE 4 A group of animals exhibit behaviors that might be classified as playing, grooming, feeding, acting aggressive, or being submissive. Psychiatric diagnosis has values like major depression, post-traumatic stress disorder, schizophrenia, and obsessive–compulsive disorder. Emotions might be classified as excitement, happiness, interest, anger, fear, or sadness. These are all examples of nominal scale data.

The *ordinal scale* applies to data that can be arranged in some order, but differences between data values either cannot be determined or are meaningless. The *ordinal level of measurement* is characterized by data that apply to categories that can be ranked. *Ordinal scale data* can be arranged in an ordering scheme.

EXAMPLE 5 Rank in the military is an example of ordinal scale data. The Holmes and Rahe scale of life stress is another example. The Holmes and Rahe scale counts the number of changes that have occurred over the past six months of a person's life. Things such as divorce, moving to a new location, loss of a job, and so on are all counted to arrive at the score. A person with a score of 250 has experienced more stress than a person with a score of 125. However, 125, the difference between 250 and 125, has no significance.

The *interval scale* applies to data that can be arranged in some order and for which differences in data values are meaningful. The *interval level of measurement* results from counting or measuring. *Interval scale data* can be arranged in an ordering scheme and differences can be calculated and interpreted. The value zero is arbitrarily chosen for interval data and does not imply an absence of the characteristic being measured. Ratios are not meaningful for interval data.

EXAMPLE 6 Temperatures are interval scale data. Differences can be calculated and interpreted. For example 90 degrees is 10 degrees higher than 80 degrees, however a temperature of 0 degrees does not represent a complete lack of heat. IQ scores and test scores represent interval level data; i.e., zero for a test score does not represent a complete lack of knowledge for the topic being studied.

The *ratio scale* applies to data that can be ranked and for which all arithmetic operations including division can be performed. Division by zero is, of course, excluded. The *ratio level of measurement* results from counting or measuring. *Ratio scale data* can be arranged in an ordering scheme and differences and ratios can be calculated and interpreted. Ratio level data have an absolute zero, and a value of zero indicates a complete absence of the characteristic of interest.

EXAMPLE 7 The number of siblings a person has is ratio level data. A value of zero means the person has no siblings. A person having four siblings has twice as many as a person having two. The reaction time under the influence of a drug is also ratio level data. A zero indicates that reaction time is absent and ratios have meanings. A reaction time of 40 seconds is twice the reaction time of 20 seconds.

EXAMPLE 8 Blood type is nominal because a blood type only indicates the group to which you belong. Finishing place in a marathon is ordinal because it gives only where you finished in the race. Temperature is interval because only differences are meaningful and zero does not indicate an absence of heat. Weight is ratio because an object that weighs 2 units is twice as heavy as an object that weighs only 1 unit.

Discrete and Continuous Variables

Discrete variables can take on a finite or a countably infinite number of values. Suppose, for example, you were counting the number of girls in families with four children. In the long run, you would find 6.25% with no girls, 25% with one girl, 37.5% with two girls, 25% with three girls, and 6.25% with all girls. (These percents will be derived when we study the binomial distribution.) This variable can take on only five values, namely 0, 1, 2, 3, or 4. Suppose you were counting the number of patients a psychologist sees until she sees her first psychotic patient. It could be 1 or 2 or 3 or … infinity. This variable is countably infinite. Both of these variables are discrete.

Continuous variables can assume values in an interval or intervals. Continuous variables do not take on a finite or countably infinite set of values. The values cannot be put into a one-to-one correspondence with the integers. Whereas discrete variables arise from counting, continuous variables arise from measuring. Discrete and continuous variables are described differently. Discrete variables are described by a table or formula that gives the values the variable assumes and their probabilities. Continuous variables are described by areas under curves.

EXAMPLE 9 One variable of interest to a hospital administrator is the length of stay (LOS) for patients at a hospital. This is a discrete variable. It is found that 50% of patients stay for 1 day, 30% stay for 2 days, 15% stay for 3 days, and 5% stay for 4 days. This variable may be described as in Table 1.1.

TABLE 1.1 Describing the Discrete Variable LOS

LOS	1	2	3	4
Percent	50%	30%	15%	5%

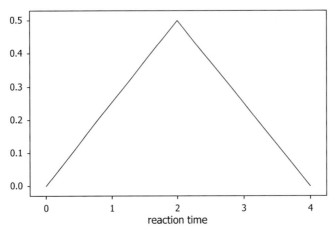

Figure 1.1 The total area under the triangle is 1 or 100%.

Contrast this discrete variable to the continuous variable reaction time when under the influence of an anti-psychotic drug. The percent of reaction times are given by the area under the graph in Figure 1.1. The reaction times are between 0 and 4 seconds. Most of the reaction times are close to 2 seconds because there is more area under the curve near 2 than near 0 or 4, for example.

Note that the area between the triangle and the reaction time axis in Figure 1.1 is $\frac{1}{2}$(base)(height) = $\frac{1}{2}(4)\left(\frac{1}{2}\right) = 1$ or 100%. This corresponds to the sum of the percents in Table 1.1 being 100%. The base is $4 - 0 = 4$ units long and the height of the triangle occurs when the reaction time is 2 and equals 0.5.

The shaded area under the graph for reaction times between 3 and 4 seconds is shown in Figure 1.2. This shaded area is the percent of reaction times between 3 and 4 seconds.

The shaded area in Figure 1.2 is a triangle having its base equal to 1 (distance from 3 to 4) and its height equal to 0.25 (the height of the triangle at reaction time = 3). The area is $\frac{1}{2}$(base)(height) = $\frac{1}{2}(1)(0.25) = 0.125$. (12.5% of the reaction times are between 3 and 4 seconds.)

The shaded area in Figure 1.3 is a trapezoid having its base equal to 1 (distance from 1 to 2) and its heights equal to 0.25 and 0.5. The area of a trapezoid is base$\left(\dfrac{\text{height 1 + height 2}}{2}\right) = 0.375$.

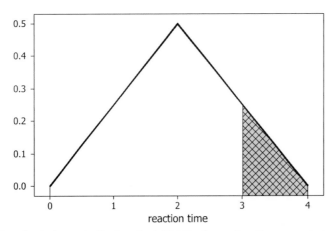

Figure 1.2 The shaded area indicates that 12.5% of reaction times are between 3 and 4.

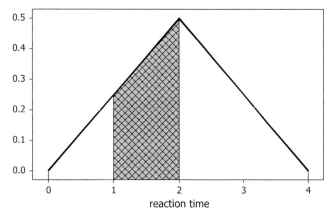

Figure 1.3 The shaded area indicates that 37.5% of reaction times are between 1 and 2.

Statistical Notation

The Greek letter Σ is used in statistics to indicate summation. Suppose the letter X is used to represent anxiety scores. The anxiety scores for five students are: $X_1 = 10$, $X_2 = 5$, $X_3 = 3$, $X_4 = 13$, and $X_5 = 19$. The symbol $\sum_{i=1}^{i=5} X_i$ which stands for $X_1 + X_2 + X_3 + X_4 + X_5$ is usually replaced by ΣX and is equal to $10 + 5 + 3 + 13 + 19 = 50$. Similarly: ΣX^2 represents $10^2 + 5^2 + 3^2 + 13^2 + 19^2 = 100 + 25 + 9 + 169 + 361 = 664$, $\Sigma(X - 10)$ represents $(10 - 10) + (5 - 10) + (3 - 10) + (13 - 10) + (19 - 10) = 0 - 5 - 7 + 3 + 9 = 0$, and $(\Sigma X)^2$ represents $(50)^2 = 2,500$.

Suppose 3 occurs 5 times, 5 occurs 3 times, 7 occurs 2 times, 9 occurs 4 times, and 10 occurs 2 times. Table 1.2 contains the anxiety scores and their *frequencies* (f).

TABLE **1.2 Anxiety Scores and Their Frequencies**

X	3	5	7	9	10
f	5	3	2	4	2

Referring to Table 1.2, the following are defined: $\Sigma Xf = (3)(5) + (5)(3) + (7)(2) + (9)(4) + (10)(2) = 15 + 15 + 14 + 36 + 20 = 100$, $\Sigma X^2 f = (9)(5) + (25)(3) + (49)(2) + (81)(4) + (100)(2) = 742$, $(Xf)^2 = (100)^2 = 10,000$.

Table 1.3 contains the number of weekly quizzes and the anxiety scores for five students.

TABLE **1.3 Anxiety Scores and Weekly Quizzes**

X	3	5	7	9	10
Y	1	1	2	3	5

Referring to Table 1.3, the following are defined: $\Sigma XY = (3)(1) + (5)(1) + (7)(2) + (9)(3) + (10)(5) = 99$, $(\Sigma X)(\Sigma Y) = (34)(12) = 408$, $(\Sigma XY)^2 = (99)^2 = 9,801$.

Statistical Software

Statistical software should be an integral part of any statistics in psychology course. Microsoft EXCEL is readily available to all college students and will save a tremendous amount of work for students and the statistical practitioner alike. EXCEL is our introduction to statistical software. We will also have occasion to use SPSS, MINITAB, and STATISTIX as the course unfolds. It will be assumed that the student is familiar with at least the fundamental structure of EXCEL.

EXAMPLE 10 The following data file was gathered on four variables: class (freshman, sophomore, junior, senior, and graduate), sex (male, female), Internet (time spent on the internet per week), and cell (time spent on the cell phone per week). The 41 records are located in A1:D42 of an EXCEL worksheet. Variable names or labels are in A1:D1. X is the variable internet time and Y is the variable cell phone time.

TABLE **1.4** **Portion of EXCEL Worksheet Containing the Data**

	A	B	C	D
1	Class	Sex	Internet	Cell
2	SO	M	15	5
3	SR	M	20	2
4	JR	M	7	2
5	SR	F	12	2
6	SR	F	25	20
7	JR	F	12	20
8	SO	M	2	2
9	SR	M	2	2
10	SR	M	15	10
11	SO	M	7	1
12	SO	M	20	15
13	JR	M	2	4
14	SO	F	10	6
15	FR	F	3	4
16	JR	F	10	10
17	GR	F	5	2
18	JR	F	6	3
19	GR	F	20	10
20	SO	M	4	2
21	JR	F	5	2
22	GR	F	10	5
23	GR	M	10	4
24	SR	M	10	15
25	SO	M	10	1
26	GR	F	15	2
27	SO	M	5	10
28	GR	F	12	12
29	SR	M	15	0
30	GR	F	3	2
31	SO	F	19	5
32	JR	F	20	25
33	SO	F	11	7
34	JR	F	10	7
35	SO	F	1	1
36	SR	F	20	10
37	SO	M	20	5
38	SR	M	20	4
39	SO	F	42	0
40	GR	F	1	3
41	GR	F	7	2
42	SR	F	25	3

Use EXCEL to find $\sum X$, $\sum Y$, $\sum XY$, $\sum X^2$, and $\sum Y^2$. The expression =SUM(C2:C42) gives 488, the value of $\sum X$. The expression =SUM(D2:D42) gives 247, the value of $\sum Y$. See Table 1.4.

7

TABLE 1.5 Computing ΣX^2, ΣY^2, and ΣXY Using EXCEL

	A	B	C	D	E	F	G
1	Class	Sex	Internet	Cell	sum x^2	sum y^2	Sum x*y
2	SO	M	15	5	225	25	75
3	SR	M	20	2	400	4	40
4	JR	M	7	2	49	4	14
5	SR	F	12	2	144	4	24
6	SR	F	25	20	625	400	500
7	JR	F	12	20	144	400	240
8	SO	M	2	2	4	4	4
9	SR	M	2	2	4	4	4
10	SR	M	15	10	225	100	150
11	SO	M	7	1	49	1	7
12	SO	M	20	15	400	225	300
13	JR	M	2	4	4	16	8
14	SO	F	10	6	100	36	60
15	FR	F	3	4	9	16	12
16	JR	F	10	10	100	100	100
17	GR	F	5	2	25	4	10
18	JR	F	6	3	36	9	18
19	GR	F	20	10	400	100	200
20	SO	M	4	2	16	4	8
21	JR	F	5	2	25	4	10
22	GR	F	10	5	100	25	50
23	GR	M	10	4	100	16	40
24	SR	M	10	15	100	225	150
25	SO	M	10	1	100	1	10
26	GR	F	15	2	225	4	30
27	SO	M	5	10	25	100	50
28	GR	F	12	12	144	144	144
29	SR	M	15	0	225	0	0
30	GR	F	3	2	9	4	6
31	SO	F	19	5	361	25	95
32	JR	F	20	25	400	625	500
33	SO	F	11	7	121	49	77
34	JR	F	10	7	100	49	70
35	SO	F	1	1	1	1	1
36	SR	F	20	10	400	100	200
37	SO	M	20	5	400	25	100
38	SR	M	20	4	400	16	80
39	SO	F	42	0	1764	0	0
40	GR	F	1	3	1	9	3
41	GR	F	7	2	49	4	14
42	SR	F	25	3	625	9	75
43			488	247	8634	2891	3479

To compute ΣX^2, ΣY^2 and ΣXY, the expression =C2^2 is entered into E2 and a click-and-drag is executed from E2 to E42. The expression =D2^2 is entered into F2 and a click-and-drag is executed from F2 to F42. The expression =C2*D2 is entered into G2 and a click-and-drag is executed from G2 to G42. The expression =SUM(E2:E42) gives ΣX^2, the expression =SUM(F2:F42) gives ΣY^2, and the expression =SUM(G2:G42) gives ΣXY. This is shown in Table 1.5. It is seen that $\Sigma X^2 = 8634$, $\Sigma Y^2 = 2891$, and $\Sigma XY = 3479$. If students are not familiar with EXCEL, they will be amazed at how quickly they learn to use it.

EXAMPLE 11 The following data file was gathered on four variables: class (freshman, sophomore, junior, senior, and graduate), sex (male, female), Internet (time spent on the internet per week), and cell (time spent on the cell phone per week). The data file shown in Table 1.6 is similar to that shown in Table 1.5, except that data were collected from a group of 38 students rather than 41. MINITAB will be used to find the same quantities as were found in Example 1.10. The data are entered into the MINITAB worksheet. The data in columns C1 and C2 are text data and the data in columns C3 and C4 are numeric. Qualitative data are also referred to as text data and quantitative data are referred to as numeric data. Text and numeric are the terms used by MINITAB.

TABLE 1.6 Data in the MINITAB Worksheet

↓	C1-T	C2-T	C3	C4
	Sex	Class	X	Y
1	m	so	2	1
2	m	so	21	5
3	f	so	15	15
4	f	so	2	10
5	m	so	12	10
6	m	jr	2	3
7	f	jr	10	15
8	m	jr	2	3
9	f	jr	3	2
10	f	jr	10	4
11	m	jr	35	30
12	f	jr	10	7
13	f	jr	5	2
14	f	jr	7	18
15	f	jr	8	7
16	m	sr	1	1
17	m	sr	7	2
18	m	sr	55	25
19	m	sr	8	8
20	m	sr	3	0
21	f	sr	10	6
22	m	sr	21	20
23	m	sr	30	0
24	f	sr	10	7
25	f	sr	15	10
26	f	sr	10	2
27	f	sr	3	15
28	f	gr	5	10
29	f	gr	10	15
30	m	gr	3	5
31	f	gr	15	7
32	f	gr	4	6
33	f	gr	22	12
34	m	gr	8	5
35	m	gr	3	2
36	f	gr	10	3
37	f	gr	8	10
38	f	gr	20	1

The text data are in columns C1-T and C2-T. MINITAB automatically supplies the T for text data. The sex data are entered in the first 38 rows of C1-T, the class data are entered into the first 38 rows of C2-T, the time spent on the internet per week is entered into the first 38 rows of C3, and the time spent on the cell phone is entered into the first 38 rows of C4. X is the variable internet time and Y is the variable cell phone time. Use MINITAB to find $\sum X$, $\sum Y$, $\sum XY$, $\sum X^2$, and $\sum Y^2$.

Table 1.7 shows the computations of the cross products XY, the computations of the squares of X, and the computations of the squares of Y. The pull-down menu **Calc → Calculator** allows the calculation of C3*C4 and the results are entered into C5. Similarly C3**2 squares the numbers in C3 and stores the results in C6; C4**2 squares the numbers in C4 and stores the results in C7. The pull-down **Calc → Column Statistics** allows the calculation of the sums of C3, C4, C5, C6, and C7. The following results are produced.

TABLE 1.7 Data Manipulations Using MINITAB

↓	C1-T	C2-T	C3	C4	C5	C6	C7
	Sex	Class	X	Y	XY	X**2	Y**2
1	m	so	2	1	2	4	1
2	m	so	21	5	105	441	25
3	f	so	15	15	225	225	225
4	f	so	2	10	20	4	100
5	m	so	12	10	120	144	100
6	m	jr	2	3	6	4	9
7	f	jr	10	15	150	100	225
8	m	jr	2	3	6	4	9
9	f	jr	3	2	6	9	4
10	f	jr	10	4	40	100	16
11	m	jr	35	30	1050	1225	900
12	f	jr	10	7	70	100	49
13	f	jr	5	2	10	25	4
14	f	jr	7	18	126	49	324
15	f	jr	8	7	56	64	49
16	m	sr	1	1	1	1	1
17	m	sr	7	2	14	49	4
18	m	sr	55	25	1375	3025	625
19	m	sr	8	8	64	64	64
20	m	sr	3	0	0	9	0
21	f	sr	10	6	60	100	36
22	m	sr	21	20	420	441	400
23	m	sr	30	0	0	900	0
24	f	sr	10	7	70	100	49
25	f	sr	15	10	150	225	100
26	f	sr	10	2	20	100	4
27	f	sr	3	15	45	9	225
28	f	gr	5	10	50	25	100
29	f	gr	10	15	150	100	225
30	m	gr	3	5	15	9	25
31	f	gr	15	7	105	225	49
32	f	gr	4	6	24	16	36
33	f	gr	22	12	264	484	144
34	m	gr	8	5	40	64	25
35	m	gr	3	2	6	9	4
36	f	gr	10	3	30	100	9
37	f	gr	8	10	80	64	100
38	f	gr	20	1	20	400	1

Sum of X
Sum of $X = 425$

Sum of Y
Sum of $Y = 304$

Sum of XY
Sum of $XY = 4995$

Sum of $X**2$
Sum of $X**2 = 9017$

Sum of $Y**2$
Sum of $Y**2 = 4266$

SOLVED PROBLEMS

Population and Sample

1. In an article, reported in *USA Today*, entitled "Research Fleshes out the Benefits of Exercise" by Nanci Hellmich, it was reported that researchers worked with 170 overweight and obese women for 2 years. The participants were given instruction on improving their eating habits, were encouraged to increase their exercise from 150 to 300 minutes per week, and received telephone calls from psychological counselors who offered guidance and encouragement. Some of the women were able to lose 5% to 7% of their starting weight by changing their eating habits. Those who lost 10% or more of their starting weight (an average of 31 pounds) were found to burn about 2,000 extra calories a week. Identify the sample and the population in this problem.

   Solution

   The sample is the 170 overweight and obese women. The population is all obese and overweight women.

2. In an article, reported in *USA Today*, entitled "East to West, Americans Are Feeling Greater Stress" by Sharon Jayson, the results of a national survey were reported in October of 2007 by the American Psychological Association (APA). A survey of 1,848 adults was conducted by Harris Interactive for the APA. Half of the participants in the study say that their stress has increased in the past five years. Among the findings: (1) 82% of the women have experienced a physical symptom of stress in the past month versus 71% of men; (2) 48% of singles say stress has hurt their social lives, compared with 34% of married couples and 38% of divorced people; (3) 52% of employees report that they have considered or made a career decision such as looking for a new job, declining a promotion, or leaving a job based on workplace stress; (4) 24% of workers with household incomes under $50,000 report that they manage their stress poorly, versus 15% with incomes of $50,000 or more; and (5) 54% of those polled reported that during the past month, they fought or argued with someone close to them: spouse or partner (32%); children (15%); parents (12%). Identify the sample and the population in this problem.

   Solution

   The sample is the 1,848 adults surveyed by Harris Interactive. The population is American adults.

3. In an article, reported in *USA Today*, entitled "Research: Red-Light Cameras Work" by Larry Copeland, the results of a study based on surveillance cameras at major intersections in 2007 were reported. The study was conducted in Philadelphia and Virginia Beach. There was a dramatic change in driver behavior when red-light cameras were used. The number of U.S. communities using these surveillance cameras increased from 19 in 1999 to 243 in 2007. Researchers found that traffic violations dropped by 36% after yellow lights were extended to give drivers more warning that the light was about to turn red. After red-light cameras were added, remaining violations dropped by 96%. Identify the sample and the population in this problem.

   Solution

   The sample is the surveillance camera results from Philadelphia and Virginia Beach. The population is all U.S. drivers.

Descriptive and Inferential Statistics

4. In the "Research: Red-Light Cameras Work" article by Larry Copeland discussed in Problem 3, one descriptive statistic that would be useful is a scatter plot of number of cameras versus year. The article includes a scatter plot like that shown in Figure 1.4 and shows that 19 cameras were in use in 1999 and 243 were in use in 2007. Estimate from the graph the number in use in 2002 and 2004.

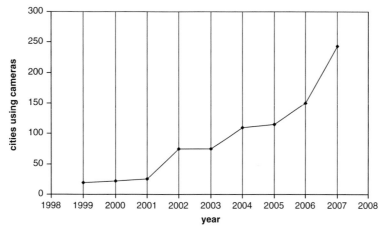

Figure 1.4 Scatter plot of camera usage versus year.

Solution

Estimating from the scatter plot, 75 cameras were in use in 2002 and 100 in 2004.

5. Percentages are descriptive statistics that are commonly used. In Problem 2 of this section, it was reported that: (1) 82% of the women in the study have experienced a physical symptom of stress in the past month versus 71% of men; (2) 48% of singles say stress has hurt their social lives, compared with 34% of married couples and 38% of divorced people; (3) 52% of employees report that they have considered or made a career decision such as looking for a new job, declining a promotion or leaving a job based on workplace stress; (4) 24% of workers with household incomes under $50,000 report that they manage their stress poorly, versus 15% with incomes of $50,000 or more, and (5) 54% of those polled report that during the past month, they fought or argued with someone close to them: spouse or partner (32%); children (15%); parents (12%). Sex and class in Table 1.4 may be summarized as follows: sex, 24 are females and 17 are males; and class, 1 is a freshman, 9 are graduate students, 8 are juniors, 13 are sophomores, and 10 are seniors. a. What percent in the sample are females? b. What percent in the sample are seniors?

Solution

a. The percent that are females is $\frac{24}{41}(100) = 58.5\%$.

b. The percent that are seniors is $\frac{10}{41}(100) = 24.4\%$.

6. The smallest (*minimum*) and the largest (*maximum*) values in a data set are descriptive statistics that are often reported. The *range* is the difference of maximum minus minimum. The 41 values of the variable "time spent on a cell phone per week" are

5	2	2	2	20	20	2	2	10	1	15	4	6	4	10	2	3	10	2
2	5	4	15	1	2	10	12	0	2	5	25	7	7	1	10	5	4	0
3	2	3																

Find the minimum, the maximum, and the range of times.

Solution

The sorted data are as follows. The sort may be performed manually or by EXCEL, or MINITAB.

0	0	1	1	1	2	2	2	2	2	2	2	2	2	2	2	3	3	3
4	4	4	4	5	5	5	5	6	7	7	10	10	10	10	10	12	15	15
20	20	25																

It is seen that the minimum is 0 hours, the maximum is 25 hours, and the range is 25 hours per week.

7. In an article entitled "Help Sought for Police after Combat" by Kevin Johnson in *USA Today*, he described a survey of 103 psychologists across the United States who treat public safety officers. The survey found that 16% of these psychologists were counseling officers who had returned from combat zones. The 16% figure is inferred to be an estimate of the percent of all psychologist in the United States who are counseling officers who have returned from combat zones. What questions should be asked about this statistical inference?

Solution

How accurate is the estimate? That is, how far off the true percent for all officers is the estimate likely to be?

Scales of Measurement

8. A computerized data file consists of several columns that correspond to values for variables. If one such column represents sex and consists of zeros and ones, where 0 represents a female and 1 represents a male, what scale of measurement is represented?

Solution

Nominal scale. The 0 and 1 only serve to categorize the variable into one of two categories. You cannot say that $1 > 0$ nor can you add 0 and 1 to get 1. Zero does not mean that none are present.

9. A computerized data file consists of several columns that correspond to values for variables. If one such column consists of the numbers 1, 2, 3, 4, or 5, where the numbers represent ratings of a teacher in a statistics in psychology class, what scale of measurement is represented (1 means excellent and 5 means poor)?

Solution

Ordinal scale. There is an ordering here. A young, untenured college professor would love to receive a 1, would be happy with a 2, and would be unhappy with a 3 or larger. However, arithmetic has no meaningful interpretation; that is, $1 + 2$ does not equal 3.

10. A computerized data file consists of several columns that correspond to values for variables. If one such column consists of test scores made in a statistics in psychology class, what scale of measurement is represented?

Solution

Interval scale. A test score of 80 is 20 points higher than a test score of 60. A test score of zero does not mean an absence of knowledge about statistics in psychology.

11. A computerized data file consists of several columns that correspond to values for variables. If one such column consists of weight gains, what scale of measurement is represented?

Solution

Ratio scale. All four mathematical operations have meaning when dealing with weight gains. There is an absolute zero. A patient who gains 4 pounds gains twice that of a patient who gains 2 pounds. A weight gain of zero means there was no weight gain at all for this patient.

Discrete and Continuous Variables

12. Identify the following psychological variables as discrete or continuous.

   a.   stress level classified as low, middle, or high

   b.   reaction time measured in seconds

    c. personality type (A or B)

    d. locus of control (internal, external)

    e. completion time for a psychological task

    Solution

    a. discrete   b. continuous   c. discrete   d. discrete   e. continuous

13. The times to complete a task are continuously and uniformly distributed between 5.0 and 15.0 seconds as shown in Figure 1.5.

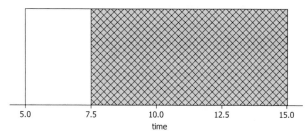

Figure 1.5 Times to complete a task is the shaded area between 7.5 seconds and 15.0 seconds.

    a. What must the height of the rectangle be so that the total area under the rectangle from 5.0 to 15.0 is 1?

    b. What percent of the tasks are completed between 7.5 seconds and 15.0 seconds?

    Solution

    a. The total area under the rectangle is base(height) = (15.0 − 5.0) (h) = 1, or 10 (h) = 1 or h = 0.1.

    b. The percent of tasks completed between 7.5 seconds and 15.0 seconds is the gray area which equals (15.0 − 7.5)(0.1) = 7.5(0.1) = 0.75 or 75%.

Statistical Notation

14. The following are scores made on a statistics for the behavioral sciences final examination:

$X_1 = 75, X_2 = 80, X_3 = 60, X_4 = 88, X_5 = 93, X_6 = 75, X_7 = 95$, and $X_8 = 55$

Find $\sum X$, $\sum X^2$, $\sum(X - 75)$, and the average on the test.

    Solution

    $\sum X = 75 + 80 + 60 + 88 + 93 + 75 + 95 + 55 = 621$

    $\sum X^2 = 5625 + 6400 + 3600 + 7744 + 8649 + 5625 + 9025 + 3025 = 49693$

    $\sum(X - 75) = 0 + 5 - 15 + 13 + 18 + 0 + 20 - 20 = 21$

    Average on the test = 621/8 = 75.25

15. A study in educational psychology collected data on a sample ($n = 5$) of middle school students. Two of the variables measured were X = hours spent watching TV per week and Y = grade in algebra. Table 1.8 gives the results of the study.

TABLE **1.8** **Results from Educational Psychology Study**

X	10	25	15	30	20
Y	80	65	85	50	75

Find the following ΣX, ΣX^2, ΣY, ΣY^2, and ΣXY using your hand-held calculator.

Solution

$\Sigma X = 10 + 25 + 15 + 30 + 20 = 100$,

$\Sigma X^2 = 100 + 625 + 225 + 900 + 400 = 2250$,

$\Sigma Y = 80 + 65 + 85 + 50 + 75 = 355$,

$\Sigma Y^2 = 6400 + 4225 + 7225 + 2500 + 5625 = 25975$,

$\Sigma XY = 800 + 1625 + 1275 + 1500 + 1500 = 6700$

16. The *linear correlation coefficient*, *r*, is a measure of the linear relationship between two variables. It is equal to $r = \dfrac{S_{XY}}{\sqrt{S_{XX}S_{YY}}}$, where $S_{XY} = \Sigma XY - \dfrac{\Sigma X \Sigma Y}{n}$, $S_{XX} = \Sigma X^2 - \dfrac{(\Sigma X)^2}{n}$, and $S_{YY} = \Sigma Y^2 - \dfrac{(\Sigma Y)^2}{n}$. Find the value of *r* for the data in Table 1.8 using your hand-held calculator. Use EXCEL to plot the data.

Solution

$$S_{XY} = 6700 - \frac{(100)(355)}{5} = -400, \quad S_{XX} = 2250 - \frac{(100)^2}{5} = 250, \quad S_{YY} = 25975 - \frac{(355)^2}{5} = 770.$$

$$r = \frac{-400}{\sqrt{(250)(770)}} = -0.912$$

Note: *r* ranges between −1 and +1. A plus sign indicates a direct relationship; that is, as *X* increases so does *Y*. A negative sign indicates a inverse relationship; that is, as *X* increases *Y* decreases. In this case the more TV watched, the lower the algebra grade. See Figure 1.6 for a plot of the data.

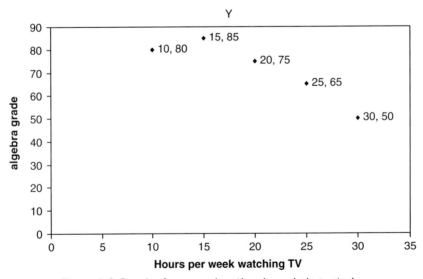

Figure 1.6 Results from an educational psychology study.

Statistical Software

17. The amount of work in computing r for Problems 15 and 16 using a hand-held calculator is substantial. Now consider a similar problem, but with a much larger sample size. Table 1.9 contains measurements of $X =$ height and $Y =$ weight for 40 individuals in a psychological study of the causes of obesity in males. Enter the data into EXCEL and compute the linear correlation coefficient between height and weight. The linear correlation coefficient is discussed in Problem 16. Also use EXCEL to make a scatter plot of the height/weight data.

TABLE 1.9 Forty Heights and Weights in a Psychological Study of Obesity

HEIGHT	WEIGHT	HEIGHT	WEIGHT	HEIGHT	WEIGHT	HEIGHT	WEIGHT
74.9	212.1	73.0	207.7	68.9	221.1	76.1	300.5
70.7	201.7	71.3	197.6	69.5	222.7	70.1	219.2
71.4	203.4	68.6	199.3	71.0	226.6	67.4	211.9
70.7	201.7	70.8	197.6	65.3	211.4	71.2	222.2
72.8	207.0	76.2	202.7	68.4	219.7	69.5	217.6
75.3	213.3	71.4	208.8	75.0	237.5	74.6	231.3
71.3	203.2	71.6	199.1	74.7	236.7	72.9	226.9
75.5	285.5	63.4	209.1	71.0	226.8	73.8	229.2
72.2	205.6	70.8	201.4	69.3	222.2	70.9	221.3
75.8	320.1	74.1	209.9	63.9	207.6	67.3	211.6

Solution

The data are entered into an EXCEL worksheet as shown in Table 1.10. The 40 heights and weights are entered into A2:B41. Labels are entered into A1:E1. The squares of the X values are computed in C2:C41 by entering =A2^2 into C2 and performing a click-and-drag from C2 to C41. The squares of the Y values are entered into D2:D41 by entering =B2^2 into D2 and performing a click-and-drag from D2 to D41. The products XY are entered into E2:E41 by entering =A2*B2 into E2 and performing a click-and-drag from E2 to E41.

ΣX is found by entering =SUM(A2:A41) in A42, ΣY is found by entering =SUM(B2:B41) in B42, ΣX^2 is found by entering =SUM(C2:C41) into C42, ΣY^2 is found by entering =SUM(D2:D41) into D42, and ΣXY is found by entering =SUM(E2:E41) into E42. $S_{XY} = \Sigma XY - \dfrac{\Sigma X \Sigma Y}{n}$ is then computed in cell A44, $S_{XX} = \Sigma X^2 - \dfrac{(\Sigma X)^2}{n}$ is computed in B44, and $S_{YY} = \Sigma Y^2 - \dfrac{(\Sigma Y)^2}{n}$ is computed in C44. Finally $r = \dfrac{S_{XY}}{\sqrt{S_{XX}S_{YY}}}$ is computed in cell A45 and is found to be 0.449. An EXCEL scatter plot of the data is shown in Figure 1.7.

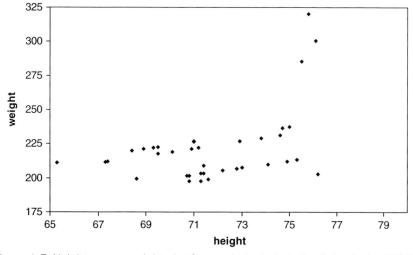

Figure 1.7 Height versus weight plot for psychological study of obesity by EXCEL.

TABLE **1.10** **EXCEL Worksheet for Computing Linear Correlation Coefficient**

	A	B	C	D	E
1	height X	weight Y	X square	Y square	XY
2	74.9	212.1	5610.01	44986.41	15886.29
3	70.7	201.7	4998.49	40682.89	14260.19
4	71.4	203.4	5097.96	41371.56	14522.76
5	70.7	201.7	4998.49	40682.89	14260.19
6	72.8	207	5299.84	42849	15069.6
7	75.3	213.3	5670.09	45496.89	16061.49
8	71.3	203.2	5083.69	41290.24	14488.16
9	75.5	285.5	5700.25	81510.25	21555.25
10	72.2	205.6	5212.84	42271.36	14844.32
11	75.8	320.1	5745.64	102464	24263.58
12	73	207.7	5329	43139.29	15162.1
13	71.3	197.6	5083.69	39045.76	14088.88
14	68.6	199.3	4705.96	39720.49	13671.98
15	70.8	197.6	5012.64	39045.76	13990.08
16	76.2	202.7	5806.44	41087.29	15445.74
17	71.4	208.8	5097.96	43597.44	14908.32
18	71.6	199.1	5126.56	39640.81	14255.56
19	63.4	209.1	4019.56	43722.81	13256.94
20	70.8	201.4	5012.64	40561.96	14259.12
21	74.1	209.9	5490.81	44058.01	15553.59
22	68.9	221.1	4747.21	48885.21	15233.79
23	69.5	222.7	4830.25	49595.29	15477.65
24	71	226.6	5041	51347.56	16088.6
25	65.3	211.4	4264.09	44689.96	13804.42
26	68.4	219.7	4678.56	48268.09	15027.48
27	75	237.5	5625	56406.25	17812.5
28	74.7	236.7	5580.09	56026.89	17681.49
29	71	226.8	5041	51438.24	16102.8
30	69.3	222.2	4802.49	49372.84	15398.46
31	63.9	207.6	4083.21	43097.76	13265.64
32	76.1	300.5	5791.21	90300.25	22868.05
33	70.1	219.2	4914.01	48048.64	15365.92
34	67.4	211.9	4542.76	44901.61	14282.06
35	71.2	222.2	5069.44	49372.84	15820.64
36	69.5	217.6	4830.25	47349.76	15123.2
37	74.6	231.3	5565.16	53499.69	17254.98
38	72.9	226.9	5314.41	51483.61	16541.01
39	73.8	229.2	5446.44	52532.64	16914.96
40	70.9	221.3	5026.81	48973.69	15690.17
41	67.3	211.6	4529.29	44774.56	14240.68
42	2852.6	8810.8	203825.24	1967591	629798.6
43					
44	1456.438	392.071	26835.584		
45	0.449008				

18. For the data in Table 1.9 use MINITAB and the pull-down **Calc → Calculator** to find ΣX, ΣX^2, ΣY, ΣY^2, and ΣXY.

Solution

The data from Table 1.9 is entered into the MINITAB worksheet in columns C1 and C2. The dialog box in Figure 1.8 shows how $X*Y$ is calculated and put into C5. Similarly, $X**2$ is calculated and put into C3 and $Y**2$ is calculated and put into C4. (** is used to square variables in MINITAB)

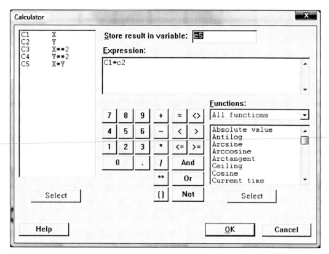

Figure 1.8 Dialog box for using Calculator of MINITAB.

The pull-down **Calc → Column Statistics** is used to calculate ΣX, ΣX^2, ΣY, ΣY^2, and ΣXY. The results are as follows.

Sum of X
Sum of $X = 2852.6$

Sum of Y
Sum of $Y = 8810.8$

Sum of X2**
Sum of $X**2 = 203825$

Sum of Y2**
Sum of $Y**2 = 1967591$

Sum of X*Y
Sum of $X*Y = 629799$

The results of the calculations are shown in Table 1.11.

19. Use the results of Problem 18, to find the linear correlation coefficient. Use MINITAB to make a scatter plot of the data.

Solution

$$r = \frac{S_{XY}}{\sqrt{S_{XX}S_{YY}}}, \text{ where } S_{XY} = \Sigma XY - \frac{\Sigma X \Sigma Y}{n}, \quad S_{XX} = \Sigma X^2 - \frac{(\Sigma X)^2}{n}, \text{ and } S_{YY} = \Sigma Y^2 - \frac{(\Sigma Y)^2}{n}.$$

$$S_{XY} = \Sigma XY - \frac{\Sigma X \Sigma Y}{n} = 629799 - \frac{(2852.6)(8810.8)}{40} = 1456.798$$

$$S_{XX} = \Sigma X^2 - \frac{(\Sigma X)^2}{n} = 203825 - \frac{(2852.6)^2}{40} = 391.831$$

TABLE 1.11   MINITAB Worksheet Showing ΣX, ΣX^2, ΣY, ΣY^2, and ΣXY

↓	C1	C2	C3	C4	C5
	X	Y	X**2	Y**2	X*Y
1	74.9	212.1	5610.0	44986	15886.3
2	70.7	201.7	4998.5	40683	14260.2
3	71.4	203.4	5098.0	41372	14522.8
4	70.7	201.7	4998.5	40683	14260.2
5	72.8	207.0	5299.8	42849	15069.6
6	75.3	213.3	5670.1	45497	16061.5
7	71.3	203.2	5083.7	41290	14488.2
8	75.5	285.5	5700.3	81510	21555.3
9	72.2	205.6	5212.8	42271	14844.3
10	75.8	320.1	5745.6	102464	24263.6
11	73.0	207.7	5329.0	43139	15162.1
12	71.3	197.6	5083.7	39046	14088.9
13	68.6	199.3	4706.0	39720	13672.0
14	70.8	197.6	5012.6	39046	13990.1
15	76.2	202.7	5806.4	41087	15445.7
16	71.4	208.8	5098.0	43597	14908.3
17	71.6	199.1	5126.6	39641	14255.6
18	63.4	209.1	4019.6	43723	13256.9
19	70.8	201.4	5012.6	40562	14259.1
20	74.1	209.9	5490.8	44058	15553.6
21	68.9	221.1	4747.2	48885	15233.8
22	69.5	222.7	4830.3	49595	15477.7
23	71.0	226.6	5041.0	51348	16088.6
24	65.3	211.4	4264.1	44690	13804.4
25	68.4	219.7	4678.6	48268	15027.5
26	75.0	237.5	5625.0	56406	17812.5
27	74.7	236.7	5580.1	56027	17681.5
28	71.0	226.8	5041.0	51438	16102.8
29	69.3	222.2	4802.5	49373	15398.5
30	63.9	207.6	4083.2	43098	13265.6
31	76.1	300.5	5791.2	90300	22868.1
32	70.1	219.2	4914.0	48049	15365.9
33	67.4	211.9	4542.8	44902	14282.1
34	71.2	222.2	5069.4	49373	15820.6
35	69.5	217.6	4830.3	47350	15123.2
36	74.6	231.3	5565.2	53500	17255.0
37	72.9	226.9	5314.4	51484	16541.0
38	73.8	229.2	5446.4	52533	16915.0
39	70.9	221.3	5026.8	48974	15690.2
40	67.3	211.6	4529.3	44775	14240.7
41					

$$S_{YY} = \Sigma Y^2 - \frac{(\Sigma Y)^2}{n} = 1967591 - \frac{(8810.8)^2}{40} = 26836.084$$

$$r = \frac{S_{XY}}{\sqrt{S_{XX} S_{YY}}} = \frac{1456.798}{\sqrt{(391.831)(26836.084)}} = 0.449.$$

A MINITAB scatter plot of the data is shown in Figure 1.9.

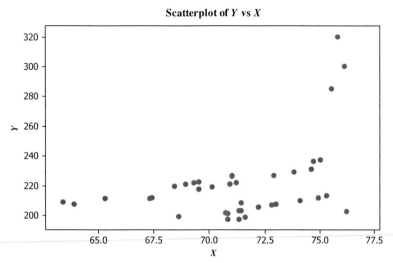

Figure 1.9 Height versus weight plot for psychological study of obesity.

20. For the data in Table 1.9, use **SPSS** and the pull-down **Transform → Compute Variables** to find XY, X^2 and Y^2.

Solution

Enter X and Y into the SPSS worksheet. Perform the pull-down **Transform → Compute Variable**. This gives Figure 1.10. In the dialog box, enter for target value XY and for numeric expression enter $X*Y$. Similarly for target value enter Xsq and for numeric expression enter $X**2$, and Ysq with $Y**2$.

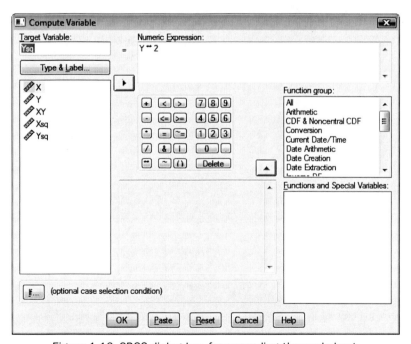

Figure 1.10 SPSS dialog box for expanding the worksheet.

Figure 1.11 shows the worksheet expanded to contain X, Y, XY, X^2, and Y^2.

	X	Y	XY	Xsq	Ysq
1	74.9	212.1	15886.29	5610.01	44986.41
2	70.7	201.7	14260.19	4998.49	40682.89
3	71.4	203.4	14522.76	5097.96	41371.56
4	70.7	201.7	14260.19	4998.49	40682.89
5	72.8	207.0	15069.60	5299.84	42849.00
6	75.3	213.3	16061.49	5670.09	45496.89
7	71.3	203.2	14488.16	5083.69	41290.24
8	75.5	285.5	21555.25	5700.25	81510.25
9	72.2	205.6	14844.32	5212.84	42271.36
10	75.8	320.1	24263.58	5745.64	102464.01
11	73.0	207.7	15162.10	5329.00	43139.29
12	71.3	197.6	14088.88	5083.69	39045.76
13	68.6	199.3	13671.98	4705.96	39720.49
14	70.8	197.6	13990.08	5012.64	39045.76
15	76.2	202.7	15445.74	5806.44	41087.29
16	71.4	208.8	14908.32	5097.96	43597.44
17	71.6	199.1	14255.56	5126.56	39640.81
18	63.4	209.1	13256.94	4019.56	43722.81
19	70.8	201.4	14259.12	5012.64	40561.96
20	74.1	209.9	15553.59	5490.81	44058.01
21	68.9	221.1	15233.79	4747.21	48885.21
22	69.5	222.7	15477.65	4830.25	49595.29
23	71.0	226.6	16088.60	5041.00	51347.56
24	65.3	211.4	13804.42	4264.09	44689.96
25	68.4	219.7	15027.48	4678.56	48268.09
26	75.0	237.5	17812.50	5625.00	56406.25
27	74.7	236.7	17681.49	5580.09	56026.89
28	71.0	226.8	16102.80	5041.00	51438.24
29	69.3	222.2	15398.46	4802.49	49372.84
30	63.9	207.6	13265.64	4083.21	43097.76
31	76.1	300.5	22868.05	5791.21	90300.25
32	70.1	219.2	15365.92	4914.01	48048.64
33	67.4	211.9	14282.06	4542.76	44901.61
34	71.2	222.2	15820.64	5069.44	49372.84
35	69.5	217.6	15123.20	4830.25	47349.76
36	74.6	231.3	17254.98	5565.16	53499.69
37	72.9	226.9	16541.01	5314.41	51483.61
38	73.8	229.2	16914.96	5446.44	52532.64
39	70.9	221.3	15690.17	5026.81	48973.69
40	67.3	211.6	14240.68	4529.29	44774.56

*Untitled1 [DataSet0] - SPSS Data Editor
File Edit View Data Transform Analyze Graphs Utilities Add-ons Wind
27 :

Figure 1.11 SPSS worksheet showing X, Y, XY, X^2, and Y^2.

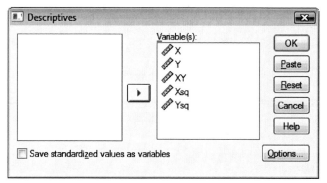

Figure 1.12 SPSS descriptive dialog box.

Descriptive Statistics

	N	Sum
X	40	2852.6
Y	40	8810.8
XY	40	629798.64
Xsq	40	203825.24
Ysq	40	1967591
Valid N (listwise)	40	

Figure 1.13 SPSS output for the sum of the five variables.

21. Refer to Problem 20. Use SPSS to find ΣX, ΣX^2, ΣY, ΣY^2, and ΣXY. Then use these sums to find the linear correlation coefficient.

Solution

Using the worksheet in Figure 1.11, give the pull-down **Analyze → Descriptive Statistics → Descriptives** and bring the five variables into the variables box (see Figure 1.12). For options, choose Sum. This produces the output shown in Figure 1.13.

The computed value of r may be completed as follows:

$$S_{XY} = \Sigma XY - \frac{\Sigma X \Sigma Y}{n} = 629799 - \frac{(2852.6)(8810.8)}{40} = 1456.798$$

$$S_{XX} = \Sigma X^2 - \frac{(\Sigma X)^2}{n} = 203825 - \frac{(2852.6)^2}{40} = 391.831$$

$$S_{YY} = \Sigma Y^2 - \frac{(\Sigma Y)^2}{n} = 1967591 - \frac{(8810.8)^2}{40} = 26836.084$$

$$r = \frac{S_{XY}}{\sqrt{S_{XX} S_{YY}}} = \frac{1456.798}{\sqrt{(391.831)(26836.084)}} = 0.449.$$

22. Use SPSS to construct a scatter plot of the data in Table 1.9.

Solution

The pull-down **Graphs → Interactive → Scatter plot** gives the plot shown in Figure 1.14.

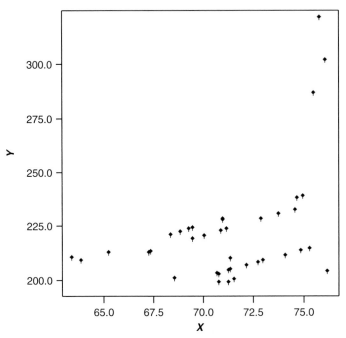

Figure 1.14 SPSS scatter plot of *X* and *Y*.

SUPPLEMENTARY PROBLEMS

Population and Sample

23. A nationwide survey of 2,900 men and women published in the *Journal of Biological Psychiatry* found that 0.6% had anorexia, 1% had bulimia, and 2.8% had a binge-eating disorder. Identify the sample and the population.

24. A study in the *New England Journal of Medicine* reported on an 18-month nationwide study of nearly 1,500 schizophrenia patients. The study compared five different antipsychotic medications for treating the condition. The study reported that about 3/4 of the patients stopped taking their medication or switched to a different medication because they felt the medication was not helping or the side effects were too much to handle. Identify the sample and the population.

25. An article in the journal *Brain, Behavior, and Immunity* studied 313 male Vietnam veterans who were part of a larger 20-year study on the effects of Agent Orange. The veterans underwent a standard psychological test to assess hostility, depression, and anger. Researchers then studied two immune system proteins known as C3 and C4. Men whose psychological screening showed the highest level of hostility, depressive symptoms, and anger had a 7.1% increase in their C3/C4 levels, while men with low levels of these psychological attributes showed no change in C3/C4 over the 20-year study. Identify the sample and the population.

Descriptive and Inferential Statistics

26. An article in the August issue (2007) of the *Journal of Pediatrics* found that 2% of children aged 8 to 17 are affected by restless legs syndrome (RLS). Give the descriptive statistic in this sentence.

27. The American Psychological Association (APA) reported that the 2001 median 12-month salary for individuals holding the Masters degree in psychology and working in research was $47,000. Explain the descriptive statistic *median*.

28. Explain the following descriptive statistics: *minimum, maximum, median, mode,* and *range*.

29. A psychologist is studying the heights and weights of men and women. If the psychologist sees a tall man, she can think of an example of a woman who is taller than the man. Similarly, if the psychologist sees a man who is overweight, she can produce an example of a woman who weighs more than the man. However, the psychologist would un-questionably accept the statement that men are taller and heavier than women. Explain how this statement is an example of inferential statistics.

30. A 1999 article in the *Journal of the American Medical Association* reported on a study of 5,888 community-dwelling senior citizens over a 10-year period. One of the findings was that 70% of the study participants showed no decline in cognitive function over the study period. What inference might this article make concerning all community-dwelling senior citizens?

31. In an article entitled "Depressed Young Adults More Likely to Start Cigarette Smoking and Other Substance Abuse," which is found at the web site medicalnewstoday.com, the following statement is found: "Depression and the initiation of cigarette, alcohol, and other drug abuse among young adults indicates that 9.4% of people aged 18 to 25, or approximately 3 million young adults in the United States experienced one or more major depressive episodes in the past year." For what size population is this inference made?

Scales of Measurement

32. Suppose the following question is part of a depression self-test:

I feel sad:　　a. never　　b. occasionally　　c. most of the time　　d. all the time
What level of measurement is the data for this question?

33. Volunteers are given a drug intended for schizophrenia patients and their reaction times are measured in traffic situations. What level of measurement are the reaction times?

34. What level of measurements are IQ scores?

35. The following question is part of a psychological study involving depression. What level of data is represented here?

Select the following that describes your use of alcohol/tobacco products:

a. alcohol only　　b. tobacco only　　c. both　　d. neither

Discrete and Continuous Variables

36. Suppose response times to a stimulus are uniformly distributed over the interval 5 to 10 seconds. For this continuous variable, construct a graph that describes the reaction times and find the time such that 50% of the response times are less than that time and 50% are greater than that time. Such a dividing value is called the *median* response time.

37. A psychologist is studying tics in boys ages 10 to 12. She measured the number of eye blinks (tics) for 1,000 children and gave the percent of the 1,000 and the number of tics. She found that the discrete variable eye blinks (tics) during a fixed period of time has the following distribution:

Tics	20	21	22	23	24	25	26	27	28	29	30
Percent	5	5	10	15	15	20	15	5	5	3	2

a.　How many children have more than 24.5 tics? How many have less than 24.5 tics?

b.　How many have 25 tics?

Statistical Notation

38. Use summation notation to express the following:

a.　$X_1^3 + X_2^3 + X_3^3 + X_4^3$

b.　$(X_1 + X_2 + X_3 + X_4)^3$

c.　$X_1^3 Y_1^3 + X_3^3 Y_3^3 + X_4^3 Y_4^3$

39. If $X_1 = 3$, $X_2 = 2$, and $X_3 = 4$ find the values of the following:

    a. ΣX^4

    b. $(\Sigma X)^4$

    c. $\Sigma \sqrt{X}$ (to 3 decimal places)

Statistical Software

40. Use SPSS and the data in Table 1.6 to find the linear correlation coefficient between time spent on the internet per week and time spent on cell phone per week. Use SPSS to construct a scatter plot for $X =$ time spent on the internet and $Y =$ time spent on cell phone per week.

CHAPTER 2

Graphing Quantitative and Qualitative Data

Frequency Distribution Tables

A study of the uric levels of the elderly appeared in the January 2007 issue of the journal *Neuropsychology* published by the American Psychology Association (APA). The results of a study of 96 seniors, aged 60 to 92, showed that those with higher levels of uric acid had lower scores when mental processing speed, verbal memory, and working memory were measured. Suppose a group of 40 elderly individuals had the uric acid levels (mg/dL) given in Table 2.1.

TABLE **2.1 Uric Acid Levels in mg/dL of 40 Elderly Individuals**

7.0	6.5	7.4	7.3	7.0	7.2	6.9	6.8	6.7	6.6
7.3	6.9	6.9	6.8	7.4	6.8	6.9	6.9	6.8	6.6
7.1	7.1	7.0	6.6	6.7	7.0	6.4	7.6	7.0	7.0
6.9	7.0	7.0	7.4	7.1	6.8	6.9	6.9	7.3	6.8

The data in this table can be brought into focus by building a *frequency distribution table*.

TABLE **2.2** **Frequency Distribution Table for Uric Acid Values**

URIC ACID VALUE	FREQUENCY	PERCENT
6.4	1	2.5
6.5	1	2.5
6.6	3	7.5
6.7	2	5.0
6.8	6	15.0
6.9	8	20.0
7.0	8	20.0
7.1	3	7.5
7.2	1	2.5
7.3	3	7.5
7.4	3	7.5
7.6	1	2.5

EXAMPLE 1 The frequency distribution table (shown in Table 2.2) is constructed by first noting every uric acid value that occurs, and then counting how many times each such number occurs. The number of times a value occurs is called the *frequency* (f) of the value. Note that the sum of the frequencies equals 40, the total number of values in Table 2.1 ($\sum f = n$). The percents for each value are obtained by dividing each frequency by 40 ($percent = (f/n)(100)$). Note that most of the uric acid values (55% of them to be exact) are equal to 6.8, 6.9, or 7.0.

The data may also be grouped into *classes*. The number of classes is usually recommended to be between 5 and 15. The rules for forming classes and the number of classes are many and varied. No one set of rules is accepted as the only correct set.

EXAMPLE 2 Suppose we decide to have 5 classes going from 6.2 to 7.8. Each class will have *width* $(7.8 - 6.2)/5 = 0.32$. The classes will be 6.20 to 6.52, 6.52 to 6.84, 6.84 to 7.16, 7.16 to 7.48, and 7.48 to 7.80. The class 6.20 to 6.52 contains 2 values and has a frequency of 2. The class 6.52 to 6.84 contains 11 values and has a frequency of 11. If all the data are tallied into all classes, we come up with Table 2.3.

TABLE **2.3** **Frequency Distribution for the Uric Acid Data with 5 Classes**

CLASS	FREQUENCY	PERCENT
6.20 to 6.52	2	5
6.52 to 6.84	11	27.5
6.84 to 7.16	19	47.5
7.16 to 7.48	7	17.5
7.48 to 7.80	1	2.5

The frequency distributions in Tables 2.2 and 2.3 are both used to present the data in Table 2.1. Either table shows that the data are more concentrated in the middle and more rarified in the tails.

Frequency Distribution Graphs

A frequency distribution may be presented graphically as a *frequency distribution polygon*. A frequency distribution polygon plots the uric acid values on the *x*-axis and the frequencies or percents on the *y*-axis. We shall now investigate the ability of EXCEL, MINITAB, and SPSS to plot frequency polygons. The EXCEL frequency distribution polygon is shown in Figure 2.1. It is a plot of the data in Table 2.2. Note that the polygon has been "tied down" by adding the points (6.3, 0) and (7.7, 0).

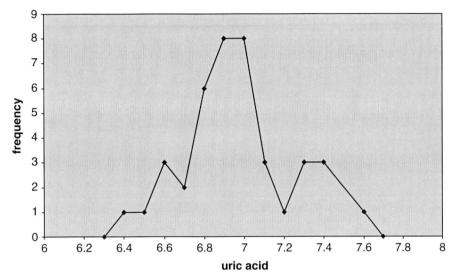

Figure 2.1 EXCEL frequency distribution polygon for the uric acid data.

A MINITAB plot of the frequency distribution polygon is shown in Figure 2.2. It is a plot of the data in Table 2.2. Note that the polygon has been "tied down" by adding the points (6.3, 0) and (7.7, 0). In this graph, the percents of the uric acid readings are plotted on the *y*-axis. In Figure 2.2, the percents are plotted on the *y*-axis.

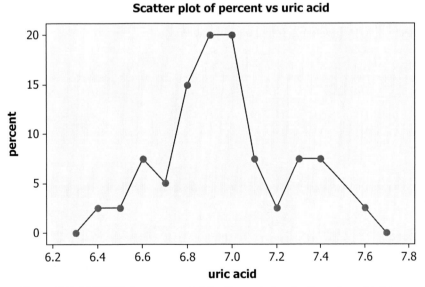

Figure 2.2 MINITAB frequency distribution polygon for the uric acid data.

The SPSS plot of the data in Table 2.2 is shown in Figure 2.3.

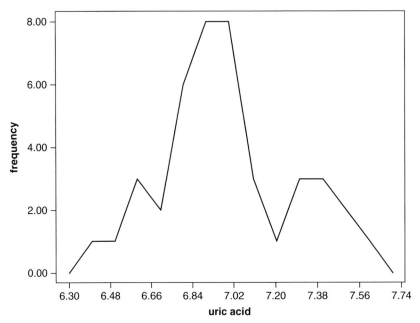

Figure 2.3 SPSS frequency distribution polygon for uric acid data.

Shape of a Frequency Distribution

Figure 2.4 gives four shapes that data often exhibit. The uric acid data in Table 2.2 favors the symmetrical shape. The plot of human lifetime data are skewed to the left. Most people have lifetimes between 60 and 80 with a few dying early and a few living into their 80s and 90s.

Age at marriage has a skewed to the right appearance. Most people marry between 20 and 35 years of age. A few marry in their 40s, a few in their 50s, and so forth.

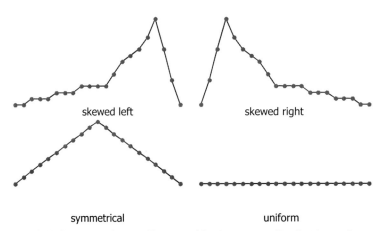

Figure 2.4 Common shapes illustrated by frequency distribution polygons.

Percentiles and Quartiles

Values that divide a set of data into 100 equal parts are called *percentiles*. They are written $P_1, P_2, \ldots, P_{99}$. Several algorithms exist for finding percentiles of sets of data. We will give one of them. First, sort your data from smallest to largest. Let p be the percentile you wish to find where p is 1 to 99. Let n be the size of your sample. Calculate the *index number*: $i = np/100$. The number i locates a position in your sorted data set. If i is a whole number, then average the ith and $(i+1)$th numbers to obtain the percentile. If i is not a whole number, round it up and choose that number in the sorted set as your percentile. In addition to percentiles, three *quartiles* are defined. The *first quartile* is the number, Q_1, which is such that 25% of the data is less than Q_1 and 75% is greater than Q_1. The first quartile is the same as P_{25}. Similarly, the *second quartile* is represented by Q_2 and is such that 50% of the data is less than Q_2 and 50% is greater than Q_2. The second quartile is the same as P_{50}. The *third quartile*, Q_3, is the same as P_{75}.

A 2007 article in the journal *Environmental Health Perspectives* reported that "safe" lead levels still reduce kids' intelligence quotients (IQs). Intelligence quotients result from psychological tests and range from 0 to above 200. The average IQ for the population is 100. A psychological study determined the IQs of a sample of 80 people and the results are shown in Table 2.4.

Suppose we wish to find the first quartile (25th percentile). First calculate $i = np/100 = 80(25)/100 = 20$. Because $i = 20$ is a whole number, go to the 20th and 21st numbers in the sorted array and average those two numbers. That is, average 93 (the 20th number in the sorted IQ scores in Table 2.4) and 93 (the 21st number in order) to get 93 as the first quartile ($Q_1 = 93$). To find the 93rd percentile, calculate $np/100 = 80(93)/100$ to get 74.4. Because this number is not a whole number, always round it up to get 75. The 75th number in the sorted array is 137 and $P_{93} = 137$. Similarly, using the above technique to find percentiles it is found that $Q_2 = 99.5$, $Q_3 = 106$, and $P_{10} = 85.5$.

TABLE 2.4 Sorted IQ Scores for 80 People

66	87	93	99	100	104	106	115
73	89	94	99	100	104	107	125
75	89	94	99	100	104	108	130
80	89	94	99	100	104	108	135
82	90	94	99	100	104	109	137
83	90	96	99	101	104	110	140
85	90	96	99	101	105	110	145
85	91	96	99	102	105	110	148
86	92	98	99	102	105	111	149
86	93	99	99	103	106	111	155

EXAMPLE 3 Use EXCEL to find the three quartiles and P_{10} and P_{93}. Enter Table 2.4 data into the 80 cells (A1:H10) of an EXCEL worksheet. The commands: =PERCENTILE(A1:H10,0.1) gives 85.9, =PERCENTILE (A1:H10,0.25) gives 93, =PERCENTILE(A1:H10,0.5) gives 99.5, =PERCENTILE(A1:H10,0.75) gives 106, and =PERCENTILE(A1:H10,0.93) gives 135.94. The EXCEL values agree or are close to the values found by the technique given above.

EXAMPLE 4 Use SPSS to find the same percentiles as found in Examples 2 and 3. The 80 IQ scores are entered into the first column of the SPSS Data editor and are given the name IQscores. The pull-down **Analyze → Descriptive Statistics → Frequencies** produces the dialog box shown in Figure 2.5. The percentiles $P_{10}, Q_1, Q_2, Q_3,$ and P_{93} are requested in the dialog box and the output shown in Figure 2.6 is given in the output window. Note that via the "by hand" technique, neither EXCEL nor SPSS give exactly the same results for the five percentiles. However, it will be found that as the data sets get larger, the results converge to the same set of results.

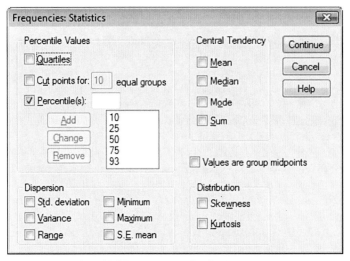

Figure 2.5 SPSS dialog box for finding percentiles.

Statistics

IQ score

N	Valid	80
	Missing	0
Percentiles	10	85.1000
	25	93.0000
	50	99.5000
	75	106.0000
	93	137.9900

Figure 2.6 SPSS output giving P_{10}, Q_1, Q_2, Q_3, and P_{93}.

Graphing Quantitative Data

With the recent developments in computer software and computer graphics (starting in 1975 but with most occurring within the past 10 years), descriptive statistics have become very important. The software produces excellent descriptive procedures for displaying data. The histogram, dot plot, box plot, and stem-and-leaf plots will be discussed in the following sections. All you need to do is put the data into a file or even a work-sheet and give the pull-down commands, and you have beautiful descriptive and graphic statistics. No graph paper, no ruler, no protractor, no compass are needed. The uric acid data from Table 2.1 and the IQ scores from Table 2.4 will be used to illustrate the graphic capabilities of SPSS, EXCEL, and MINITAB in the following sections.

Dot Plots

An SPSS *dot plot* of the IQ scores in Table 2.4 is given in Figure 2.7. Use the pull-down **Graph → Interactive → Dot**.

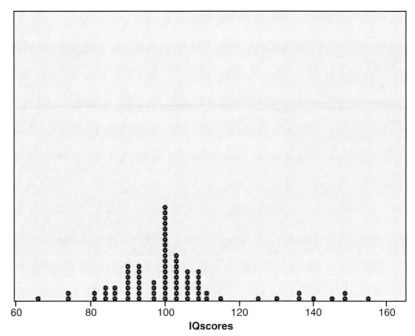

Figure 2.7 SPSS dot plot of IQ scores in Table 2.4.

The MINITAB dot plot in Figure 2.8 gives a dot for each occurrence of the IQ score. Use the pull-down **Graph → Dotplot**. The dot plot shows the distribution of the IQ scores. The distribution shows that most IQs are between 80 and 120. There are a few that are higher (over 120) and a few that are lower (below 80).

Dot plot of IQ score

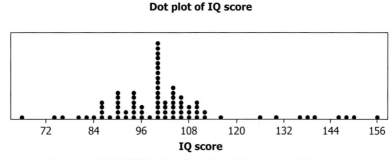

Figure 2.8 MINITAB dot plot of the IQ scores in Table 2.4.

Stem-and-Leaf Displays

The MINITAB stem-and-leaf plot of the IQs in Table 2.4 is given by the pull-down **Graph → stem-and-leaf** and it is shown in Figure 2.9.

Stem-and-Leaf Display: IQ score

The MINITAB *stem-and-leaf plot* is composed of three columns. The first column is a cumulative count from the top and from the bottom. From the top, the cumulative counts are 1, 3, 14, and 40. From the bottom, the cumulative counts are 1, 5, 8, 9, 15, and 40. From the top, the first number is 66. The stem is 6 and the leaf is 6. The second row has two numbers 73 and 75. The stem here is 7 and the leaves are 3 and 5. The cumulative count in the second row is 3 because 3 numbers 66, 73, and 75 have a stem of 6 or 7. The third row contains a cumulative count of 14. There are 14 numbers with a stem of 6, 7, or 8. The stem is the number

```
Stem-and-leaf of IQ score N = 80
Leaf Unit = 1.0

    1       6       6
    3       7       35
   14       8       02355667999
   40       9       0001233444466689999999999
   40      10       00000112234444445555667889
   15      11       000115
    9      12       5
    8      13       057
    5      14       0589
    1      15       5
```

Figure 2.9 MINITAB stem-and-leaf plot.

of tens in the number and the leaf is the number of ones in the number. For example 66 contains 6 tens and 6 ones. The stem is 6 and the leaf is 6. The *stem-and-leaf plot* shows not only the shape of the distribution but the actual numbers that make up the distribution.

Histograms

An SPSS *histogram* of the IQ scores is given in Figure 2.10. This histogram is composed of 15 *classes* extending from 60 to 160. Each class has a *class width* equal to 6-2/3 IQ units.

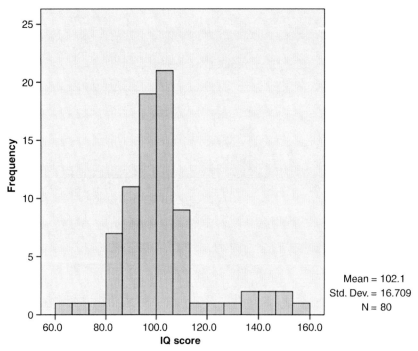

Mean = 102.1
Std. Dev. = 16.709
N = 80

Figure 2.10 SPSS histogram of IQ scores.

Box Plots

To understand a *box plot*, we need to learn a lot of new terms. First, recall that the three quartiles for the IQ data were $Q_1 = 93.0$, $Q_2 = 99.5$, and $Q_3 = 106.0$. The *inter-quartile range* (IQR) is $Q_3 - Q_1 = 106 - 93 = 13$.

Two *inner fences* and two *outer fences* are defined. The *lower outer fence* is $Q_1 - 3$ IQR or $93 - 3(13) = 54$, the *lower inner fence* is $Q_1 - 1.5$ IQR or $93 - 1.5(13) = 73.5$, the *upper inner fence* is $Q_3 + 1.5$ IQR or $106 + 1.5(13) = 125.5$, and the *upper outer fence* is $Q_3 + 3$ IQR or $106 + 3(13) = 145$.

Lower Outer	Lower Inner	Upper Inner	Upper Outer
Fence	Fence	Fence	Fence
54	73.5	125.5	145

Numbers outside the outer fences are called *outliers*, that is, numbers less than 54 or greater than 145. Numbers between the inner and outer fences are called *potential outliers*, that is, numbers between 54 and 73.5 and numbers between 125.5 and 145. The data from Table 2.4 are reproduced below to help clarify the discussion.

66	87	93	99	100	104	106	115
73	89	94	99	100	104	107	125
75	89	94	99	100	104	108	130
80	89	94	99	100	104	108	135
82	90	94	99	100	104	109	137
83	90	96	99	101	104	110	140
85	90	96	99	101	105	110	145
85	91	96	99	102	105	110	148
86	92	98	99	102	105	111	149
86	93	99	99	103	106	111	155

Note that: 66 and 73 are between the lower outer fence and the lower inner fence, 130, 135, 137, 140, and 145 are between the upper inner fence and the upper outer fence, and 148, 149, and 155 are beyond the upper outer fence. Note that the four fences are invisible fences. They do not show up in the box plot itself. The SPSS generated box plot is shown in Figure 2.11. *Outliers* are shown as vertical lines above the numbers and

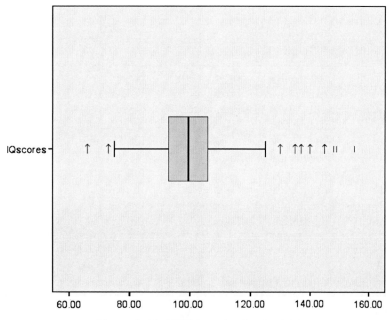

Figure 2.11 SPSS box plot for the IQ data.

potential outliers are identified with arrows pointing upward above the numbers. The left side of the box is above the IQscore Q1 and the right side of the box is above the IQscore Q3. The vertical line inside the box is above Q2.

A *whisker* extends on the left side of the box to the smallest number that is not below the lower inner fence. Seventy-five is the smallest number that does not cross the lower inner fence. The end of the left whisker is above 75. Another *whisker* extends from the right side of the box to the largest IQ score that does not exceed the upper inner fence. The end of the right whisker is above 125. Note that *potential outliers* are identified for IQ scores of 66, 73, 130, 135, 137, 140, and 145. *Outliers* are identified for IQ scores of 148, 149, and 155.

Graphing Qualitative Data

Psychologists often encounter qualitative data when doing research. People are classified as: male or female, depressed or non-depressed, smokers or non-smokers. University students may be classified as freshmen, sophomores, juniors, or seniors. These data are at the nominal or interval level. The data may be grouped into a frequency distribution. The *pie chart* or *bar chart* is the usual graphical technique used to display the data. For a pie chart, the categories are represented as pieces of a pie. Because a pie is circular, it can be thought of as encompassing 360 degrees. Each category is represented as a piece of the pie. The angle associated with the category is a percent of 360 degrees. For example if 30% of a class is seniors, the angle of the piece of pie associated with seniors is (0.30)(360) = 108 degrees. A *bar chart* is made up of rectangular bars. Each category is represented as a bar whose height is usually the frequency of the category.

Pie Charts and Bar Charts

A study reported in the *British Medical Journal* (*BMJ*) in September 2004 reported on a study of 1,018 men and women, ages 65 to 79 years. The study classified the participants as to alcohol consumption: no alcohol, frequent consumption (several times a month), or infrequent consumption (less than one time per month). The study found that those who drank no alcohol or drank frequently were both twice as likely to have mild cognitive impairment in old age than those who drank infrequently. Suppose a similar study was conducted and the following data were obtained.

TABLE 2.5 **Alcohol Usage**

None	Infrequently	Infrequently	None	Infrequently
Frequently	Frequently	Frequently	Frequently	Infrequently
Infrequently	None	Frequently	None	Frequently
Infrequently	Infrequently	Infrequently	Infrequently	Infrequently
Frequently	None	None	Infrequently	None
Infrequently	Infrequently	Infrequently	None	Infrequently
None	Infrequently	None	Frequently	Infrequently
Frequently	Infrequently	Frequently	Infrequently	Frequently
Frequently	Infrequently	Infrequently	Frequently	Infrequently
Infrequently	Frequently	Frequently	Infrequently	Frequently

EXAMPLE 5 Create an SPSS pie chart for the data in Table 2.5. The data are entered into the first column and the pull-down **Graphs → Interactive → Pie → Simple** gives the pie chart shown in Figure 2.12. The angles for the pieces of the pie chart are none, (0.20)(360) = 72 degrees; frequently, (0.32)(360) = 115.2 degrees; and infrequently, (0.48)(360) = 172.8 degrees.

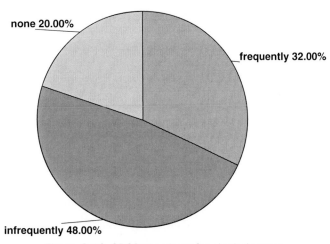

Figure 2.12 SPSS pie chart for alcohol usage.

EXAMPLE 6 A frequency distribution shows that 10 respondents in the study are classified as none, 16 are classified as frequently, and 24 are classified as infrequently. Use EXCEL to form a bar chart.

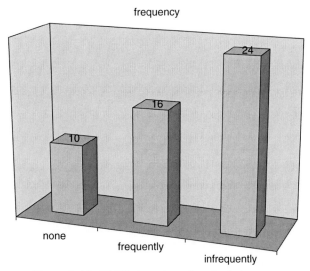

Figure 2.13 EXCEL bar chart for alcohol usage.

The data are first summarized into a frequency distribution and then the chart wizard is used to construct the bar chart shown in Figure 2.13.

SOLVED PROBLEMS

Frequency Distribution Tables

1. A 2006 article entitled "Loneliness Is a Unique Predictor of Age-Related Differences in Systolic Blood Pressure" in the journal *Psychology and Aging* found that loneliness is a major risk factor in increasing blood pressure in older Americans. Table 2.6 contains typical systolic readings in older Americans experiencing loneliness.

TABLE **2.6 Systolic Blood Pressure Values in Seniors Experiencing Loneliness**

144	149	158	148	140	160	160	148	152	145
147	153	147	149	158	161	158	149	140	143
149	154	157	152	161	153	143	139	161	148
149	148	154	160	145	126	134	150	136	144
144	155	148	159	159	149	147	139	131	153
136	148	163	133	154	158	153	144	149	145
145	138	166	166	145	143	147	153	164	145
146	141	155	144	147	155	138	158	153	158
156	137	152	164	142	146	145	168	148	139
135	151	154	152	155	144	150	138	163	151

Form a frequency distribution consisting of the unique values in Table 2.6 and their frequencies.

Solution

SYSTOLIC	FREQUENCY	PERCENT	SYSTOLIC	FREQUENCY	PERCENT
126	1	1	149	7	7
131	1	1	150	2	2
133	1	1	151	2	2
134	1	1	152	4	4
135	1	1	153	6	6
136	2	2	154	4	4
137	1	1	155	4	4
138	3	3	156	1	1
139	3	3	157	1	1
140	2	2	158	6	6
141	1	1	159	2	2
142	1	1	160	3	3
143	3	3	161	3	3
144	6	6	163	2	2
145	7	7	164	2	2
146	2	2	166	2	2
147	5	5	168	1	1
148	7	7			

2. Group the data in Problem 1 into 9 *classes*, each having *class width* equal to 5. Start the first class at 124.5.

Solution

TABLE **2.7 Systolic Blood Pressures Grouped Into 9 Classes**

SYSTOLIC	FREQUENCY	PERCENT
124.5–129.5	1	1
129.5–134.5	3	3
134.5–139.5	10	10
139.5–144.5	13	13
144.5–149.5	28	28
149.5–154.5	18	18
154.5–159.5	14	14
159.5–164.5	10	10
164.5–169.5	3	3

Frequency Distribution Graphs

3. Use SPSS to plot a frequency polygon for the distribution shown in Problem 2.

Solution

First find the *class midpoints* by averaging the class limits. The first class midpoint is $(124.5 + 129.5)/2 = 127$. The second class midpoint is $(129.5 + 134.5)/2 = 132$. The remaining class midpoints are 137, 142, 147, 152, 157, 162, and 167. Two other points, 132 and 172, are added on the *x*-axis to tie down the frequency polygon and obtain Table 2.8.

TABLE **2.8 Class Midpoints for Systolic Blood Pressures**

MIDPOINT	PERCENT
122	0
127	1
132	3
137	10
142	13
147	28
152	18
157	14
162	10
167	3
172	0

The SPSS plot of the points in Table 2.7 is shown in Figure 2.14.

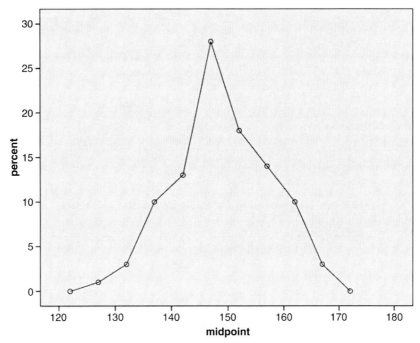

Figure 2.14 SPSS scatter plot for the systolic blood pressures in Table 2.6.

4. Use EXCEL to construct a frequency polygon for the data in Table 2.6.

Solution

Assuming that the data have been put into classes to obtain Table 2.7, and then midpoints found as in Table 2.8, the chart wizard of EXCEL is used to construct Figure 2.15.

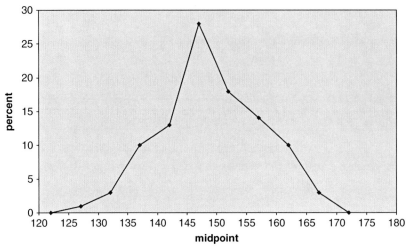

Figure 2.15 EXCEL scatter plot for the systolic blood pressures in Table 2.6.

Shape of a Frequency Distribution

5. What shape do the systolic blood pressures have as revealed by the frequency polygon plots in Figures 2.14 and 2.15?

   Solution

   The distribution of systolic blood pressures for the elderly shown in Figures 2.14 and 2.15 is symmetrical.

6. What shape frequency distribution would the heights of a large group of adult males and adult females have?

   Solution

   The shape would be a *bimodal shape*. The distribution would have peaks near 163 centimeters because of the women in the group, and 178 centimeters because of the men in the group. The two peaks are called modes and because there are two peaks the distribution is called a *bimodal distribution*.

Percentiles and Quartiles

7. In a psychological experiment, response time was measured for 60 participants given a stimulant and is given in Table 2.9.

TABLE **2.9 Response Times When Under the Influence of a Stimulant**

4.59	5.51	4.75	5.96	4.43	4.15
5.26	5.87	4.16	5.18	4.24	4.42
5.61	5.08	4.15	5.14	5.78	3.40
4.74	4.55	5.11	4.27	4.67	4.34
5.22	4.69	5.70	5.73	5.25	4.50
4.79	5.55	4.75	4.95	5.11	5.88
4.42	5.03	4.31	4.29	5.46	5.21
5.27	5.23	5.16	4.06	5.39	3.97
5.26	4.82	4.44	4.48	5.08	5.14
4.92	5.55	5.85	5.80	5.34	5.72

Find P_{15}, Q_1, P_{67}, and P_{91} using the technique described earlier.

Solution

First we need to sort the data. The sorted data are as follows.

3.40	4.34	4.69	5.08	5.25	5.61
3.97	4.42	4.74	5.11	5.26	5.70
4.06	4.42	4.75	5.11	5.26	5.72
4.15	4.43	4.75	5.14	5.27	5.73
4.15	4.44	4.79	5.14	5.34	5.78
4.16	4.48	4.82	5.16	5.39	5.80
4.24	4.50	4.92	5.18	5.46	5.85
4.27	4.55	4.95	5.21	5.51	5.87
4.29	4.59	5.03	5.22	5.55	5.88
4.31	4.67	5.08	5.23	5.55	5.96

To find P_{15}, calculate $np/100 = 60(15)/100 = 9$. The 15th percentile is the average of the 9th and 10th observations or $(4.29 + 4.31)/2 = 4.30$.

To find P_{25}, calculate $np/100 = 60(25)/100 = 15$. The first quartile is the average of the 15th and 16th observations or $(4.44 + 4.48)/2 = 4.46$.

To find P_{67}, calculate $np/100 = 60(67)/100 = 40.2$. The 67th percentile is the 41st data value in the sorted array or 5.25.

To find P_{91}, calculate $np/100 = 60(91)/100 = 54.6$. The 91st percentile is the 55th data value in the sorted array or 5.78.

8. Use MINITAB to find P_{15}, Q_1, P_{67}, and P_{91}.

Solution

Enter the data from Table 2.9 into column C1 of the MINITAB worksheet.

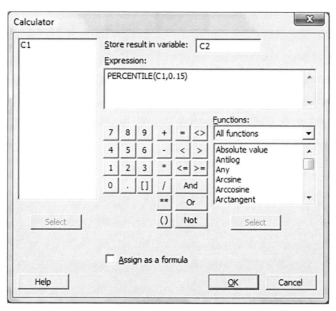

Figure 2.16 MINITAB dialog box for computing P_{15}.

The pull-down **Calc → Calculator** gives the dialog box shown in Figure 2.16, which is completed as shown to compute P_{15}. The answer is given in Column C2 of the MINITAB worksheet as 4.29. Similarly, MINITAB gives $Q_1 = 4.45$, $P_{67} = 5.25$, and $P_{91} = 5.79$. The answers are close to those found using the technique given in the book, but are not exactly the same.

9. Use EXCEL to find P_{15}, Q_1, P_{67}, and P_{91}.

Solution

A portion of the EXCEL worksheet is shown in Figure 2.17 for computing P_{15}, Q_1, P_{67}, and P_{91}. The answers are close to those found using the technique given in the book and MINITAB, but are not exactly the same.

	A	B	C	D	E	F
1	4.59	5.51	4.75	5.96	4.43	4.15
2	5.26	5.87	4.16	5.18	4.24	4.42
3	5.61	5.08	4.15	5.14	5.78	3.4
4	4.74	4.55	5.11	4.27	4.67	4.34
5	5.22	4.69	5.7	5.73	5.25	4.5
6	4.79	5.55	4.75	4.95	5.11	5.88
7	4.42	5.03	4.31	4.29	5.46	5.21
8	5.27	5.23	5.16	4.06	5.39	3.97
9	5.26	4.82	4.44	4.48	5.08	5.14
10	4.92	5.55	5.85	5.8	5.34	5.72
11						
12	4.307	PERCENTILE(A1:F10,0.15)				
13	4.47	PERCENTILE(A1:F10,0.25)				
14	5.2406	PERCENTILE(A1:F10,0.67)				
15	5.7645	PERCENTILE(A1:F10,0.91)				

Figure 2.17 EXCEL worksheet for computing P_{15}, Q_1, P_{67}, and P_{91}.

10. Use SPSS to find P_{15}, Q_1, P_{67}, and P_{91}.

Solution

The SPSS pull-down **Analyze → Descriptive Statistics → Frequencies** gives the dialog box shown in Figure 2.18, which is completed as shown. The output is shown in Figure 2.19.

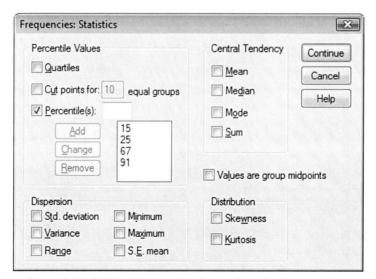

Figure 2.18 SPSS dialog box for finding P_{15}, Q_1, P_{67}, and P_{91}.

Statistics

time

N	Valid	60
	Missing	0
Percentiles	15	4.2930
	25	4.4500
	67	5.2474
	91	5.7902

Figure 2.19 SPSS output showing P_{15}, Q_1, P_{67}, and P_{91}.

Dot Plots

11. A MINITAB dot plot of the response times given in Table 2.9 is shown in Figure 2.20. Refer to the dot plot in Figure 2.20 to answer the following questions concerning the response times.

    a.   What is the maximum response time?

    b.   What is the minimum response time?

    c.   How many of the 60 response times are between 4.90 and 5.25 seconds, including 4.90 and 5.25?

Solution

    a.   5.95 seconds

    b.   3.40 seconds

    c.   18

Dot plot of time

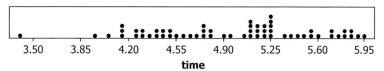

time

Figure 2.20 MINITAB dot plot of the response times under the influence of the stimulant.

12. Use SPSS to create a dot plot the systolic blood pressures in Table 2.6.

    a.   What is the maximum systolic blood pressure?

    b.   What is the minimum systolic blood pressure?

    c.   What is the most frequently occurring value or values and what is their frequency?

Solution

    a.   168

    b.   126

    c.   Three values occur with a frequency of 7: 145, 148, and 149

The SPSS dotplot is shown in Figure 2.21.

Stem-and-Leaf Displays

13. A stem-and-leaf plot of the systolic blood pressures in Table 2.6, generated by STATISTIX, is given in Figure 2.22.

    a.   Interpret the numbers in the first column of the stem-and-leaf display.

    b.   Which number occurs most often?

    c.   What shape does the distribution have?

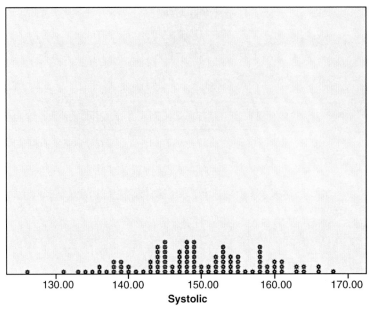

Figure 2.21 SPSS dot plot of the systolic blood pressures in Table 2.6.

```
Statistix 8.1
Stem-and-Leaf Plot of systolic
Leaf Digit Unit = 1                     Minimum   126.00
12   6   represents 126.              Median    149.00
                                        Maximum   168.00

     Stem      Leaves
    1    12    6
    4    13    134
   14    13    5667888999
   27    14    0012333444444
  (28)   14    5555555667777788888889999999
   45    15    00112222333333334444
   27    15    55556788888899
   13    16    0001113344
    3    16    668

100 cases included   0 missing cases
```

Figure 2.22 STATISTIX stem-and-leaf display of the blood pressure data in Table 2.6.

Solution

a. Starting with the top, the 1 means there is one number less than or equal to 126; the 4 means there are 4 numbers less than or equal to 134; the 14 means there are 14 numbers equal to or less than 139; the 27 means there are 27 numbers less than or equal to 144; the (28) means there are 28 numbers in the class that contains 145, 146, 147, 148, or 149. Going to the bottom of the column, the 3 means that there are 3 numbers that are 166 or higher; the 13 means there are 13 numbers that are 160 or higher; the 27 means there are 27 numbers that are 155 or higher; and the 45 means there are 45 numbers that are 150 or higher.

b. 145, 148, and 149 occur 7 times

c. Symmetrical

14. Use SPSS to create a stem-and-leaf plot for the systolic blood pressure data in Table 2.6. How is this plot different from the STATISTIX plot in Problem 13?

Solution

```
Systolic Stem-and-Leaf Plot

Frequency    Stem &  Leaf

 1.00 Extremes     (=<126)
 1.00          13 .  1
 1.00          13 .  3
 2.00          13 .  45
 3.00          13 .  667
 6.00          13 .  888999
 3.00          14 .  001
 4.00          14 .  2333
13.00          14 .  4444445555555
 7.00          14 .  6677777
14.00          14 .  88888889999999
 4.00          15 .  0011
10.00          15 .  2222333333
 8.00          15 .  44445555
 2.00          15 .  67
 8.00          15 .  88888899
 6.00          16 .  000111
 2.00          16 .  33
 2.00          16 .  44
 2.00          16 .  66
 1.00          16 .  8

Stem width:      10
Each leaf:     1 case(s)
```

Figure 2.23 SPSS plot for the data in Table 2.6.

The SPSS pull-down menu **Analyze → Descriptive Statistics → Explore** gives the Explore dialog box from which the stem-and-leaf plot may be chosen. The SPSS plot is shown in Figure 2.23. The stems are 130, 140, 150, or 160. The leaves are 0 through 9, the number of ones. The first column is simply the frequency for that row. The rows contain numbers with leaves 0 or 1, 2 or 3, 4 or 5, 6 or 7, and 8 or 9. The STATISTIX stem-and-leaf plot has rows which have leaves 0, 1, 2, 3, or 4 or leaves 5, 6, 7, 8, or 9.

Histograms

15. Construct a STATISTIX histogram of the systolic blood pressure data in Table 2.6.

   a. What shape does the histogram have?

   b. What is the class width?

   ### Solution

   The pull-down **Statistics → Summary Statistics → Histogram** gives the histogram shown in Figure 2.24. The histogram has a symmetrical shape. The class width is 3 units.

16. Construct a MINITAB histogram for the blood pressure data in Table 2.6.

   ### Solution

   The pull-down **Graph → Histogram** is used to construct the histogram for the data after the data is entered into column C1. The Histogram is shown in Figure 2.25.

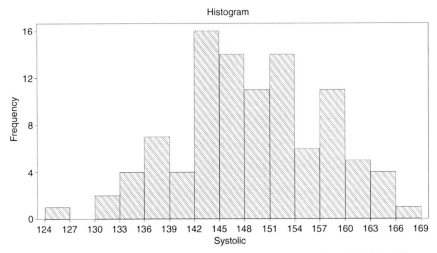

Figure 2.24 STATISTIX histogram of the blood pressure data in Table 2.6.

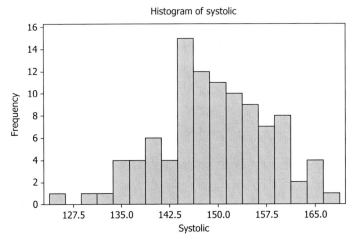

Figure 2.25 MINITAB histogram of the blood pressure data in Table 2.6.

Box Plots

17. A MINITAB box plot for the data in Table 2.6 is shown in Figure 2.26. From Figure 2.26, give the following: Q_1, Q_2, Q_3, and the identified outlier and comment on the outlier. Give the inner and outer fences.

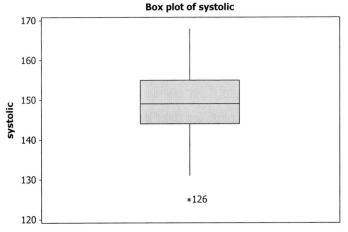

Figure 2.26 MINITAB box plot of the blood pressure data in Table 2.6.

Solution

Q_1 is 144, Q_2 is 149, and Q_3 is 155. The outlier is 126. The outlier is lower than we would expect from a group of lonely elderly people who tend to have elevated blood pressures.

Lower outer fence = $Q_1 - 3IQR = 144 - 3(155 - 144) = 111$

Lower inner fence = $Q_1 - 1.5(11) = 144 - 16.5 = 127.5$

Upper inner fence = $Q_3 + 1.5(11) = 155 + 16.5 = 171.5$

Upper outer fence = $Q_3 + 3(11) = 188$

The 126 is between 111 and 127.5 and is called a potential outlier.

18. Using the software package STATISTIX, the pull down **Statistics → Summary Statistics → Box and Whisker plots** gives the dialog box shown in Figure 2.27, which is completed as shown. The data are the response time data shown in Table 2.9.

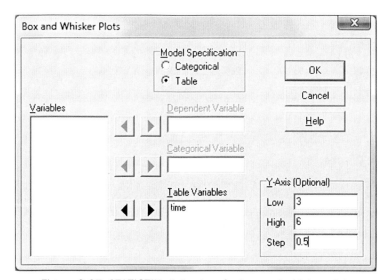

Figure 2.27 STATISTIX dialog box for box and whisker plot.

The output is shown in Figure 2.28. From Figure 2.28, give the following: Q_1, Q_2, Q_3, and the inner and outer fences. Show that none of the data falls below the lower inner fence and none of the data falls above the upper inner fence.

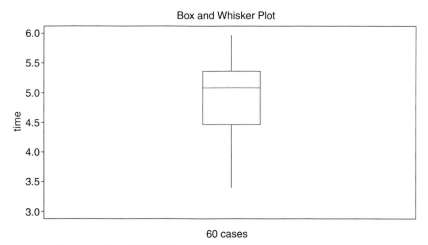

Figure 2.28 STATISTIX box and whisker plot response times.

Solution

Q_1 is 4.45, Q_2 is 5.08, and Q_3 is 5.38.

Lower outer fence = $Q_1 - 3IQR = 4.45 - 3(5.38 - 4.45) = 4.45 - 3(0.93) = 1.66$

Lower inner fence = $Q_1 - 1.5(0.93) = 4.45 - 1.40 = 3.05$

Upper inner fence = $Q_3 + 1.5(0.93) = 5.38 + 1.40 = 6.78$

Upper outer fence = $Q_3 + 3(0.93) = 5.38 + 2.79 = 8.17$

The sorted data are reproduced below.

3.40	4.34	4.69	5.08	5.25	5.61
3.97	4.42	4.74	5.11	5.26	5.70
4.06	4.42	4.75	5.11	5.26	5.72
4.15	4.43	4.75	5.14	5.27	5.73
4.15	4.44	4.79	5.14	5.34	5.78
4.16	4.48	4.82	5.16	5.39	5.80
4.24	4.50	4.92	5.18	5.46	5.85
4.27	4.55	4.95	5.21	5.51	5.87
4.29	4.59	5.03	5.22	5.55	5.88
4.31	4.67	5.08	5.23	5.55	5.96

None of the data falls outside the inner fences. There are no potential outliers nor outliers.

Pie Charts and Bar Charts

19. In a psychological study of marriage, the participants were classified as: married, single, divorced, or separated. The study involved 250 participants who were classified as shown in Table 2.10. Use MINITAB to construct a pie chart and STATISTIX to construct a bar chart of the data in Table 2.10. Confirm the percents given in the MINITAB pie chart.

TABLE 2.10   Categories in Marriage Study

CATEGORY	FREQUENCY
Married	80
Single	40
Divorced	70
Separated	60

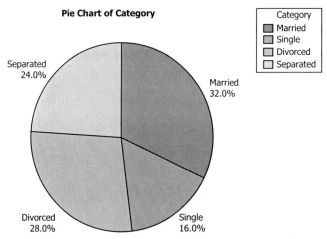

Figure 2.29 MINITAB pie chart of data in Table 2.10.

Solution

The pull-down **Graph → Pie Chart** gives the pie chart shown in Figure 2.29.

The percents are obtained as follows: separated (60/250) = 0.24 or 24%, married (80/250) = 0.32 or 32%, single (40/250) = 0.16 or 16%, and divorced (70/250) = 0.28 or 28%.

The STATISTIX pull-down **Statistics → Summary Statistics → Error Bar Chart** gives the bar chart shown in Figure 2.30.

Figure 2.30 STATISTIX barchart of the data in Table 2.10.

20. A group of 200 adults were classified into four categories as shown in Figure 2.31.

    a. How many male and females were in the study?

    b. How many were smokers in the study?

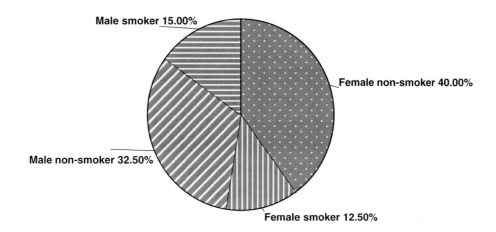

Figure 2.31 SPSS Pie Chart.

Solution

    a. 47.5% of the 200 or 95 were males and 52.5% of the 200 or 105 were females.

    b. 27.5% of the 200 or 55 were smokers.

SUPPLEMENTARY PROBLEMS

Frequency Distribution Tables

21. A psychological study that was searching for causes of dementia in the elderly recorded the ages of the women in their study. The ages are given in Table 2.11.

TABLE 2.11 Ages of 150 Elderly Women

73	77	93	76	75	82	82	78	87	79
74	78	90	76	85	87	103	85	83	78
74	86	72	88	77	71	81	72	78	93
71	90	76	103	89	73	87	84	83	73
94	108	75	86	89	95	75	83	70	78
79	79	90	70	74	87	76	98	74	97
97	102	98	82	86	90	83	75	72	79
91	76	89	78	77	95	82	77	71	89
88	77	81	84	73	82	70	74	75	81
89	94	105	72	80	94	77	88	85	79
78	70	89	76	75	84	72	74	79	70
77	82	76	73	75	82	73	77	74	70
79	80	70	89	86	87	87	97	75	91
73	78	101	83	73	73	82	89	86	97
88	83	77	98	80	86	76	71	82	81

Group the data into the following 10 classes: 68.5 to 72.5, 72.5 to 76.5, 76.5 to 80.5, 80.5 to 84.5, 84.5 to 88.5, 88.5 to 92.5, 92.5 to 96.5, 96.5 to 100.5, 100.5 to 104.5, and 104.5 to 108.5.

22. Group the data in Table 2.11 so that the each class is a single unique number.

Frequency Distribution Graphs

23. Use the frequency distribution you obtained in Problem 21 and use the class midpoint and the frequency for each class to obtain a set of 10 points. Add the points (66.5, 0) and (110.5, 0) to tie down the frequency distribution polygon. Plot a scatter plot using STATISTIX. What is the basic difference between a scatter plot and a frequency polygon?

24. Use the frequency distribution obtained in Problem 22 and EXCEL to plot a frequency distribution polygon for the age data in Table 2.11.

Shape of Frequency Distributions

25. What shape do the frequency distribution polygons have in Problems 23 and 24?

26. What is the main difference between the graphs in Problems 23 and 24?

Percentiles and Quartiles

27. Use MINITAB to find P_{10}, Q_3, P_{83}, and P_{99} for the age data in Table 2.11.

28. Use SPSS to find P_{10}, Q_3, P_{83}, and P_{99} for the age data in Table 2.11.

29. Use EXCEL to find P_{10}, Q_3, P_{83}, and P_{99} for the age data in Table 2.11.

30. Use STATISTIX to find P_{10}, Q_3, P_{83}, and P_{99} for the age data in Table 2.11.

Dot Plots

31. Use MINITAB to construct a dot plot for the ages in Table 2.11.

32. Consider the dot plot in Problem 31. What percent of the sample are older than 100?

Stem-and-Leaf Displays

33. Use SPSS to construct a stem-and-leaf diagram for the age data in Table 2.11. Explain what the row
17.00   7 . 66666666777777777 means.

34. A psychological study of people entering their retirement years was designed. One of the variables measured was the amount of savings each of the participants had . The following is a MINITAB stem-and-leaf display of their savings. Note that the leaf unit is 10000. This means that the row 7   4   4579 represents 440000, 450000, 470000 and 490000 and that 7 retirement amounts are 490000 or smaller, for example. Answer the following by considering Figure 2.32.

    a.   What is the smallest retirement account?

    b.   What is the largest retirement account?

    c.   What retirement account is in middle of the retirement accounts?

    d.   What is the range of the retirement accounts?

```
         Stem-and-Leaf Display: C1

         Stem-and-leaf of C1   N  = 35
         Leaf Unit = 10000
             1         1     1
             3         2     36
             3         3
             7         4     4579
            11         5     0478
            17         6     145667
            (7)        7     1357899
            11         8     13
             9         9     448
             6        10     45
             4        11     4
             3        12     11
             1        13     5
```

Figure 2.32 MINITAB stem-and-leaf of amounts in retirement accounts.

Histograms

35. Use MINITAB and the data in Figure 2.32 to construct a histogram for the retirement accounts.

36. Use SPSS and the data in Figure 2.32 to construct a histogram for the retirement accounts.

Box Plots

37. Construct a box plot using MINITAB for the data in Figure 2.32.

38. Construct a box plot using SPSS for the data in Figure 2.32.

Pie Charts and Bar Charts

39. A section of the Statistics for the Behavioral Sciences course has 300 students. Their classifications are given by the EXCEL pie chart shown in Figure 2.33.

    a.   Give the numbers in each classification.

    b.   Give the angle of the piece of the pie representing each classification.

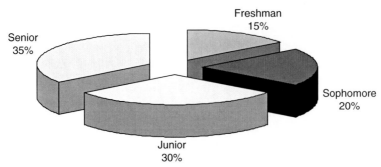

Figure 2.33 EXCEL pie chart showing classification of students in Statistics for the Behavioral Sciences course.

40. In a psychology of world religion study, peoples' religion was classified as: Islam, Judaism, Buddhism, Animism, Christianity, and Hinduism. The participants in the study were classified into one of the six religions as shown in Figure 2.34. Give the proportion for each group.

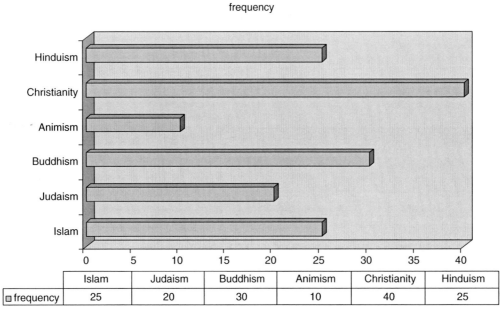

	Islam	Judaism	Buddhism	Animism	Christianity	Hinduism
frequency	25	20	30	10	40	25

Figure 2.34 EXCEL bar chart for psychology of world religion study.

CHAPTER 3

Central Tendency

Mean

When searching for a single number to represent a group of numbers, the measure that often comes to mind is the *mean*. When you have a sample, you find the mean by adding the values and dividing by the number of values you added up. This mean is referred to as the sample mean and is represented by *M*. It is found by the adding the sample values and dividing by the number of values, $\sum X/n$. That is, the *sample mean* is $M = \sum X/n$.

> **EXAMPLE 1** A Basic Psychology class is composed of 30 students and the class takes a final exam with the scores shown in the partial EXCEL worksheet in Figure 3.1.

	A	B	C	D	E	F	G
1	68	50	65	83	72		
2	67	67	80	47	81		
3	64	76	62	74	59		
4	75	66	55	82	65		
5	75	88	83	61	78		
6	67	77	67	65	72		
7							
8	2091	69.7					

Figure 3.1 EXCEL worksheet containing test scores.

The scores are entered into A1:E6. The sum is found by entering =SUM(A1:E6) into cell A8. The sample mean is found by entering =A8/30 into cell B8. The sample mean of the scores is 69.7. When Jane Doe, the instructor of the Basic Psychology class, is asked "How did your class score on the final exam?," she would likely answer by stating that the average score was close to 70. If this group of 30 students is regarded as a population, the mean is found the same way but the mean is represented by the Greek letter μ (pronounced mu). The *population mean* is $\mu = \sum X/N$. Note that a lower case letter *n* is used for the sample size and an upper case *N* is used for the population size. Whether the 30 numbers is a sample or a population depends on what you are using the numbers to do. If you are thinking of the class as representative of all basic psychology classes taught at Midwestern University then it would be a sample. If you are interested only in this class, it would be a population.

Median

A second measure of central tendency is the *median*. The median is the number that divides a set of data so that half is above the median and half is below the median. It is the same as the fiftieth percentile, P_{50}, or the second quartile, Q_2, of the set of data. To find the median, sort your data so that they are ascending or descending. If the number of data values is odd, choose the middle value. If the amount of data is even, then average the two points nearest the middle.

EXAMPLE 2 Find the median of the test scores given in Figure 3.1.

Figure 3.2 shows the data from Figure 3.1 in A1:A30 and the same data sorted in C1:C30. The cell below C30 is selected, the symbol ⬇ is double clicked, and the data is sorted. The 15th and 16th values are 67 and 68 and their average is 67.5. This is the median. Note that 50% of the data is above 67.5 and half is below 67.5. The mean (69.7) and the median (67.5) are very close for this data set. There is no universally accepted symbol for the median. It is usually simply called *sample median* if it is found for a sample and *population median* if it is found for a population.

Microsoft Excel - Book1			
File Edit View Insert Format Tools			
C31		*fx*	
A	B	C	D
68		47	
67		50	
64		55	
75		59	
75		61	
67		62	
50		64	
67		65	
76		65	
66		65	
88		66	
77		67	
65		67	
80		67	
62		67	
55		68	
83		72	
67		72	
83		74	
47		75	
74		75	
82		76	
61		77	
65		78	
72		80	
81		81	
59		82	
65		83	
78		83	
72		88	

Figure 3.2 Sorting data in an EXCEL worksheet.

Mode

The *mode* of a set of data is the most frequently occurring value in a set of data, if only one exists. A set of data may not have a mode at all, or it may have more than one data value that occurs most often. A set with two values that occur most often is referred to as *bimodal*, and a set of data with three values that occur most often is referred to as *trimodal*. The term *multimodal* is often used for data having more than one mode. The best approach to finding the mode of a quantitative data set is to sort the data first and then the mode or modes will be easy to find.

> **EXAMPLE 3** The mode of the test scores given in Figure 3.2 is 67 because this score occurs with a frequency of 4 and no other test score occurs as often.

The terms *modal category* or *modal class* is often used with qualitative data. This is simply the category or class that occurs most frequently.

> **EXAMPLE 4** Figure 3.3 gives the results of a study of alcohol usage. In this study the class or category labeled **infrequently** would be referred to as the modal class.

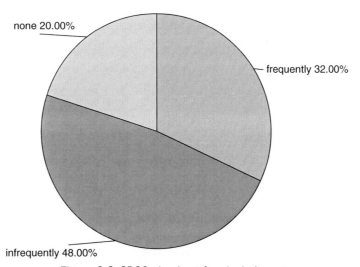

Figure 3.3 SPSS pie chart for alcohol usage.

Choosing the Correct Measure of Central Tendency

The most widely used measure of central tendency is the mean. However, there are situations where the median or mode is more appropriate. There are theoretical relationships connecting the mean and standard deviation. For example, the *empirical rule* states that for a normal distribution, there is approximately 68% of the distribution within one standard deviation of the mean, approximately 95% of the distribution within two standard deviations of the mean, and over 99% of the distribution within three standard deviations of the mean. *Chebyshev's theorem* is another theoretical result connecting the mean and standard deviation. The median is more appropriate when variables are highly skewed. Consider the following example involving a skewed measure.

> **EXAMPLE 5** The following is a sample of salaries for a group of consulting psychologists (in thousands of dollars): 60, 185, 70, 75, and 65. The mean salary is 91 thousand and the median salary is 70 thousand. The median is much more representative of the salaries of the group.

Other examples where the median is more representative than the mean is: the price of homes, the age at marriage, and the time spent on the internet per week. Some get hooked on the internet and spend an enormous amount of time on it. Also, for *open ended distributions*, the median is more appropriate.

EXAMPLE 6 A group of 50 rats are timed in a psychological experiment as to the time it takes them to make their way through a maze. The times are given in Table 3.1.

TABLE 3.1 Times to Transverse a Maze

TIME	FREQUENCY
1	5
2	7
3	25
4	8
More than 5	5

The median is the average of the 25th and 26th time to transverse the maze. Both the 25th and 26th times are 3 minutes. The median time is 3 minutes. You cannot give the mean time because you do not know the times of the 5 who took more than 5 minutes. Similarly, if a data set has an open class at the low side of the distribution, you may be able to give the median but not the mean.

In some instances the mode may be the more appropriate measure. The mode is always appropriate for data at the nominal level. The mean and median are not appropriate for nominal level data.

EXAMPLE 7 In a psychological study of adult relationships, the study participants were divided into four groups as shown in Figure 3.4. The modal group would be the **married** group since it has the highest percent.

When discrete data that take on only integral values are collected, the researcher may prefer a measure that also takes on only integral values.

Pie Chart of Category

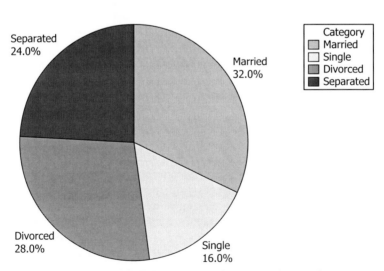

Figure 3.4 MINITAB pie chart of relationships study.

EXAMPLE 8 In a research study involving families, the number of children per family is one variable of interest. A study involved 300 families and the number of children per family had the distribution shown in Table 3.2.

It is not possible to calculate the mean because of the **more than 5** category. The median is the average of the 150th and 151st values which is $(3 + 4)/2 = 3.5$. The mode is 3. We would say that the modal number of children per family is 3 for the 300 families. The mode is the only one of the three measures of central tendency that is a whole number.

TABLE 3.2 Children per Family

CHILDREN PER FAMILY	NUMBER OF FAMILIES
2	60
3	90
4	65
5	50
More than 5	35

Central Tendency Measures and Their Relationship to the Shape of the Distribution

Figure 3.5 shows four common distribution shapes encountered in psychological studies.

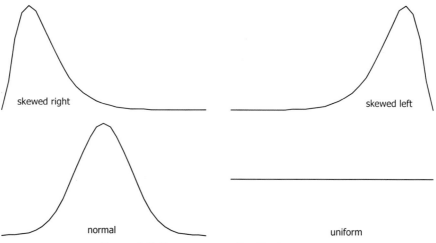

Figure 3.5 Four common distribution curves.

Skewed right

The mean > median. An example is age at time of marriage. Most people marry between ages 20 and 35, but a few are in their 40s, 50s, 60s, 70s, 80s and 90s. A particularly hard test will have grades that are skewed to the right.

Skewed left

The median > mean. An example is human lifetimes. Most people live to be between 55 and 85 years olf, but a few early deaths occur giving a skew to the left. A particularly easy test will have grades that are skewed to the left.

Normal

The mean = median = mode. An example is the heights of adult males. The mean, the median, and the mode are all about 70 inches. The normal is a symmetrical distribution.

Uniform

The mean = median. There is no mode. An example is a random number generator that generates random numbers between 1 and 10. Each of the numbers between 1 and 10 are equally likely to occur. The mean = median = 5.5.

Note that the mode occurs at the high point of the curve except in the case of the uniform distribution which has no high point.

Measures of Central Tendency and Statistical Software

The measures of central tendency are included in the routine called descriptive statistics in software packages. For the data shown in Figure 3.1, stack the data in any open column of MINITAB, SPSS, EXCEL, or STATISTIX to obtain the measures of central tendency.

The following output is from EXCEL. It is obtained by using the pull down **Tools → Data Analysis → Descriptive Statistics**.

SCORE	
Mean	69.7
Standard Error	1.804942
Median	67.5
Mode	67
Standard Deviation	9.886075
Sample Variance	97.73448
Kurtosis	−0.12021
Skewness	−0.33065
Range	41
Minimum	47
Maximum	88
Sum	2091
Count	30

The mean, median, range, minimum, maximum, sum, and count have previously been discussed. Most of the other measures will be discussed in future chapters.

The following output is from MINITAB. It is obtained by using the pull-down **Stat → Basic Statistics → Display Descriptive Statistics**

Descriptive Statistics: Score

Variable	Total Count	Mean	Sum	Minimum	Q1	Median	Q3	Maximum	Range
score	30	69.70	2091.00	47.00	64.75	67.50	77.25	88.00	41.00

Variable	Mode	N for Mode
score	67	4

The following output is obtained from SPSS by using the pull-down **Analyze → Descriptive Statistics → Descriptives**.

Descriptive Statistics

	N	RANGE	MINIMUM	MAXIMUM	SUM	MEAN
Scores	30	41	47	88	2091	69.70
Valid N (listwise)	30					

The following output is obtained from STATISTIX by using the pull-down **Statistics → Summary Statistics → Descriptive Statistics**.

STATISTIX 8. **Descriptive Statistics**

	Score
N	30
Sum	2091
Mean	69.700
Minimum	47.000
1st Quartile	64.750
Median	67.500
3rd Quartile	77.250
Maximum	88.000

MINITAB, SPSS, and STATISTIX allow you to request other descriptive statistics. Notice that the only requirement is that you stack the data in a column and give the correct pull-down for the software being used to get the descriptive statistics you desire.

SOLVED PROBLEMS

Mean, Median, and Mode

1. **Sports psychology** is an important subject that involves the interaction between exercise and psychology. Suppose we wished to investigate the outcomes of the 41 super bowls that have been played through 2007. The results of those games are shown in Figure 3.6. Answer the following questions concerning the super bowls through 2007. Use EXCEL to answer the questions.

Microsoft Excel - Book1

File Edit View Insert Format Tools Data Window Help

P33

	A	B	C	D	E
1	Year	Winner	Winning score	Loser	Losing score
2	1967	Green Bay	35	Kansas City	10
3	1968	Green Bay	33	Oakland	14
4	1969	N Y Jets	16	Baltimore Colts	7
5	1970	Kansas City	23	Minnesota	7
6	1971	Baltimore Colts	16	Dallas	13
7	1972	Dallas	24	Miami	3
8	1973	Miami	14	Washington	7
9	1974	Miami	24	Minnesota	7
10	1975	Pittsburgh	16	Minnesota	6
11	1976	Pittsburgh	21	Dallas	17
12	1977	Oakland	32	Minnesota	14
13	1978	Dallas	27	Denver	10
14	1979	Pittsburgh	35	Dallas	31
15	1980	Pittsburgh	31	Los Angeles	19
16	1981	Oakland	27	Philadelphia	10
17	1982	San Francisco	26	Cincinnati	21
18	1983	Washington	27	Miami	17
19	1984	L A Raiders	38	Washington	9
20	1985	San Francisco	38	Miami	16
21	1986	Chicago	46	New England	10
22	1987	N Y Giants	39	Denver	20
23	1988	Washington	42	Denver	10
24	1989	San Francisco	20	Cincinnati	16
25	1990	San Francisco	55	Denver	10
26	1991	N Y Giants	20	Buffalo	19
27	1992	Washington	37	Buffalo	24
28	1993	Dallas	52	Buffalo	17
29	1994	Dallas	30	Buffalo	13
30	1995	San Francisco	49	San Diego	26
31	1996	Dallas	27	Pittsburgh	17
32	1997	Green Bay	35	New England	21
33	1998	Denver	31	Green Bay	24
34	1999	Denver	34	Atlanta	19
35	2000	St. Louis	23	Tennessee	16
36	2001	Baltimore Ravens	34	N Y Giants	7
37	2002	New England	20	St. Louis	17
38	2003	Tampa Bay	48	Oakland	21
39	2004	New England	32	Carolina	29
40	2005	New England	24	Philadelphia	21
41	2006	Pittsburgh	21	Seattle	10
42	2007	Indianapolis	29	Chicago	17

Figure 3.6 Partial EXCEL worksheet of super bowl results.

   a.   What is the mean number of points scored by the wining teams in Figure 3.6?

   b.   What is the mean number of points scored by the losing teams in Figure 3.6?

   c.   What is the minimum number of points scored by the winning teams in Figure 3.6?

   d.   What is the minimum number of points scored by the losing teams in Figure 3.6?

   e.   What is the maximum number of points scored by the winning teams in Figure 3.6?

   f.   What is the maximum number of points scored by the losing teams in Figure 3.6?

Solution

   a.   In any empty cell enter =AVERAGE(C2:C42). The answer is 30.51.

   b.   In any empty cell enter =AVERAGE(E2:E42). The answer is 15.17.

   c.   In any empty cell enter =MIN(C2:C42). The answer is 14.

   d.   In any empty cell enter =MIN(E2:E42). The answer is 3.

   f.   In any empty cell enter =MAX(C2:C42). The answer is 55.

   g.   In any empty cell enter =MAX(E2:E42). The answer is 31.

2. In a 2005 issue of the *Journal of Social Issues* an article entitled "Watching More TV Increases Seniors' Negative Views of Aging," it was reported that seniors watch an average of 21 hours of TV per week. Suppose a similar study gave the data in Table 3.3. Find the following measures of central tendency: mean, median, and mode.

TABLE 3.3 Time Spent by Seniors Watching TV

23	17	21	22	28
18	25	26	22	13
23	13	21	25	11
19	31	23	11	16
18	25	16	31	30

Solution

Mean = 21.12 hours, median = 22 hours, bimodal = 23 and 25 hours with frequency = 3.

3. Figure 3.7 is a pie chart of the super bowl winners from Figure 3.6. Teams that have only one win are placed into the category **Other**. Give the mode or modes for winners in the super bowl.

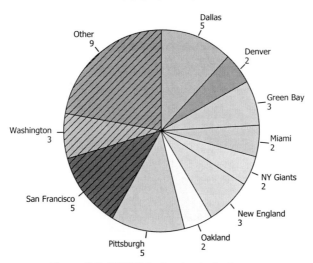

Figure 3.7 MINITAB pie chart of winners.

Solution

The variable winner is trimodal: San Francisco, Dallas, and Pittsburgh each have 5 wins.

4. The following are scores made on a stress test by 20 individuals:

54 41 55 60 43 49 47 60 56 51 47 55 46 52 53 50 55 58 49 55

If the scores are sorted, the results are

41 43 46 47 47 49 49 50 51 52 53 54 55 55 55 55 56 58 60 60

The sum of the data is 1035.33.

Find the mean, median, and mode.

Solution

The mean is the sum divided by 20 or 1035.33/20 = 51.8.

The median is (52 + 53)/2 = 52.5.

The mode is 55.

5. Sometimes data are given in grouped form and the raw data are no longer available. Consider the stress test scores given in Table 3.4.

Find the center of each category and assume all the scores are located at the center of the category. These values are referred to as the *class midpoints*. The class midpoints are 35.5, 45.5, 55.5, 65.5, 75.5, and 85.5. An approximation to the mean is found by assuming 35.5 occurred 10 times, 45.5 occurred 15 times, and so forth. The mean is referred to as the *grouped mean*. Find the grouped mean for the data in Table 3.4.

TABLE 3.4 Stress Test Score Distribution

STRESS TEST SCORE	FREQUENCY
30.5 – 40.5	10
40.5 – 50.5	15
50.5 – 60.5	25
60.5 – 70.5	20
70.5 – 80.5	20
80.5 – 90.5	10

Solution

The solution using EXCEL is shown in Figure 3.8. The midpoints are entered into A2:A7; the frequencies are entered into B2:B7. The expression =A2*B2 is entered into C2 and a click-and-drag is performed from C2 to C7. The expression =SUM(C2:C7) in C8 gives the sum as 6100. The expression = C8/100 in C9 gives the grouped mean as 61.

6. Refer to the data in Table 3.4. The category with the highest frequency is called the *modal class*. The *mode of the grouped data* is given as the class midpoint of the modal class. Find the *modal class* and the *mode of the grouped data* for the data in Table 3.4.

Solution

The class 50.5–60.5 is the modal class and mode of the grouped data is 55.5.

Choosing the Correct Measure of Central Tendency

7. A sports psychologist is studying baseball players. One of the factors that she included in the study is the salaries of the players. In order to include a representative measure of salary, which of the measures of central tendency should she use for the salary of a typical baseball player?

	A	B	C
1	midpoint	frequency	product
2	35.5	10	355
3	45.5	15	682.5
4	55.5	25	1387.5
5	65.5	20	1310
6	75.5	20	1510
7	85.5	10	855
8			6100
9			61

Figure 3.8 Using EXCEL to find a grouped mean.

Solution

The median of the salaries would be more representative of the salary of a typical baseball player. There are only a few of the players who are making salaries in the millions. Most earn under a million.

The web site http://asp.usatoday.com/sports/baseball/salaries contains a listing of the top 25 baseball player salaries for 2007. Some of the salaries are astronomical. The high salaries of a few players gives a distribution that is highly skewed to the right. This causes the mean to be far to the right of the median and not representative of all major league baseball players.

8. A psychologist administers the Myers-Briggs type indicator to several thousand individuals and classifies the individuals into one of 16 types. What is a good choice for the measure of central tendency?

Solution

You could use the mode. Suppose the personality type ISFJ is the most frequently occuring of the 16 Myers-Briggs type indicators. This is the modal type and we would give it as a measure of central tendency. The mean and the median are not appropriate.

Central Tendency Measures and Their Relationship to the Shape of the Distribution

9. Figure 3.9 shows the times required for 20 rats to find their way to food through a maze.

a. Classify the distribution in Figure 3.9 as skewed to the right, skewed to the left, symmetrical, or uniform.

b. Find the median, mean, and mode.

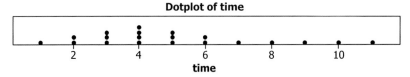

Figure 3.9 MINITAB dot plot of times for rats to find food in a maze.

Solution

a. The distribution is skewed to the right.

b.   Descriptive statistics: time:

Variable	Mean	Minimum	Median	Maximum	Mode	N for Mode
time	5.100	1.000	4.500	11.000	4	4

Note that mode < median < mean.

10. Figure 3.10 shows the times required for 20 rats to find their way to food through a maze.

a.   Classify the distribution in Figure 3.10 as skewed to the right, skewed to the left, symmetrical, or uniform.

b.   Find the median, mean, and mode.

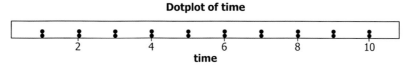

Dotplot of time

Figure 3.10 MINITAB dot plot of times for rats to find food in a maze.

Solution

a.   The distribution is uniform.

b.   Descriptive statistics: time:

Variable	Mean	Minimum	Median	Maximum	Mode	N for Mode
time	5.500	1.000	5.500	10.000	1, 2, 3, 4	2

The data contain at least five mode values. Only the smallest four are shown.

Note that MINITAB states that the data has at least 4 modes. It actually has 10. We say that it does not have a mode if it has more than three values tied for the mode.

Mean = median, and the distribution has no mode.

11. Figure 3.11 shows the times required for 20 rats to find their way to food through a maze.

a.   Classify the distribution as skewed to the right, skewed to the left, symmetrical, or uniform.

b.   Find the median, mean, and mode.

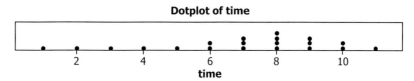

Dotplot of time

Figure 3.11 MINITAB dot plot of times for rats to find food in a maze.

Solution

a.   The distribution is skewed to the left.

b.   Descriptive statistics: time:

Variable	Mean	Median	Mode	N for Mode
time	6.900	7.500	8	4

Note that mean < median < mode.

12. Figure 3.12 shows the times required for 20 rats to find their way to food through a maze.

    a.   Classify the distribution shown in Figure 3.12 as skewed to the right, skewed to the left, symmetrical, or uniform.

    b.   Find the median, mean, and mode.

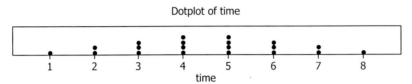

Figure 3.12 MINITAB dot plot of times for rats to find food in a maze.

Solution

    a.   The distribution is symmetrical about 4.5.

    b.   Descriptive statistics: time:

Variable	Mean	Minimum	Median	Maximum	Mode	N for Mode
time	4.500	1.000	4.500	8.000	4, 5	4

Note that mean = median.

Measures of Central Tendency and Statistical Software

13. *Kurtosis* is the degree of peakedness of a distribution, usually taken relative to a normal distribution. The kurtosis is positive for a distribution with a high peak, negative for a flat-topped distribution, and zero for a normal distribution. The *skewness* measure is positive for a distribution that is skewed to the right, negative for a distribution that is skewed to the left, and 0 if there is no skew. Find the *kurtosis* and *skewness* of the data shown in Figure 3.12 using MINITAB.

    Solution

    The data in Figure 3.12 is placed into column C1. Using only the descriptive statistics pull-down and choosing the options only for kurtosis and skewness we get the following measures.

    Descriptive Statistics: time

Variable	Skewness	Kurtosis
time	0.00	−0.53

    The data has no skewness and therefore the skewness measure is 0. The −0.53 value means the distribution tends to be less peaked than the normal.

14. *Kurtosis* is the degree of peakedness of a distribution, usually taken relative to a normal distribution. The kurtosis is positive for a distribution with a high peak, negative for a flat-topped distribution, and zero for a normal distribution. The *skewness* measure is positive for a distribution that is skewed to the right and negative for a distribution that is skewed to the left. Find the *kurtosis* and *skewness* of the data shown in Figure 3.10 using EXCEL.

    Solution

    If the data in Figure 3.10 is placed in A1:A20 of an EXCEL worksheet, the command =SKEW(A1:A20) gives −5.19403E-17 which is 0 for all practical purposes. This means there is no skewness to the distribution. The command =KURT(A1:A20) gives −1.224 which means this distribution is much flatter than the one for which data are given in Figure 3.12.

15. *Kurtosis* is the degree of peakedness of a distribution, usually taken relative to a normal distribution. The kurtosis is positive for a distribution with a high peak, negative for a flat-topped distribution, and zero for a normal distribution. The *skewness* measure is positive for a distribution that is skewed to the right and negative for a distribution that is skewed to the left. Find the *kurtosis* and *skewness* of the data shown in Figure 3.11 using SPSS.

Solution

The skewness measure is −0.727 and the kurtosis measure is −0.120. The skewness tells us that the distribution is skewed to the left. The −0.120 tells us that the distribution is not as peaked as a normal distribution.

Statistics

time

N	Valid	20
	Missing	0
Skewness		−0.727
Std. Error of Skewness		0.512
Kurtosis		−0.120
Std. Error of Kurtosis		0.992

16. *Kurtosis* is the degree of peakedness of a distribution, usually taken relative to a normal distribution. The kurtosis is positive for a distribution with a high peak, negative for a flat-topped distribution, and zero for a normal distribution. The *skewness* measure is positive for a distribution that is skewed to the right and negative for a distribution that is skewed to the left. Find the *kurtosis* and *skewness* of the data shown in Figure 3.9 using STATISTIX.

Solution

STATISTIX gives 0.6712 for the skewness for the right skewed distribution. It gives -0.3779 for the kurtosis. This tells us this distribution is not as peaked as the normal.

```
Statistix 8.1

Descriptive Statistics

Variable      Skew        Kurtosis
time        0.6712       -0.3779
```

17. Before working Problem 17, it is recommended that the student work Problems 13 through 16. Looking at the data represented in Figure 3.13, one would guess that the skewness is 0 because the distribution is not skewed. One would also guess that the kurtosis value would be positive and quite a bit larger than 0, because this distribution has a much steeper peak than the normal distribution shown in Figure 3.5. Use MINITAB, EXCEL, and SPSS to find skewness and kurtosis.

Solution

MINITAB
Descriptive Statistics: time
```
 Variable    Skewness    Kurtosis
 time          0.00        2.98
```
EXCEL
=SKEW(A2:A21) = 0
=KURT(A2:A21) = 2.98
SPSS

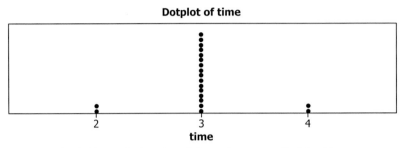

Statistics

time

N	Valid	20
	Missing	0
Skewness		0.000
Std. Error of Skewness		0.512
Kurtosis		2.980
Std. Error of Kurtosis		0.992

Dotplot of time

time

Figure 3.13 MINITAB dot plot of times for rats to find food in a maze.

SUPPLEMENTARY PROBLEMS

Mean, Median, and Mode

18. Give the central measure (mean, median, and mode) that you think would be most representative for each of the following sets of data.

     a.   Incomes of all individuals who have acted in films in the past year.

     b.   Heights of adult females.

     c.   A data set consisting of the class (freshman, sophomore, junior, or senior) to which each person belongs in Beginning Psychology at Midwestern University.

19. Find the minimum, the maximum, the sum, and the mean of the uric acid levels of seniors over 70 in the following data:

     7.0 7.3 7.1 6.9 6.5 6.9 7.1 7.0 7.4 6.9 7.0 7.0 7.3 6.8 6.6 7.4
     7.0 7.4 6.7 7.1 7.2 6.8 7.0 6.8 6.9 6.9 6.4 6.9 6.8 6.9 7.6 6.9
     6.7 6.8 7.0 7.3 6.6 6.6 7.0 6.8

20. Sort the data in Problem 19; give the 20th and 21st values in the sorted array and give the median uric acid level.

21. Give the frequency distribution of the uric acid readings in Problem 19 and pick out the mode of the uric acid readings.

22. The following are systolic blood pressures in individuals having borderline high blood pressure. They are involved in a psychological experiment to see if transcendental meditation can reduce elevated blood pressures.

     155   152   154   148   149   152   160   159   133   166   144   164
     152   140   158   161   145   159   154   145   147   142   155   160
     161   153   126   149   158   143   155   146   144   160   158   143
     134   147   153   147   138   145   150   148   149   139   150   139
     144   153   158   168   138   152   140   161   136   131   149   164
     153   148   163   145   143   148   144   153   145   145   158   139
     151

     Find the minimum, the maximum, the sum, and the mean systolic blood pressure for the group.

23. Sort the data in Problem 22; give the 37th value in the sorted array and give the median uric acid level.

24. Give the frequency distribution of the systolic blood pressure readings in Problem 22 and pick out the mode of the systolic blood pressure readings from the frequency values.

Choosing the Correct Measure of Central Tendency

25. The following are the salaries of the Kansas City Royals baseball players for the 2007 season from the web site sports.espn.go.com/mlb/teams/salaries?team=kan.

7400000	5000000	4000000	2000000	2000000
1800000	1250000	712500	625000	550000
500000	440000	423000	422000	417000
416000	407000	400500	392500	382500
380000	380000	380000	380000	380000

Find the mean and median salary. Which is the more typical salary?

26. Suppose the onset symptoms of 200 juvenile diabetics were listed with the following results. Many juvenile diabetics exhibited more than one of the symptoms.

  a. Give the modal symptom.

  b. What measure of central tendency might you give as a symptom of diabetes?

TABLE 3.5 Symptoms Exhibited by Juvenile Diabetics

SYMPTOM	PERCENT EXHIBITING
Frequent Urination	80
Numbness in arms	75
Extreme thirst	90
Extreme hunger	75
Weight Loss	60
Blurred vision	55
Extreme Fatigue	40
Diabetic coma	15

Central Tendency Measures and Their Relationship to the Shape of the Distribution

27. Suppose a data set consisting of stress test scores are all bunched together with only a few of the scores extremely high. Which of the measures of central tendency is the least appropriate to use?

28. You are reading a research paper about a group of criminals that have committed murder and you come across the statement that the hostility scores made by the group have a mean, a median, and a mode that are roughly equal. What do you know about the shape of the distribution of the hostility scores?

29. (*True or False*) A set of data has a mean, median, and mode that are very close to each other. Furthermore, the skewness and kurtosis measures given by software are both close to 0. You may conclude that the data are likely from a normal distribution.

30. An article in the July 2007 issue of the journal *Neuropsychology* pointed out that, in many cases, tests used to diagnose learning disability, progressive brain disease, or impairment from head injury need to be given more than one time to get an accurate measure of a person's mental functioning. Suppose a test used to diagnose learning disability is given 10 times to J. Doe with the scores shown in the SPSS dot plot in Figure 3.14. What measure of central tendency would you use?

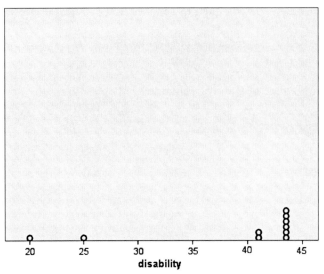

Figure 3.14 Learning disability scores for J. Doe.

31. Refer to Problem 30. Suppose the learning disability scores were as shown in Figure 3.15. What measure of central tendency would you use?

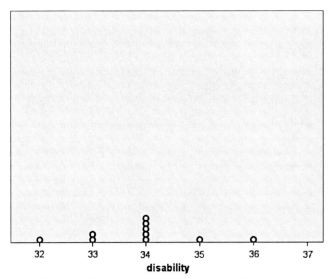

Figure 3.15 Learning disability scores for J. Doe.

32. Refer to Problem 30. Suppose the learning disability scores were as shown in Figure 3.16. What measure of central tendency would you use?

Measures of Central Tendency and Statistical Software

33. Find all the descriptive statistics given by MINITAB for the data in Table 3.6.

34. Find all the measures of central tendency given by SPSS for the data in Table 3.6.

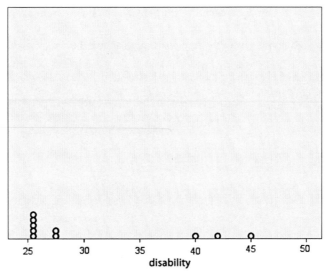

Figure 3.16 Learning disability scores for J. Doe

TABLE **3.6 Response Times of Rats in a Psychology Laboratory**

5.26	5.87	4.16	5.18	4.24	4.42
5.61	5.08	4.15	5.14	5.78	3.40
4.74	4.55	5.11	4.27	4.67	4.34
5.22	4.69	5.70	5.73	5.25	4.50
4.79	5.55	4.75	4.95	5.11	5.88
4.42	5.03	4.31	4.29	5.46	5.21
5.27	5.23	5.16	4.06	5.39	3.97
5.26	4.82	4.44	4.48	5.08	5.14
4.92	5.55	5.85	5.80	5.34	5.72

35. Find the descriptive statistics given by STATISTIX for the data in Table 3.6.

36. Find the descriptive statistics given by EXCEL for the data in Table 3.6.

Odds and Ends

37. The distribution of exercise times for a group of persons being studied for stress reduction by a psychologist has a normal distribution with mean 300 minutes. Find the median, mode, skewness, and kurtosis measures for the distribution.

38. Rarely, a psychological researcher may encounter a measure of central tendency called the *harmonic mean*. Suppose the researcher has a set of data: $X_1, X_2, \ldots, X_n$. The *harmonic mean* is defined to be

$H = \dfrac{n}{\Sigma \dfrac{1}{X}}$. Use EXCEL to find the *harmonic mean* of the response times in Table 3.6.

39. Rarely, a psychological researcher may encounter a measure of central tendency called the *geometric mean*. Suppose the researcher has a set of data: $X_1, X_2, \ldots, X_n$. The *geometric mean* is defined to be $G = \sqrt[n]{X_1 X_2 \cdots X_n}$. Use EXCEL to find the *geometric mean* of the response times in Table 3.6.

40. The following inequality may be shown algebraically to be true. (If you feel like your algebra is extremely good, try it.) Show that it holds for the data in Table 3.6.

$$H \leq G \leq M$$

Variability

Range

One of the simplest measures of variability is the *range*. The *range* is the largest value in a data set minus the smallest value or *maximum – minimum*. It has the drawback of involving only two values and does not involve the remaining numbers in the data set.

EXAMPLE 1 A study involving the use of cell phones by 21 college students was conducted. Twenty-one students were asked the number of hours per week they spent talking on a cell phone. Consider the three different sets of data for such a study as shown by the dot plots in Figure 4.1: Set 1 is spread from 0 to 20 at 1 hour intervals. Set 2 has 0, 4 with a frequency of three, 8 with a frequency of three, 10 with a frequency of seven, 12 with a frequency of three, 16 with a frequency of three, and one 20. Set 3 has 0, 8 with a frequency of four, 10 with a frequency of eleven, 12 with a frequency of four, and one 20. The dispersion or variability is decreasing from set 1 to set 3.

Dotplot of Dataset 1, Dataset 2, Dataset 3

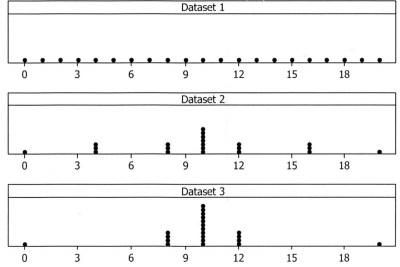

Figure 4.1 Comparing the variability of three different data sets.

The range is $20 - 0 = 20$ in all three cases but the variability is obviously not the same.

Variance and Standard Deviation of Samples and Populations

A measure of variation that involves every point in the data set is the *variance* and *standard deviation*. These measures look at the variability of the data points about the mean. The mean for each of the data sets in

Figure 4.1 is 10. Figure 4.2 shows the three data sets in Figure 4.1, the *deviations about the mean* and the *squares of the deviations about the mean* in an EXCEL worksheet. Columns A, B, and C are concerned with data set 1. The data are shown in A2:A22. Column B shows the *deviations about the mean*. The entry =A2−10 is entered into B2 and a click-and-drag from B2 to B22 calculates the deviations from the mean. In B23 the expression =SUM(B2:B22) gives the *sum of the deviations about the mean*. It is seen that the sum of the deviations about the mean is 0. This is always the case. The deviations about the mean are squared in column C. The expression =B2^2 is entered into C2 and a click-and-drag is performed from C2 to C22. In C23 the expression =SUM(C2:C22) gives the *sum of the squares of the deviations about the mean*.

Microsoft Excel - Book1

File Edit View Insert Format Tools Data Window Help

R14

	A	B	C	D	E	F	G	H	I	J	K	L
1	X	X - M	(X - M)^2		X	X - M	(X - M)^2		X	X - M	(X - M)^2	
2	0	-10	100		0	-10	100		0	-10	100	
3	1	-9	81		4	-6	36		8	-2	4	
4	2	-8	64		4	-6	36		8	-2	4	
5	3	-7	49		4	-6	36		8	-2	4	
6	4	-6	36		8	-2	4		8	-2	4	
7	5	-5	25		8	-2	4		10	0	0	
8	6	-4	16		8	-2	4		10	0	0	
9	7	-3	9		10	0	0		10	0	0	
10	8	-2	4		10	0	0		10	0	0	
11	9	-1	1		10	0	0		10	0	0	
12	10	0	0		10	0	0		10	0	0	
13	11	1	1		10	0	0		10	0	0	
14	12	2	4		10	0	0		10	0	0	
15	13	3	9		10	0	0		10	0	0	
16	14	4	16		12	2	4		10	0	0	
17	15	5	25		12	2	4		10	0	0	
18	16	6	36		12	2	4		12	2	4	
19	17	7	49		16	6	36		12	2	4	
20	18	8	64		16	6	36		12	2	4	
21	19	9	81		16	6	36		12	2	4	
22	20	10	100		20	10	100		20	10	100	
23		0	770			0	440			0	232	
24			38.5				22				11.6	
25			6.204837				4.690416				3.405877	
26												

Figure 4.2 Deviations about the mean (*M*) and deviations about *M* squared.

The sample variance is calculated in C24 by =C23/20 and the sample standard deviation is computed in C25 by =SQRT(C24). The same procedure is performed for data set 2 in columns E, F, and G, and for data set 3 in columns I, J, and K. Summarizing, the variance of a set of sample data consisting of *n* observations is represented by $S^2 = \dfrac{\Sigma(X - M)^2}{n - 1}$ and the standard deviation is given by $S = \sqrt{\dfrac{\Sigma(X - M)^2}{(n - 1)}}$. If the data are considered a population, the variance is represented by σ^2 and the standard deviation is represented by σ. The only difference in calculations is that division is by *N*, the population size, rather than (*n* − 1), one less than the sample size. Summarizing, the population variance is $\sigma^2 = \dfrac{\Sigma(X - \mu)^2}{N}$ and the population standard deviation is $\sigma = \sqrt{\dfrac{\Sigma(X - \mu)^2}{N}}$. The EXCEL worksheet in Figure 4.2 shows how to carry out the formula for S^2 and S. Note that, when comparing Figures 4.1 and 4.2, the following is clear: **The greater the dispersion in the data, the larger the computed value of variance or standard deviation.**

There exist built-in routines for calculating variance and standard deviation. In Figure 4.3, data set 1 is entered in A2:A22, data set 2 is entered into C2:C22, and data set 3 is entered into E2:E22. Then =VAR(A2:A22) in A24 gives S^2 for data set 1, =STDEV(A2:A22) in A25 gives S for data set 1, =VARP(A2:A22) in A28 gives σ^2 if the data are considered a population, and =STDEVP(A2:A22) in A29 gives σ. The figure shows similar computations for the other two data sets. The answers in Figure 4.3 are the same as found in Figure 4.2.

	A	B	C	D	E	F
1	X		X		X	
2	0		0		0	
3	1		4		8	
4	2		4		8	
5	3		4		8	
6	4		8		8	
7	5		8		10	
8	6		8		10	
9	7		10		10	
10	8		10		10	
11	9		10		10	
12	10		10		10	
13	11		10		10	
14	12		10		10	
15	13		10		10	
16	14		12		10	
17	15		12		10	
18	16		12		12	
19	17		16		12	
20	18		16		12	
21	19		16		12	
22	20		20		20	
23						
24	38.5		22		11.6	
25	6.204837		4.690416		3.405877	
26						
27						
28	36.66667		20.95238		11.04762	
29	6.055301		4.577377		3.323796	
30						

Figure 4.3 Using EXCEL Built-in routines to find S^2, S, σ^2, and σ.

Alternate Formula for Variance and Standard Deviation

It can be shown algebraically that $S^2 = \dfrac{\Sigma(X-M)^2}{n-1}$ may be also expressed as follows:

$$S^2 = \frac{\Sigma X^2 - \dfrac{(\Sigma X)^2}{n}}{(n-1)} \text{ and that } \sigma^2 = \frac{\Sigma X^2 - \dfrac{(\Sigma X)^2}{n}}{N}.$$ This has been called the *computing* or *short cut form*

of the formula for the variance. It is the preferable form to use if the student is finding the variance of a set of messy data having many decimal values on a hand-held calculator. Today, psychologists usually use software to find the variance of a set of data.

EXAMPLE 2 Find the variance and standard deviation of data set 1 in Figure 4.1, first treating the data as a sample and next treating it as a population. The computation is shown in Figure 4.4. Enter the data from data set 1 in A2:A22. The sum of the X values are computed in A24 by using =SUM(A2:A22). This gives 210. The sum of the X values squared are found by entering =A2^2 into B2 and performing a click-and-drag from B2 to B22. The sum of the X^2 values are found by using =SUM(B2:B22) in B24. At this point ΣX is in A24 and ΣX^2 is in B24.

The sample variance $S^2 = \dfrac{\Sigma X^2 - \dfrac{(\Sigma X)^2}{n}}{(n-1)}$ is computed by entering =(B24–A24^2/21)/20 into D3. We see that the sample variance is 38.5. The sample standard deviation is found by entering =SQRT(D3) into E3. We see that the sample standard deviation is 6.2048.

The population variance $\sigma^2 = \dfrac{\Sigma X^2 - \dfrac{(\Sigma X)^2}{N}}{N}$ is computed by entering =(B24–A24^2/21)/21 into D6. The population variance is 36.67. The population standard deviation is found by entering =SQRT(D6) in E6. The population standard deviation is 6.0553.

The variance and the standard deviation may be found using either of the two formulas. As stated before, psychologist usually use computer software to find the variance and standard deviation today, and the computing formula is not as relevant as it once was.

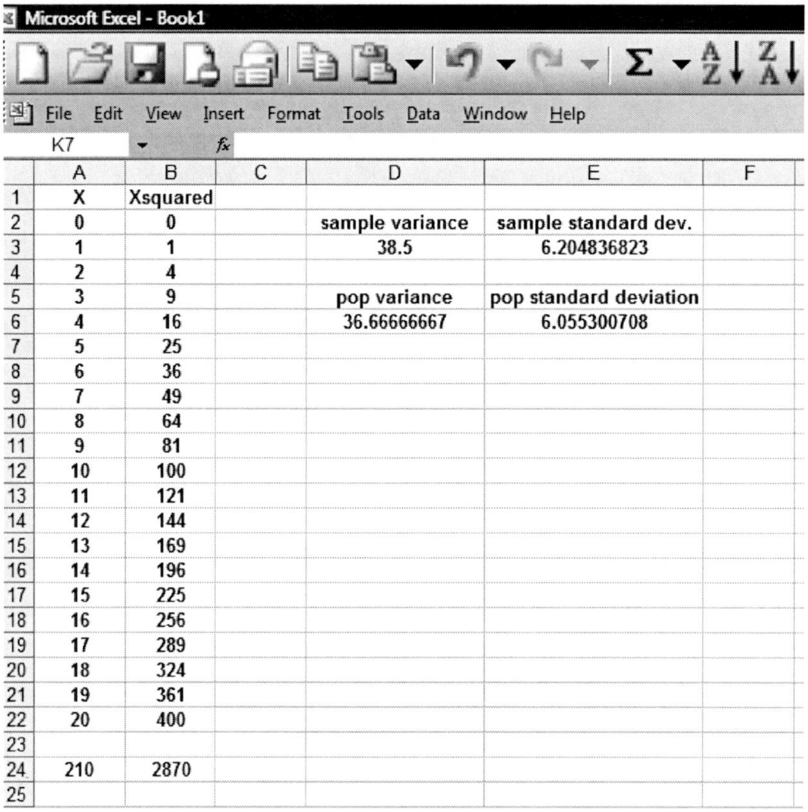

	A	B	C	D	E	F
1	X	Xsquared				
2	0	0		sample variance	sample standard dev.	
3	1	1		38.5	6.204836823	
4	2	4				
5	3	9		pop variance	pop standard deviation	
6	4	16		36.66666667	6.055300708	
7	5	25				
8	6	36				
9	7	49				
10	8	64				
11	9	81				
12	10	100				
13	11	121				
14	12	144				
15	13	169				
16	14	196				
17	15	225				
18	16	256				
19	17	289				
20	18	324				
21	19	361				
22	20	400				
23						
24	210	2870				
25						

Figure 4.4 Calculating variance/standard deviation using the shortcut formula.

Properties of the Variance and the Standard Deviation

Some properties of the variance and standard deviation will now be given and then illustrated with examples.

1. The variance and standard deviation is 0 for a data set consisting of the same constant value.

2. Adding or subtracting a constant value from the values in a data set does not change the variance or standard deviation of the original data.

3. Multiplying each value by a constant multiplies the variance by the square of the constant and the standard deviation by the constant.

4. Chebyshev's theorem states that at least $\left(1-\dfrac{1}{k^2}\right)100\%$ of the data is between $\mu - k\sigma$ and $\mu + k\sigma$. If $k = 2$, then at least 75% of the data is between $\mu - 2\sigma$ and $\mu + 2\sigma$. If $k = 3$, then at least 89% of the data is between $\mu - 3\sigma$ and $\mu + 3\sigma$.

EXAMPLE 3 Figure 4.5 is an EXCEL illustration of the properties of the variance and standard deviation of a data set. Data set 1 consists of the constant value (1) in A2:A11. The variance is given by =VARP(A2:A11) in A13 and is 0. The standard deviation is given by =STDEVP(A2:A11) in A14 and is 0.

	A	B	C	D	E
	data set 1	data set 2	data set 3	data set 4	
1					
2	1	1	11	10	
3	1	3	13	30	
4	1	5	15	50	
5	1	7	17	70	
6	1	5	15	50	
7	1	10	20	100	
8	1	9	19	90	
9	1	9	19	90	
10	1	8	18	80	
11	1	11	21	110	
12					
13	0	9.36	9.36	936	
14	0	3.0594117	3.0594117	30.594117	
15					

Figure 4.5 Illustration of the properties of σ^2 and σ.

Data set 2 is a data set having $\sigma^2 = 9.36$ and $\sigma = 3.0594117$ computed in B13 and B14. Data set 3 has 10 added to each value in Data set 2. The variance is given in C13 and the standard deviation is given in C14. Note that they are not changed. Data set 4 consists of each value in data set 2 multiplied by 10. Note that for data set 4 the variance of data set 4 is 10^2 times the variance of data set 2. The standard deviation of data set 4 is 10 times the standard deviation of data set 2.

Interquartile and Semi-interquartile Range

The *interquartile range* (IQR) is defined as $Q_3 - Q_1$ and the *semi-interquartile range* is defined as $\dfrac{1}{2}(Q_3 - Q_1)$. The box plots for the data sets given in Figure 4.1 are shown in Figure 4.6. The *interquartile range* for the different data sets is simply the width of the box in Figure 4.6, which equals $Q_3 - Q_1$. For data set 1, the width of the box is 15.5 – 4.5 = 11.0 units; for data set 2, the width of the box is 12 – 8 = 4 units; and for data set 3, the width of the box = 11 – 9 = 2. The semi-interquartile range for data set 1 is 5.5, for data set 2 the semi-interquartile range is 2, and for data set 3 the semi-interquartile range = 1. In this example, the *semi-interquartile* range is the distance from the line in the center of the box to either side of the box.

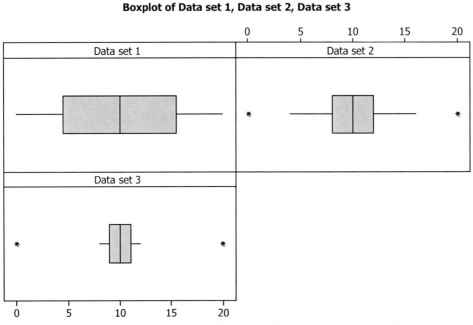

Boxplot of Data set 1, Data set 2, Data set 3

Figure 4.6 Graphical comparison of interquartile and semi-interquartile range.

The interquartile range is simply the spread of the middle 50% of the data and the semi-interquartile range is one-half the spread of the middle 50% of the data.

Mean Deviation

The *mean deviation* is defined as the average of the absolute deviations from the mean. The *mean deviation* is found as follows: Mean deviation $= \dfrac{\Sigma |X - M|}{n}$. The bars in the formula indicate absolute value or value without the sign considered.

EXAMPLE 4 Find the mean deviation for the three data sets shown in Figure 4.1. Figure 4.7 shows the three data sets in columns A, C, and E. The expression =ABS(A2–10) in B2 computes the absolute value of the difference between the value in A2 and the mean, which is 10. A click-and-drag from B2 to B22 computes all the absolute values in the numerator of the expression for mean deviation. The expression =SUM(B2:B22)/21 in B23 computes the mean deviation. The mean deviation equals 5.238 for data set 1.

	A	B	C	D	E	F	G
1	X	|X - M|	X	|X - M|	X	|X - M|	
2	0	10	0	10	0	10	
3	1	9	4	6	8	2	
4	2	8	4	6	8	2	
5	3	7	4	6	8	2	
6	4	6	8	2	8	2	
7	5	5	8	2	10	0	
8	6	4	8	2	10	0	
9	7	3	10	0	10	0	
10	8	2	10	0	10	0	
11	9	1	10	0	10	0	
12	10	0	10	0	10	0	
13	11	1	10	0	10	0	
14	12	2	10	0	10	0	
15	13	3	10	0	10	0	
16	14	4	12	2	10	0	
17	15	5	12	2	10	0	
18	16	6	12	2	12	2	
19	17	7	16	6	12	2	
20	18	8	16	6	12	2	
21	19	9	16	6	12	2	
22	20	10	20	10	20	10	
23		5.2380952		3.2380952		1.714286	
24							

Figure 4.7 Computing the mean deviation using EXCEL.

Similarly, the mean deviation for data set 2 is 3.238 and for data set 3 is 1.714.

Comparing Measures of Variability

Figure 4.1 shows the three data sets we have been illustrating. Data set 1 is quite spread out and variable, data set 2 is less variable and less spread out, and data set 3 is the least variable of the three. In order to quantify these appearances, we introduced several measures of variability. These measures are summarized in Table 4.1. For all the measures, as the data becomes less spread out and less variable, the measures become smaller in numerical value. The most widely used of the measures given is the standard deviation.

TABLE **4.1** **Comparing Measures of Variability**

	VARIABILITY MEASURES					
	VARIANCE	STANDARD DEVIATION	RANGE	INTERQUARTILE RANGE(IQR)	SEMI-IQR	MEAN DEVIATION
Data set 1	38.5	6.2	20	11	5.5	5.3
Data set 2	22	4.7	20	4	2	3.2
Data set 3	11.6	3.4	20	2	1	1.7

Measures of Variability and Statistical Software

Today, most practitioners of statistics use statistical software to compute measures of variation and, most likely, they use EXCEL for this calculation. We shall take an example and use EXCEL, MINITAB, SPSS, and STATISTIX to obtain the various measures of variability.

EXAMPLE 5 Table 4.2 contains the response times of rats in a psychology laboratory. Find various measures of variation of the data using MINITAB, SPSS, and STATISTIX.

TABLE **4.2 Response Times of Rats in a Psychology Laboratory**

5.26	5.87	4.16	5.18	4.24	4.42
5.61	5.08	4.15	5.14	5.78	3.40
4.74	4.55	5.11	4.27	4.67	4.34
5.22	4.69	5.70	5.73	5.25	4.50
4.79	5.55	4.75	4.95	5.11	5.88
4.42	5.03	4.31	4.29	5.46	5.21
5.27	5.23	5.16	4.06	5.39	3.97
5.26	4.82	4.44	4.48	5.08	5.14
4.92	5.55	5.85	5.80	5.34	5.72

MINITAB has all the measures of variation except mean deviation. The pull-down **Stat → Basic Statistics → Display Descriptive Statistics** gives the dialog box shown in Figure 4.8. The checked routines are requested.

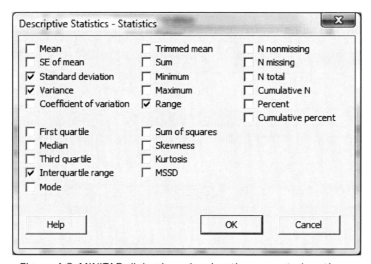

Figure 4.8 MINITAB dialog box showing the requested routines.

The following MINITAB output is produced.

Descriptive Statistics: times

```
Variable   StDev    Variance   Range    IQR
times      0.5760   0.3318     2.4800   0.8825
```

When using SPSS, enter your data in the first column of the worksheet. Then the pull-down **Analyze →** **Descriptive Statistics → Frequency** gives the dialog box shown in Figure 4.9.

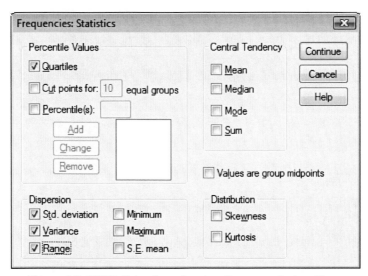

Figure 4.9 SPSS dialog box showing the requested routines.

The SPSS output is as follows:

Statistics

time

N	Valid	54
	Missing	61
Std. Deviation		0.57602
Variance		0.332
Range		2.48
Percentiles	25	4.4700
	50	5.0950
	75	5.3525

The IQR is 5.35 – 4.47 = 0.88 and the semi-IQR is 0.44. SPSS does not give the mean deviation.

When STATISTIX is used, the data are entered into the worksheet. The pull-down **Statistics → Summary** **Statistics → Descriptive Statistics** gives the dialog box shown in Figure 4.10.

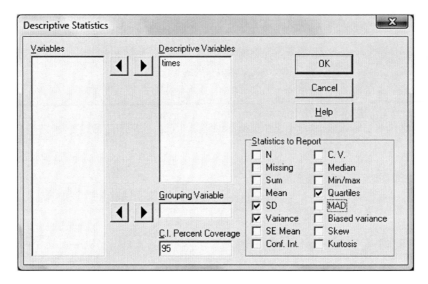

Figure 4.10 STATISTIX dialog box showing requested routines.

The following output is produced.

```
Statistix 8.1
Descriptive Statistics

Variable   SD        Variance   1st Quarti   3rd Quarti
times      0.5760    0.3318     4.4700       5.3525
```

The IQR and the semi-IQR are computable from Q_1 and Q_3. The mean deviation is not given.

SOLVED PROBLEMS

Range

1. Twenty rats are randomly divided into two groups. Reaction times, when taking drug A and drug B, are measured for experiment 1 with the results shown in Table 4.3.

TABLE **4.3** **Reaction Times for Drug A and Drug B in Experiment 1**

DRUG A	DRUG B
48	40
49	47
52	48
48	46
54	42
51	42
47	44
52	43
50	43
49	45

a. Compute the means for both groups for experiment 1.

b. Construct dot plots for both groups on the same graph for experiment 1.

c. Find the range for both drugs in experiment 1.

Solution

a. Mean for drug A group = 50, mean for drug B group = 44.

b. The dot plots for experiment 1 are shown in Figure 4.11.

c. Range for drug A group = 7, range for drug B group = 8.

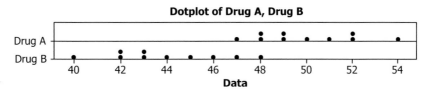

Figure 4.11 MINITAB dot plot of reaction times for drugs A and B in experiment 1.

2. Twenty rats are randomly divided into two groups. Reaction times, when taking drug A and drug B, are measured for experiment 2 with the results shown in Table 4.4.

a. Compute the means for both groups for experiment 2.

b. Construct dot plots for both groups on the same graph for experiment 2.

c. Find the range for both drugs in experiment 2.

TABLE **4.4 Reaction Times for Drug A and Drug B in Experiment 2**

DRUG A	DRUG B
68	51
49	55
57	50
45	76
43	54
68	26
55	17
52	19
22	26
41	66

Solution

a. Mean for drug A group = 50, mean for drug B group = 44.

b. The dot plots for experiment 2 are shown in Figure 4.12.

c. Range for drug A group = 46; range for drug B group = 59.

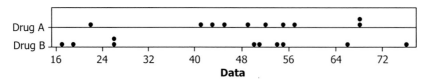

Figure 4.12 MINITAB dot plot of reaction times for Drugs A and B in experiment 2.

3. Consider Problems 1 and 2 and answer the following questions.

   a. Drug A had a mean reaction time of 50 and drug B had a mean reaction time of 44, a difference of 6 on the average for both experiments. In which of the two experiment is it clearer that the means differ?

   b. In terms of the range, what can you say about the variability?

   c. When comparing means in experiments, what effect does variability have on the comparisons?

   ### Solution

   a. The difference is much clearer in experiment 1.

   b. The variability of reaction times for drug A, as measured by the range, is 46/7 = 6.57 times greater in experiment 2 than in experiment 1. The variability of reaction times for drug B as measured by the range is 59/8 = 7.38 times greater in experiment 2 than in experiment 1.

   c. Experiments with high variability cloud the picture. It becomes much harder to compare means when the variability is high.

Variance and Standard Deviation of Samples and Populations

4. Refer to Problem 1.

   a. Construct box plots for both groups on the same graph for experiment 1.

   b. Find the variance for both drug groups for experiment 1.

   ### Solution

   a. The box plot for experiment 1 is shown in Figure 4.13.

   b. The STATISTIX output below gives the standard deviation and variance for both drug groups.

```
Statistix 8.1
```

Descriptive Statistics

Variable	N	Mean	SD	Variance
DrugA	10	50.000	2.2111	**4.8889**
DrugB	10	44.000	2.4944	**6.2222**

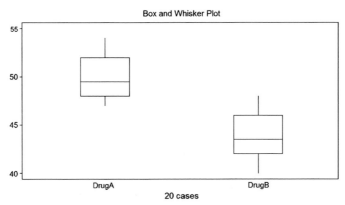

Figure 4.13 STATISTIX box plot of reaction times for drugs A and B—experiment 1.

5. Refer to Problem 2.

a. Construct box plots for both groups on the same graph for experiment 2.

b. Find the variance for both drug groups for experiment 2.

Solution

a. The box plot for experiment 2 is shown in Figure 4.14.

b. The STATISTIX output below gives the standard deviation and variance for both drug groups in experiment 2.

```
Statistix 8.1
```

Descriptive Statistics

Variable	N	Mean	SD	Variance
DrugA	10	50.000	13.606	**185.11**
DrugB	10	44.000	20.591	**424.00**

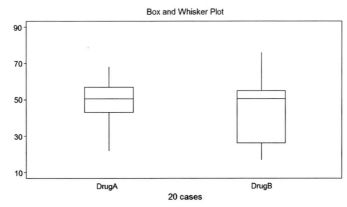

Figure 4.14 STATISTIX box plot of reaction times for drugs A and B—experiment 2.

6. Consider Problems 4 and 5 and answer the following questions.

    a. Drug A had a mean reaction time of 50 and drug B had a mean reaction time of 44, a difference of 6 on the average for both experiments. Look at the box plots for both experiments. In which case is the difference in means clear and in which case is the difference in means not so clear?

    b. In terms of the variance, what can you say about the variability?

    c. When comparing means in experiments, what effect does variability have on the comparisons?

    Solution

    a. The difference is much clearer in experiment 1.

    b. The variability of reaction times for drug A as measured by the variance is $185.11/4.89 = 37.8$ times greater in experiment 2 than in experiment 1. The variability of reaction times for drug B as measured by the variance is $424.0/6.22 = 68.2$ times greater in experiment 2 than in experiment 1. The ratio of standard deviations for drug A is $13.606/2.211 = 6.15$ and the ratio of standard deviations for drug B is $20.591/2.494 = 8.26$.

    c. Experiments with high variability cloud the picture. It becomes much harder to compare means when the variability is high.

Properties of the Variance and the Standard Deviation

7. A stress test administered to 5 policemen gave the following scores: 50, 50, 50, 50, and 50. For this sample find the range, variance, standard deviation, IQR, semi-IQR, and the mean deviation.

    Solution

    Range = maximum – minimum = $50 - 50 = 0$.

    The mean of the five scores is 50. $S^2 = \dfrac{\Sigma(X - M)^2}{n - 1} = \dfrac{\Sigma(50 - 50)^2}{n - 1} = 0$.

    The standard deviation is 0. Because $Q_1 = 50$ and $Q_3 = 50$, IQR and semi-IQR $= 0$.

    The mean deviation $= \dfrac{\Sigma|X - M|}{n} = 0$, because all the absolute deviations are 0.

    All the measures of variation are 0 for a set of data that consists of the same value.

8. A property of variance is $\text{Var}(aX + b) = a^2\text{Var}(X)$ or $\text{SD}(aX + b) = a\text{SD}(X)$. Illustrate this property with an example.

    Solution

    Enter the set of data: 10, 11, 17, 13, and 21 into EXCEL as shown in Figure 4.15.

	A	B	C
	B10		f_x
	A	B	C
1	X	2X + 5	
2	10	25	
3	11	27	
4	17	39	
5	13	31	
6	21	47	
7			
8	20.8	83.2	
9	4.560702	9.121403	
10			

Microsoft Excel – Book1 · File Edit View Insert Form

Figure 4.15 EXCEL illustration of $\text{Var}(aX + b) = a^2\text{Var}(X)$.

The values of *X* are entered into A2:A6. The values of $aX + b = 2X + 5$ are entered into B2:B6. The variance of *X* is given by =VAR(A2:A6) and is equal to 20.8 shown in A8. The variance of $2X + 5$ is given by =VAR(B2:B6) and is shown in B8. Note that $\text{Var}(2X + 5) = 2^2\text{Var}(X)$. Likewise =STDEV(A2:A6) in A9 gives SD(*X*) and =STDEV(B2:B6) in B9 gives SD($2X + 5$). Note that $\text{SD}(2X + 5) = 2\text{SD}(X)$, illustrating but not proving that $\text{Var}(aX + b) = a^2\text{Var}(x)$ and $\text{SD}(aX + b) = a\text{SD}(X)$. Note also the new notation for standard deviation and variance.

9. The Bortner instrument for measuring type A personality was given to ten individuals with the results: 40, 45, 47, 50, 51, 53, 55, 55, 58, and 60. Find the mean and standard deviation and determine what percent of the scores were within two standard deviations of the mean, and what percent were within three standard deviations of the mean. How do these percents compare with Chebyshev's theorem which says the percents must be at least 75% and 89%?

Solution

The mean is 51.40 and the standard deviation is 6.13. Two standard deviations below the mean is $51.40 - 2(6.13) = 39.14$ and two standard deviations above the mean is $51.40 + 2(6.13) = 63.66$. We see that all ten numbers fall within two standard deviations of the mean. Therefore, 100% of the data falls within two standard deviations of the mean. If we go three standard deviations on either side of the mean, this would again include all the data. So we see that at least 75% is within two and at least 89% is within three standard deviations of the mean. Remember Chebyshev's theorem gives a lower boundary on how much of the data falls within two or three standard deviations. There may be more and this is the case here.

Interquartile Range and Semi-interquartile Range

10. Find the semi-IQR for the drug A reaction times in experiment 1 (see Table 4.3 in Problem 1) and drug A reaction times in experiment 2 (see Table 4.4 in Problem 2). Use EXCEL to solve this problem.

Solution

The drug A reaction times from experiment 1 are entered into A2:A11 and the drug A reaction times from experiment 2 are entered into C2:C11 (see Figure 4.16).

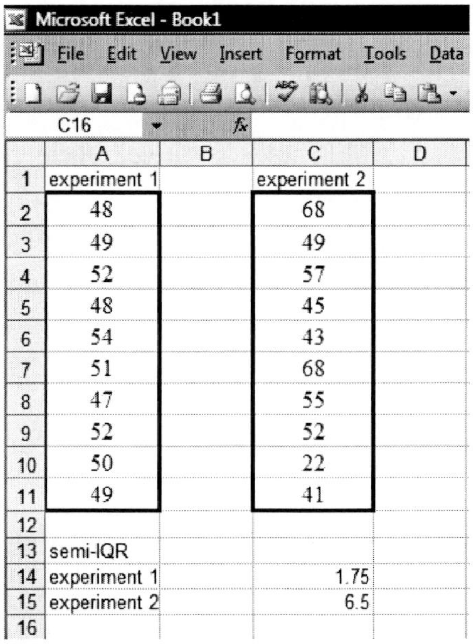

Figure 4.16 Calculating semi-IQR using EXCEL.

The semi-IQR for drug A reaction times from experiment 1 are calculated in C14 as =0.5* (PERCENTILE(A2:A11,0.75)-PERCENTILE(A2:A11,0.25)) and equals 1.75.

The semi-IQR for drug A reaction times from experiment 2 are calculated in C15 as =0.5* (PERCENTILE(C2:C11,0.75)-PERCENTILE(C2:C11,0.25)) and equals 6.5.

11. Find the semi-IQR for the drug B reaction times in experiment 1 (see Table 4.3 in Problem 1) and drug B reaction times in experiment 2 (see Table 4.4 in Problem 2). Use EXCEL to solve this problem.

Solution

The Drug B reaction times from experiment 1 are entered into A2:A11 and the drug B reaction times from experiment 2 are entered into C2:C11 (see Figure 4.17).

The semi-IQR for drug B reaction times from experiment 1 are calculated in C14 as =0.5* (PERCENTILE(A2:A11,0.75)-PERCENTILE(A2:A11,0.25)) and equals 1.75.

The semi-IQR for drug B reaction times from experiment 2 are calculated in C15 as =0.5* (PERCENTILE(C2:C11,0.75)-PERCENTILE(C2:C11,0.25)) and equals 14.375.

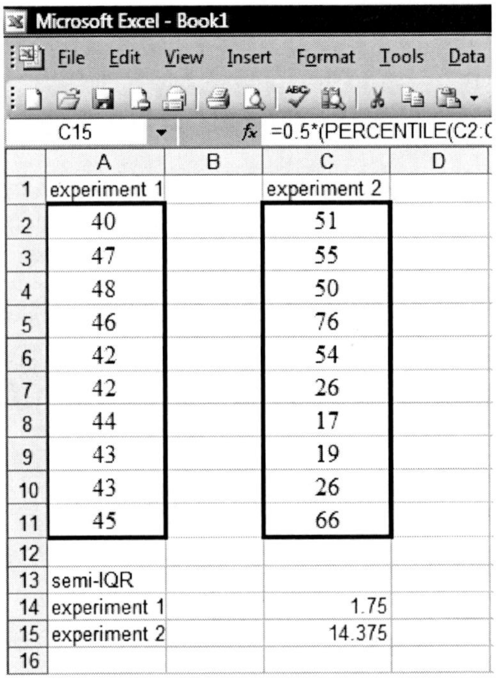

Figure 4.17 Calculating semi-IQR using EXCEL.

Measures of Variability and Statistical Software

12. A study of the psychological effect of TV on 20 children was made. One question that was asked involved the number of TVs per household. Consider the four distributions of TVs per household shown in Table 4.5 for the 20 children.

TABLE **4.5 Four Distributions of TVs per Household**

TVs PER HOUSEHOLD	DIST 1	DIST 2	DIST 3	DIST 4
1	0	4	2	3
2	0	4	4	4
3	20	4	8	6
4	0	4	4	4
5	0	4	2	3

Construct histograms for these four distributions. Rank the four distributions from 1 to 4 with respect to the variability of the distribution.

Solution

Histograms of the four distributions are shown in Figure 4.18.

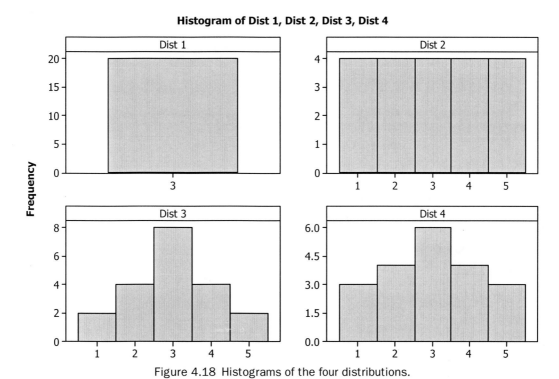

Figure 4.18 Histograms of the four distributions.

Most spread = distribution 2, next = distribution 4, next = distribution 3, least = distribution 1.

13. Use SPSS to compute the standard deviation for all four distributions to test your answer in Problem 12.

Solution

Descriptive Statistics

	N	MINIMUM	MAXIMUM	MEAN	STD. DEVIATION
Dist 1	20	3.00	3.00	3.0000	0.00000
Dist 2	20	1.00	5.00	3.0000	1.45095
Dist 3	20	1.00	5.00	3.0000	0.79472
Dist 4	20	1.00	5.00	3.0000	1.29777
Valid N (listwise)	20				

14. Construct box plots for the four distributions in Problem 12 and compare them.

Solution

Note that when IQR is used to measure the variability of the middle 50% of the distributions, there is no difference in distributions 2, 3, and 4. There is no variation in the middle 50% of the first distribution.

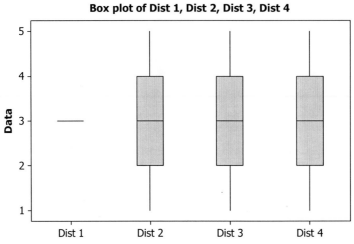

Figure 4.19 Box plots of the four distributions.

15. Use MINITAB to compute the IQR for the four distributions.

> *Solution*
>
> **Descriptive Statistics: Dist 1, Dist 2, Dist 3, Dist 4**
>
> ```
> Variable    IQR
> Dist1       0.000000
> Dist2       2.000
> Dist3       2.000
> Dist4       2.000
> ```

SUPPLEMENTARY PROBLEMS

Range

16. The number of dreams that a sample of 30 individuals reported having during a given week is shown in Table 4.6.

TABLE 4.6   **Number of Dreams Reported during a Given Week per Person**

15	6	14	18	1	19	22	15	0	7
9	2	21	1	7	5	6	23	4	3
7	13	18	15	18	7	11	23	8	16

Find the range for the data in Table 4.6.

17. A set of data on dreams reports a range of 27. If the data have a minimum number of dreams equal to 7, what is the maximum number of dreams in the data set?

18. A set of data on dreams reports a range of 17. If the data have a maximum number of dreams equal to 35, what is the minimum number of dreams in the data set?

Variance and Standard Deviation of Samples and Populations

19. A data set consisting of ten observations has $\Sigma X = 20$ and $\Sigma X^2 = 40$. What can you conclude about the standard deviation of the data?

20. For the data in Table 4.6 compute the standard deviation, first considering the data as a sample and then considering the data as a population. Then compute the percent absolute difference in S and (σ as follows: $(\sigma - S)/\sigma) \times 100\%$.

21. Use EXCEL and both forms of the sample standard deviation formula to compute the standard deviation of the following data: 10, 20, 30, 40, 50, 60, 70, 80, 90, 100.

Properties of the Variance and the Standard Deviation

22. Approximate relationships exist between certain of the measures of variation. For example, the following approximate relationship exists between the mean deviation and the standard deviation: **Mean deviation/ standard deviation** is approximately 0.8. Compute the ratio, **mean deviation/standard deviation**, for the data in Table 4.6.

23. Approximate relationships exist between certain of the measures of variation. For example, the following approximate relationship exists between the semi-interquartile range and the standard deviation: **Semi-interquartile range/standard deviation is approximately 0.67.** Compute the ratio, **semi-interquartile range/standard deviation,** for the data in Table 4.6.

24. Approximate relationships exist between certain of the measures of variation. For example, the following relationship often exists between the range and the standard deviation: **Range/6 < standard deviation < Range/4.** See if this approximate relationship holds for the data in Table 4.6.

The Interquartile and Semi-interquartile Range

25. A data set is skewed to the right. It has minimum equal to 10.5, 25th percentile equal to 15.25, median equal to 18.55, 75th percentile equal to 25.75, and maximum equal to 30.05. Find the semi-interquartile range for this set of data.

26. A large set of data has semi-interquartile range equal to 3.5. If the third quartile is 25.75, find the value of the first quartile.

Measures of Variability and Statistical Software

27. A test to determine student attitudes toward statistics is administered to senior psychology students. Low scores indicate a negative attitude toward statistics, and a high score indicates a positive attitude toward statistics. The researcher is interested not only in the mean attitude but the amount of variation in the attitude. Scores range from 20 to 100. Table 4.7 gives the attitude scores.

TABLE 4.7 Scores on Attitude Toward Statistics by Psychology Majors

59	59	72	68	55	68	48	60	51	49
53	65	73	65	53	56	58	63	60	62
60	50	71	69	65	71	67	65	63	57
60	68	67	75	58	57	54	72	74	60
45	60	65	67	70	62	46	70	71	72
57	58	57	56	63	53	58	62	48	50
52	65	66	50	64	52	66	68	64	68
57	58	68	58	60	58	60	64	56	55
63	63	58	59	62	65	54	62	61	61
55	65	64	62	71	67	57	73	65	55

a. Use SPSS to box plot the data in Table 4.7.

b. Find the mean and standard deviation of the scores.

28. a.   Use MINITAB to box plot the data in Table 4.7.

     b.   Find the mean and standard deviation of the scores.

29. a.   Use STATISTIX to box plot the data in Table 4.7.

     b.   Find the mean and standard deviation of the scores.

30. a.   Use EXCEL to histogram the data in Table 4.7

     b.   Use EXCEL to find the mean and standard deviation.

CHAPTER 5

Z-Scores

Z-Scores

A *z-score* is computed by taking an observation from a data set and subtracting from that observation the mean of the data set, and then dividing that difference by the standard deviation of the data set.

> **EXAMPLE 1** Figure 5.1 shows a data set in A2:A11, the mean of the data set in B13, and the standard deviation in B14. This is a set of test scores made in an advanced psychology course along with their z-scores.

If the observation 60 is selected from the data set, and the mean 66.3 is subtracted from the observation, we get the difference −6.3. Now divide that difference by the standard deviation 17.98796 to get the z-score −0.35. This *transformation* may be described as follows: z-score = (60 − 66.3)/17.98796 = −0.35. If this transformation is performed on each value in the data set, we get the z-scores shown in B2:B11. The z-score may be interpreted as follows: The score 60 made on the test is −0.35 standard deviations below the mean score made on the test. Similarly, the score 95 made on the test is approximately 1.6 standard deviations above the mean of the test. The computation of the z-score may be generally described as follows: For a sample, the z-score = $\dfrac{X - M}{S}$ and for a population, the z-score = $\dfrac{X - \mu}{\sigma}$.

	Microsoft Excel - Book1		
	A	B	C
1	X	Z-score	
2	75	0.483657	
3	60	-0.35023	
4	80	0.761621	
5	55	-0.6282	
6	38	-1.57327	
7	85	1.039584	
8	70	0.205693	
9	95	1.595512	
10	45	-1.18413	
11	60	-0.35023	
12			
13	M	66.3	
14	S	17.98796	
15			

Figure 5.1 Calculating z-scores using EXCEL.

EXAMPLE 2 For a dream study, the mean number of dreams per week was 15, and the standard deviation was 5. An individual in the study who had 25 dreams had a z-score of $\frac{25-15}{5} = 2$. This individual had a number of dreams that was 2 standard deviations above the mean for the group.

A *z-score* gives the location of any *raw score*, X, in the distribution of raw scores. If the sign of the z-score is positive, X is above the mean of the raw scores and if it is negative, X is below the mean of the raw scores. The numerical value of the z-score tells how many standard deviations the raw score is from the mean of the distribution.

What Effect Does Transforming the Raw Scores to Z-Scores Have on the Shape of the Distribution?

The shape of the z-score distribution will be the same as the shape of the raw score distribution. When the kurtosis and skewness are calculated, it is clear that the shapes of the two distributions are the same because these values are the same for both distributions. The MINITAB calculation of kurtosis and skewness for the two distributions in Figure 5.1 are

Descriptive Statistics: z-scores, x

```
Variable    Skewness    Kurtosis
z-scores    -0.02       -0.78
x           -0.02       -0.78
```

The two distributions are shown in Figures 5.2 and 5.3.

We say that the shape of the distribution has been preserved under the transformation z-score $= \frac{X-\mu}{\sigma}$ for a population or z-score $= \frac{X-M}{S}$ for a sample.

Dotplot of x

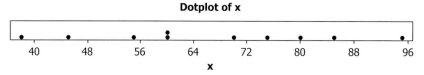

Figure 5.2 Shape of the raw scores distribution.

Dotplot of z-scores

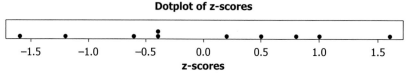

Figure 5.3 Shape of the z-scores distribution.

Mean and Standard Deviation of the Z-Scores

Suppose a set of sample data has mean equal to M and standard deviation equal to S, what are the mean and standard deviation of the z-scores = $\frac{X-M}{S}$ corresponding to the raw scores.

EXAMPLE 3 In a study, about dreams, the data shown in Table 5.1 was collected. Find the z-score for each raw score. Then, find the sum of the z-scores, the mean of the z-scores and the standard deviation of the z-scores using EXCEL.

TABLE 5.1 Number of Dreams Reported during a Given Week per Person

15	6	14	18	1	19	22	15	0	7
9	2	21	1	7	5	6	23	4	3
7	13	18	15	18	7	11	23	8	16

The data in Table 5.1 are entered into A2:A31 of an EXCEL worksheet as shown in Figure 5.4. The mean of the raw scores is found in D2 by entering =AVERAGE(A2:A31). The standard deviation of the raw scores

Microsoft Excel - Book1

File Edit View Insert Format Tools Data Window Help

Q7 fx

	A	B	C	D	E	F
1	Dreams	Z-scores				
2	15	0.540626		11.13333333	M	
3	9	-0.29828		7.152204065	S	
4	7	-0.57791				
5	6	-0.71773		4.66057E-08	mean of Z-scores	
6	2	-1.277		1.000000009	SD of Z-scores	
7	13	0.260992		1.39817E-06	Sum of Z-scores	
8	14	0.400809				
9	21	1.379528				
10	18	0.960077				
11	18	0.960077				
12	1	-1.41681				
13	15	0.540626				
14	1	-1.41681				
15	7	-0.57791				
16	18	0.960077				
17	19	1.099894				
18	5	-0.85754				
19	7	-0.57791				
20	22	1.519345				
21	6	-0.71773				
22	11	-0.01864				
23	15	0.540626				
24	23	1.659162				
25	23	1.659162				
26	0	-1.55663				
27	4	-0.99736				
28	8	-0.43809				
29	7	-0.57791				
30	3	-1.13718				
31	16	0.680443				
32						

Figure 5.4 EXCEL verification that the mean of z-scores = 0 and the standard deviation of the z-scores = 1.

is found in D3 by entering =STDEV(A2:A31). The z-scores are computed by entering =(A2–11.1333)/7.1522 into B2 and doing a click-and-drag from B2 to B31.

The expression =AVERAGE(B2:B31) in D5 computes the mean of the z-scores (0.0000000466) and the expression =STDEV(B2:B31) in D6 computes the standard deviation of the z-scores (1.000000009). The expression =SUM(B2:B31) in D7 computes the sum of the z-scores (0.0000014).

Theoretically, the following is true for both samples and populations: **The mean of the z-scores is 0, the standard deviation of the z-scores is 1, and the sum of the z-scores is 0.** The above results are off slightly due to round-off error.

Converting Z-Scores to Raw Scores

In this chapter so far, we have been concerned with having a set of raw scores and wishing to convert these to z-scores. There are occasions when we wish to do the reverse. We have a set of z-scores and we wish to convert them to raw scores. In order to accomplish this we need to solve the equation, z-score $= \dfrac{X - \mu}{\sigma}$, for X.

Simply multiply both sides of this equation by σ and then add μ to both sides. We obtain the following equation: $X = \mu + \text{z-score}\,(\sigma)$.

> **EXAMPLE 4** Suppose a population measure of IQ has a mean equal to 100 and standard deviation equal to 15 and we want to know what IQ scores correspond to z-scores of –2, –1, 1, and 2. Using the equation $X = \mu + \text{z-score}\,(\sigma)$, we find for z-score = –2, $X = 100 - 2(15) = 70$. We say that a raw score that is 2 standard deviations below the mean is 70. Similarly, a raw score that is 1 standard deviation below the mean is 85, a raw score that is 1 standard deviation above the mean is 115, and a z-score that is 2 standard deviations above the mean is 130.

Converting a Distribution with Mean = M_1 and Standard Deviation = σ_1 to a Distribution Having Mean = M_2 And Standard Deviation = σ_2

> **EXAMPLE 5** A researcher develops a new stress test that measures the stress a person is experiencing. The test has 20 questions with 5 responses to each question. For example, one of the questions is:
>
> My interaction with fellow employees at my job causes me:
>
> 1. no stress at all
> 2. very little stress
> 3. once a month I feel somewhat stressed
> 4. a moderate amount of stress daily
> 5. I am under continuous stress

The scores range from 20 to 100 when the responses to the questions are summed. The higher the score, the more stressed the person taking the test. The scores made by a sample of 25 are shown in Table 5.2.

TABLE **5.2 Raw Scores Made on a Stress Test**

39	41	34	83	30
38	54	47	58	89
88	56	40	88	61
47	40	34	38	80
35	41	74	71	44

	A	B	C	D	E
1	Testscore	Z-score		Standardized	
2	39	-0.76555		80.86128309	
3	38	-0.81659		79.58536863	
4	88	1.735244		143.3810917	
5	47	-0.35726		91.06859878	
6	35	-0.96969		75.75762525	
7	41	-0.66348		83.41311201	
8	54	0		100	
9	56	0.102073		102.5518289	
10	40	-0.71451		82.13719755	
11	41	-0.66348		83.41311201	
12	34	-1.02073		74.48171079	
13	47	-0.35726		91.06859878	
14	40	-0.71451		82.13719755	
15	34	-1.02073		74.48171079	
16	74	1.020732		125.5182892	
17	83	1.480061		137.0015194	
18	58	0.204146		105.1036578	
19	88	1.735244		143.3810917	
20	38	-0.81659		79.58536863	
21	71	0.867622		121.6905458	
22	30	-1.22488		69.37805294	
23	89	1.78628		144.6570061	
24	61	0.357256		108.9314012	
25	80	1.326951		133.173776	
26	44	-0.51037		87.24085539	
27					
28	54	M		100	
29	19.59379	S		25.00000196	
30					

Figure 5.5 Computing standardized scores with mean = 100 and standard deviation = 25.

The test designer would like the test to have a mean of 100 and a standard deviation of 25. Reassign the scores so the test has a mean of 100 and a standard deviation of 25.

The raw scores in Table 5.2 are entered in A2:A26 in Figure 5.5. The mean of the raw scores is computed in A28 and is 54. The standard deviation is computed in A29 and is 19.59379. The z-scores corresponding to the raw scores are computed in B2:B26. The z-scores are changed to *standardized scores* with a mean equal to 100 and standard deviation equal to 25 in D2:D26. The standardized scores are formed by entering =100+B2*25 into D2 and performing a click-and-drag from D2 to D26. The mean of the standardized scores is 100 and the standard deviation of the standardized scores is 25. The scores in D2:D26 are called the *standardized scores.*

Figure 5.6 and the skewness and kurtosis values below the figure confirm that the shapes of the distributions are preserved under the z transformation.

Notice that the raw score 54, the mean z-score 0, and the mean standardized score 100, all line up under one another on the graph in Figure 5.6.

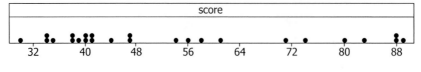

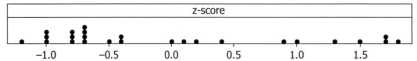

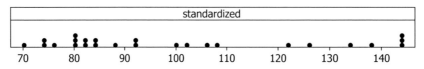

Figure 5.6 Dot plot of raw scores, z-scores, and standardized scores.

Descriptive Statistics: score, z-score, standardized score

Variable	Skewness	Kurtosis
score	0.70	-0.98
z-score	0.70	-0.98
standardized score	0.70	-0.98

The standardized scores are shown in Table 5.3. The mean of the standardized scores is 100 and the standard deviation is 25.

TABLE 5.3 Standardized Scores for the Stress Test

81	83	74	137	69
80	100	91	105	145
143	103	82	143	109
91	82	74	80	133
76	83	126	122	87

SOLVED PROBLEMS

Z-Scores

1. If $M = 15$ and $S = 3$, find the z-score corresponding to the following raw scores.
   a. $X = 21$ b. $X = 12$ c. $X = 15$

   Solution

   a. $Z = \dfrac{21 - 15}{3} = 2.00$ b. $Z = \dfrac{12 - 15}{3} = -1.00$ c. $Z = \dfrac{15 - 15}{3} = 0.00$

2. If $\mu = 70$ and $\sigma = 4$, find the z-score corresponding to the following raw scores.
   a. $X = 72$ b. $X = 60$ c. $X = 75$

   Solution

   a. $Z = \dfrac{72 - 70}{4} = 0.50$ b. $Z = \dfrac{60 - 70}{4} = -2.50$ c. $Z = \dfrac{75 - 70}{4} = 1.25$

3. Joe received a grade of 80 on an Introductory Psychology test taught by Dr. French and Jane received a 70 on a Introductory Psychology test taught by Dr. Hendricks. In terms of z-scores, which student actually scored higher? The mean and standard deviation for Dr. French's class were 75 and 10, and the mean and standard deviation for Dr. Hendricks class were 60 and 5.

Solution

Joe's z-score was $\dfrac{X - \mu}{\sigma} = \dfrac{80 - 75}{10} = 0.5$ and Jane's z-score was $\dfrac{70 - 60}{5} = 2.0$.

Jane actually scored better because she was 2 standard deviations above the mean and Joe's score was only 0.5 standard deviations above the mean. Even though Joe scored 10 points higher than Jane, Jane's score was higher in terms of z-scores.

4. A stress test is given and the mean score is reported as 100. Your score on the test was 90 and you know you were 2 standard deviations below the mean. What was the standard deviation on the stress test?

Solution

M is 100, $X = 90$, and z-score $= -2.0$. We wish to know the standard deviation. Solving the z-score equation for S, $S = \dfrac{X - M}{z - \text{score}} = \dfrac{90 - 100}{-2} = 5.$

What Effect Does Transforming the Raw Scores to Z-Scores have on the Shape of the Distribution?

5. A study of 16 adult males recorded their heights; a dot plot of their heights is given in Figure 5.7.

Dot plot of heights

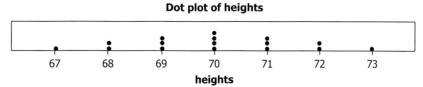

Figure 5.7 Dot plot of heights of adult males.

    a. Find the mean and standard deviation.

    b. What shape is the distribution?

Solution

    a.   The mean is 70 and the standard deviation is 1.633.

    b.   The distribution is symmetrical about 70.

6. Transform the heights to z-scores in Problem 5. Construct MINITAB dot plots for both the height distribution and their z-score distribution on the same graph. Use MINITAB to calculate the skewness and kurtosis for both the height and the z-score distributions. What effect does the transformation have on the shape of the heights distribution?

Solution

Enter the heights from Figure 5.7 into C1 of the MINITAB worksheet. Then use the pull-down **Calc →** **Calculator** and fill out the Calculator dialog box as shown in Figure 5.8. This will calculate the z-scores for the heights and put them in column C2. Then construct a dot plot for both the heights and their z-values. This gives Figure 5.9. The kurtosis and skewness output gives the same values for both dot plots.

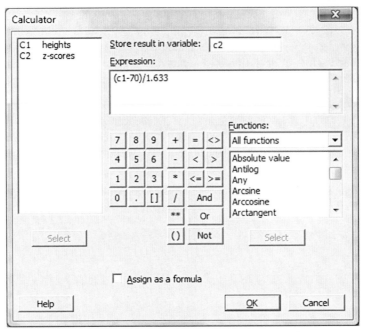

Figure 5.8 Calculating z-scores for heights using the MINITAB calculator.

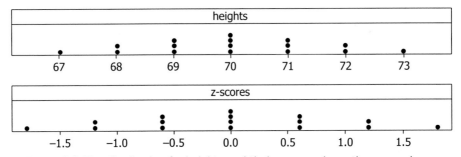

Figure 5.9 The distribution for heights and their z-scores have the same shape.

Descriptive Statistics: heights, z-scores

Variable	N	N*	Mean	StDev	Skewness	Kurtosis
heights	16	0	70.000	1.633	-0.00	-0.46
z-scores	16	0	0.000	1.000	-0.00	-0.46

7. Dr. Becker's Introductory Psychology class performed according to the *U* distribution on his first test. That is, he had a lot of low grades and a lot of high grades on the test. The dot plot of the grades is shown in Figure 5.10.

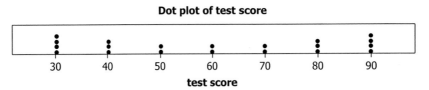

Figure 5.10 *U* distribution of test scores.

Find the mean and standard deviation of this sample.

Solution

The mean is 60 and the standard deviation is 22.94.

8. Transform the test scores to z-scores in Problem 7. Construct MINITAB dot plots for both the test score distribution and their z-score distribution on the same graph. Use MINITAB to calculate the skewness and kurtosis values for both the test scores and the z-score distributions. What effect does the transformation have on the shape of the test scores distribution?

Solution

Enter the test scores from Figure 5.10 into C1 of the MINITAB worksheet. Then use the pull-down **Calc →** **Calculator** and fill out the Calculator dialog box as shown in Figure 5.11. This will calculate the z-scores for the test scores and put them in column C2. Then construct a dot plot for both the test scores and their z-values. This gives Figure 5.12. The kurtosis and skewness output gives the same values for both dot plots.

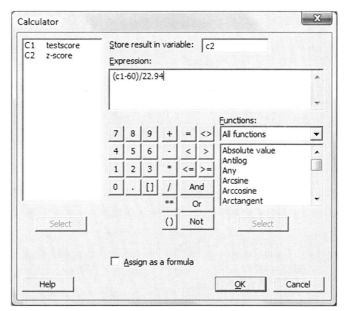

Figure 5.11 Calculating z-scores for test scores.

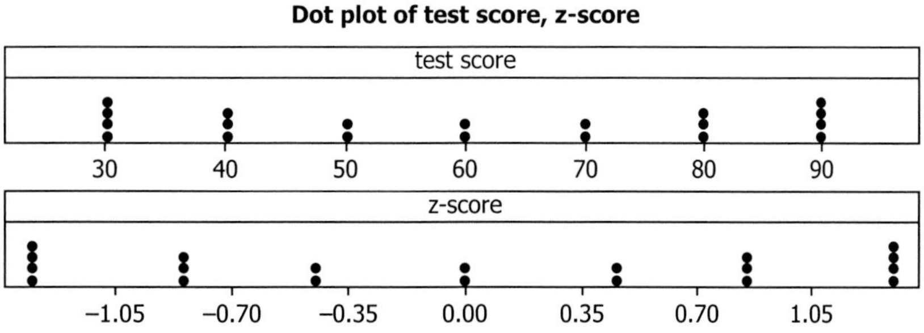

Dot plot of test score, z-score

Figure 5.12 The distributions for test scores and their z-scores have the same shape.

Descriptive Statistics: test score, z-score

Variable	Mean	StDev	Skewness	Kurtosis
testscore	60.00	22.94	-0.00	-1.59
z-score	0.000	1.000	0.00	-1.59

Mean and Standard Deviation of the Z-Scores

9. Confirm that the sum of the z-scores = 0, mean of the z-scores = 0, and the standard deviation of the z-scores = 1 for the heights in Figure 5.7 using EXCEL.

Solution

The solution is shown in Figure 5.13. The z-scores for heights are computed in B2:B17. The functions, =SUM(B2:B17), is given in D2, =AVERAGE(B2:B17) is given in D3, and =STDEV(B2:B17) in D4.

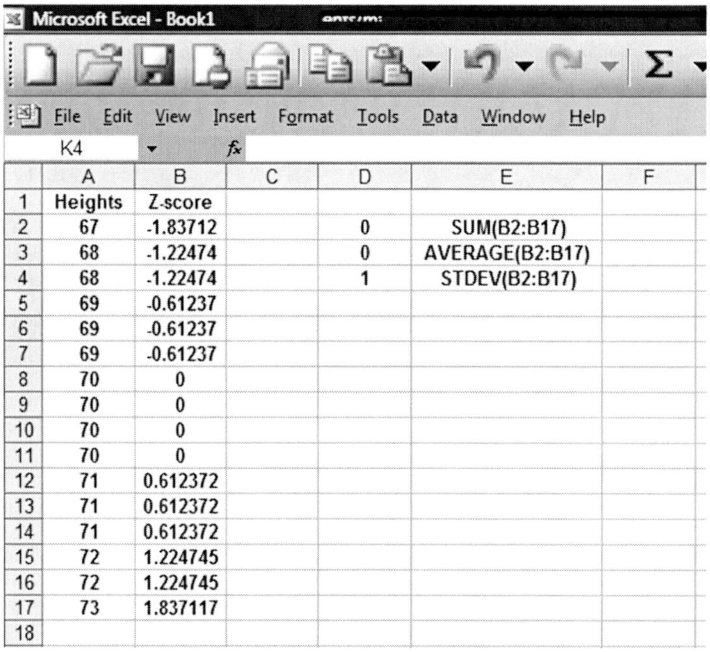

	A	B	C	D	E	F
1	Heights	Z-score				
2	67	-1.83712		0	SUM(B2:B17)	
3	68	-1.22474		0	AVERAGE(B2:B17)	
4	68	-1.22474		1	STDEV(B2:B17)	
5	69	-0.61237				
6	69	-0.61237				
7	69	-0.61237				
8	70	0				
9	70	0				
10	70	0				
11	70	0				
12	71	0.612372				
13	71	0.612372				
14	71	0.612372				
15	72	1.224745				
16	72	1.224745				
17	73	1.837117				
18						

Figure 5.13 Sum, mean, and standard deviation for z-scores of adult male heights.

10. Confirm that the sum of the z-scores = 0, mean of the z-scores = 0, and the standard deviation of the z-scores = 1 for the test scores in Figure 5.10. Use MINITAB.

Solution

The test scores and the corresponding z-scores are shown in Figure 5.14. The descriptive statistics (sum, mean, and standard deviation) for the z-scores are shown following Figure 5.14.

Descriptive Statistics: z-scores

Variable	Mean	StDev	Sum
z-scores	0.000	1.000	0.000

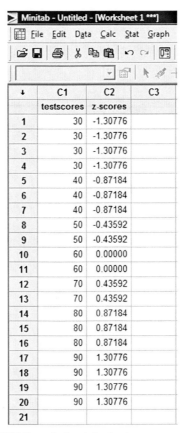

Figure 5.14 MINITAB worksheet for test scores and their z-scores.

11. The sample of stress scores in Table 5.4 have a mean equal to 100 and a standard deviation equal to 25. Use SPSS to confirm that the z-scores for the stress scores have a sum = 0, a mean = 0, and a standard deviation = 1.

TABLE **5.4** **Scores for the Stress Test**

81	83	74	137	69
80	100	91	105	145
143	103	82	143	109
91	82	74	80	133
76	83	126	122	87

Solution

Enter the stress test scores in the first column of the SPSS data sheet. Then use the pull-down **Transform →**
Compute Variable. Fill in the Compute Variable dialog box as shown in Figure 5.15.

The stress scores and their corresponding z-scores are shown in Figure 5.16. When the descriptive statistics of sum, mean, and standard deviation are requested, Figure 5.17 results. Note that the sum is not exactly 0, the mean is not exactly 0, and the standard deviation is not exactly 1. This is due to round-off error.

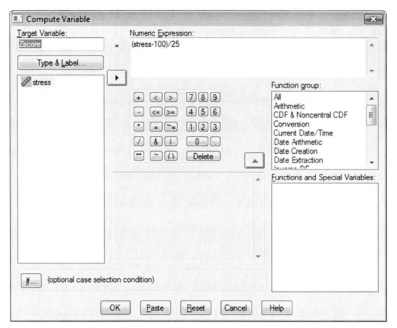

Figure 5.15 SPSS dialog box for computing z-scores from raw stress scores.

	stress	Zscore	var
1	81	-.76	
2	80	-.80	
3	143	1.72	
4	91	-.36	
5	76	-.96	
6	83	-.68	
7	100	.00	
8	103	.12	
9	82	-.72	
10	83	-.68	
11	74	-1.04	
12	91	-.36	
13	82	-.72	
14	74	-1.04	
15	126	1.04	
16	137	1.48	
17	105	.20	
18	143	1.72	
19	80	-.80	
20	122	.88	
21	69	-1.24	
22	145	1.80	
23	109	.36	
24	133	1.32	
25	87	-.52	
26			

Figure 5.16 SPSS data sheet showing stress scores and their z-scores.

Statistics

z-score

N	Valid	25
	Missing	0
Mean		−0.0016
Std. Deviation		1.00210
Sum		−0.04

Figure 5.17 SPSS output for mean, standard deviation, and sum of z-scores.

12. The sample dream data in Table 5.5 have a mean equal to 11.1333 and a standard deviation equal to 7.1522. Use STATISTIX to confirm that the z-scores for the dream data have a sum = 0, a mean = 0, and a standard deviation = 1.

TABLE 5.5 Number of Dreams Reported during a Given Week per Person

15	6	14	18	1	19	22	15	0	7
9	2	21	1	7	5	6	23	4	3
7	13	18	15	18	7	11	23	8	16

Solution

The STATISTIX dialog box requesting the z-scores is shown in Figure 5.18.

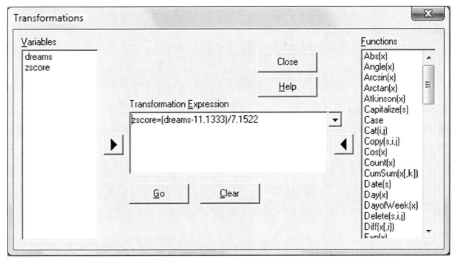

Figure 5.18 STATISTIX dialog box for transformation of dreams to z-scores.

The STATISTIX output is as follows.

```
Statistix 8.1

Descriptive Statistics

Variable     Sum            Mean           SD
dreams       334            11.133         7.1522
zscore       1.398E-04      4.661E-06      1.0000
```

The sum of the z-scores is 0.0001398, the mean of the z-scores is 0.000004661, and the standard deviation of the z-scores is 1.0000. The z-scores for the dream data have a sum = 0, a mean = 0, and a standard deviation = 1, except for rounding errors.

Converting Z-Scores to Raw Scores

13. Suppose a population measure of IQ has a mean equal to 100 and standard deviation equal to 25. What IQ scores correspond to z-scores of a. −2 b. −1, c. 1, and d. 2.

> **Solution**
>
> a. $X = \mu + \text{z-score}(\sigma) = 100 + (-2)(25) = 50$. Similarly, b. $X = 75$, c. $X = 125$, and d. $X = 150$.

14. A population has a mean $= 35$ and a standard deviation $= 4$. Find the X score corresponding to a. z-score $= -1.5$, b. z-score $= -0.5$, c. z-score $= 0.5$, and d. z-score $= 1.5$.

> **Solution**
>
> a. $X = \mu + \text{z-score}(\sigma) = 35 + (-1.5)(4) = 29$. Similarly, b. $X = 33$, c. $X = 37$, and d. $X = 41$.

15. A population has standard deviation equal to 3.3 and the observation $X = 104$ has a standard score equal to 0.75. Find the mean of the set of data.

> **Solution**
>
> Solving $X = \mu + \text{z-score}(\sigma)$ for μ gives $\mu = X - \text{z-score}(\sigma)$ or $\mu = 104 - 0.75(3.3) = 101.525$.

16. A stress test has a population mean of 100 and a population standard deviation of 20. You are told that your score on the test has a z-score that equals 2.5. What is your score on the stress test?

> **Solution**
>
> $X = \mu + \text{z-score}(\sigma) = 100 + 2.5(20) = 150$

Converting a Distribution with Mean $= \mu_1$ and Standard Deviation $= \sigma_1$ to a Distribution Having Mean $= \mu_2$ and Standard Deviation $= \sigma_2$

17. A set of scores has a mean of 93.5 and a standard deviation of 13.7. Describe in words how to convert the set of scores to a new set of scores with a mean of 75 and a standard deviation of 10.

> **Solution**
>
> Convert the original set of scores to z-scores by the transformation z-score $= (X - 93.5)/13.7$. Now convert those z-scores to a new set of scores by the transformation $X = 75 + \text{z-score}(10)$. The new set of standardized scores will have mean $= 75$ and standard deviation $= 10$.

18. A student scores 58 on a test taken by 100 psychology students; the mean of the 100 scores is 52 and the standard deviation is 6. If the instructor wishes to transform the scores so that the mean is 100 and the standard deviation is 25, what would be the new score for the student who scored 58.

> **Solution**
>
> The z-score for the student who scored 58 is $\dfrac{X - M}{S} = \dfrac{58 - 52}{6} = 1$. The student's new score on the
>
> transformed set of scores would be $X = 100 + (1)(25) = 125$.

19. Ten scores made on a Beginning Psychology test are as follows: 10, 20, 30, 40, 50, 60, 70, 80, 90, and 100. Transform these scores so that the new scores have a mean equal to 50 and a standard deviation equal to 5. Give the transformed scores to one decimal place.

> **Solution**
>
> The original scores are entered into A2:A11 in Figure 5.19. The z-scores are formed by entering =(A2−A$13)/A$14 into B2 and clicking-and-dragging from B2 to B11. Then enter =50+B2*5 into C2 and do a click-and-drag from C2 to C11. These are the new scores. Note that in the expression =(A2−A$13)/A$14, the $ character keeps the mean and the standard deviation form changing as we drag.

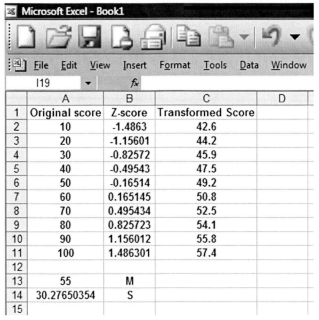

Figure 5.19 Transforming scores using EXCEL.

20. In Problem 19, show that the transformed scores have a mean of 50 and a standard deviation of 5.

Solution

In Figure 5.19, if =AVERAGE(C2:C11) is entered into any available cell and returned, 50 appears. If =STDEV(C2:C11) is entered into any other cell and returned, 5 appears.

SUPPLEMENTARY PROBLEMS

Z-Scores

21. A sample consists of 500 members and has a mean equal to 48.0 and a standard deviation equal to 6.5. Find the z-score for the observation $X = 53.7$.

22. A population has $\mu = 65.5$ and $\sigma = 3.5$. Find the z-score corresponding to $X = 60.0$.

23. Describe a z-score.

24. You are given that the mean of sample is 85, the observation is 95, and the z-score is equal to -1.0. What is wrong with the given information?

What Effect Does Transforming the Raw Scores to Z-Scores Have on the Shape of the Distribution?

25. If the kurtosis measure is -0.5 and the skewness measure is 1.0 for a sample, what is the kurtosis and skewness measure of the z-scores for the sample?

26. Find the kurtosis and skewness of the sample: 1, 2, 2, 3, 3, 3, 3, 4, 4, 5 and find the kurtosis and skewness of the z-scores for the sample.

27. If a data set has a distribution that is skewed to the right, what can you say about the distribution of the z-scores?

28. If you transform a set of z-scores to a set of observations having a mean of 10 and a standard deviation of 3, what will the relation of the measures of kurtosis and skewness be between the two sets?

Mean and Standard Deviation of the Z-Scores

29. If a sample is replaced by its z-scores, what will the sum of the z-scores be?

30. If a sample is replaced by its z-scores and the mean of all the z-scores is found, what will the mean equal?

31. If a data set is replaced by its z-scores and the standard deviation of all the z-scores is found, what will the standard deviation equal?

32. For the following sample (0.1, 0.2, 0.3, 0.4, 0.5, 0.6, 0.7, 0.8, 0.9, 1.0), the mean is 0.55 and the standard deviation is 0.302765. Find the z-scores and their mean and standard deviation.

Converting Z-Scores to Raw Scores

33. A sample has a mean of 25 and a standard deviation of 5. What observation in the data set corresponds to z-score = 0.75?

34. An observation X is chosen from a population. Find X if the z-score corresponding to X is 1.

35. An observation X is chosen from a population. Find X if the z-score corresponding to X is 0.

36. (*True or False*) $X = 0$ always corresponds to z-score = mean.

Converting a Distribution with Mean = μ_1 and Standard Deviation = σ_1 to a Distribution Having Mean = μ_2 and Standard Deviation = σ_2

37. Explain in words how any set of data having mean a and standard deviation b can be converted to a data set having mean c and standard deviation d.

38. A distribution has mean 70 and standard deviation 7.4. This distribution is to be standardized to a distribution having mean 100 and standard deviation 15. What will the scores 65 and 80 in the non-standardized system become in the standardized system?

39. A distribution has mean 50 and standard deviation 5. This distribution is to be standardized to a distribution having mean 100 and standard deviation 15. What will the scores 45 and 60 in the non-standardized system become in the standardized system?

40. Five psychology students score 40, 45, 50, 55, 100 on a senior level test. Give the scores on a standardized scale having $\mu = 100$ and $\sigma = 15$. Show the mean and standard deviation on both the non-standardized and the standardized scales.

CHAPTER 6

Elementary Probability

Experiment, Sample Space, Events, and Probability

We shall lay the groundwork for discussing the important topic of probability in this section. First, we must present some related terms and their definitions before defining what probability means. An *experiment* is defined as any procedure whose outcome cannot be predicted with certainty. Examples of experiments are rolling a die, tossing a coin, selecting a student at random from a psychology class, determining the stress level of several individuals, and so forth. The examples that we shall give will often deal with games of chance because students are familiar with them. A *sample space* is the set of possible outcomes when an experiment is performed. An *event* is a subset of the sample space.

> **EXAMPLE 1** Consider the *experiment* of rolling a balanced die (see Figure 6.1). The *sample space* consists of six faces with dots on them. The *event*, an even number turns up, consists of the faces with 2, 4, or 6 dots. Many games of chance consist of outcomes that are equally likely. In this case each of the faces with 1, 2, 3, 4, 5, or 6 dots are equally likely to turn up.

Figure 6.1 The experiment of rolling a balanced die.

If an experiment consists of n equally likely outcomes and event A consists of k of these outcomes, the *probability of event A* is defined as $P(A) = \frac{k}{n}$. The equally likely outcome definition of probability is only one of many definitions of probability. The probability that an even number turns up when the die is rolled is

$$P(A) = \frac{3}{6} = 0.5 \text{ or } 50\%.$$

EXAMPLE 2 A card is selected at random from a deck consisting of 52 cards (see Figure 6.2). The event A is the event of selecting a face card. The sample space consists of 52 outcomes and event A consists of 12 of these outcomes as shown by the gray part of Figure 6.2. The probability of event A occurring is $P(A) = \frac{12}{52} = 0.23$ or 23%. There is a 23% chance that you will select a face card when you pick a card at random from a deck of cards.

A♣	2♣	3♣	4♣	5♣	6♣	7♣	8♣	9♣	10♣	J♣	Q♣	K♣
A♦	2♦	3♦	4♦	5♦	6♦	7♦	8♦	9♦	10♦	J♦	Q♦	K♦
A♥	2♥	3♥	4♥	5♥	6♥	7♥	8♥	9♥	10♥	J♥	Q♥	K♥
A♠	2♠	3♠	4♠	5♠	6♠	7♠	8♠	9♠	10♠	J♠	Q♠	K♠

Figure 6.2 The sample space for selecting one card at random from a deck of 52.

A♣	2♣	3♣	4♣	5♣	6♣	7♣	8♣	9♣	10♣	J♣	Q♣	K♣
A♦	2♦	3♦	4♦	5♦	6♦	7♦	8♦	9♦	10♦	J♦	Q♦	K♦
A♥	2♥	3♥	4♥	5♥	6♥	7♥	8♥	9♥	10♥	J♥	Q♥	K♥
A♠	2♠	3♠	4♠	5♠	6♠	7♠	8♠	9♠	10♠	J♠	Q♠	K♠

Figure 6.3 Illustration of the *additive rule*.

The Additive Rule and Mutually Exclusive Events

Many times events are connected by **or**. It seems reasonable that we would add the probabilities of events when connected by **or**. Consider the following example.

EXAMPLE 3 A card is selected at random from a deck consisting of 52 cards (see Figure 6.3). Event A is the event that a red card is selected and event B is that a face card is selected. Event A (a red card) is represented by underlining in Figure 6.3. That is, each of the diamonds and hearts are underlined. Event B (a face card) is represented by gray shading. The probability of event A is $P(A) = \frac{26}{52}$ and the probability of event B is $P(B) = \frac{12}{52}$. The probability that the card is red or a face card is represented by $P(A \text{ or } B)$. If we count the cards that are red or a face card, we see that the probability, $P(A \text{ or } B) = \frac{32}{52}$. Notice that if we add, $P(A)$ and $P(B)$, we get $\frac{38}{52}$. We see that when $P(A)$ and $P(B)$ are added, the part that has underlining and gray shading is added twice and must be subtracted once. The part with underlining and gray shading is A and B. This example illustrates the *additive rule*.

$$P(A \text{ or } B) = P(A) + P(B) - P(A \text{ and } B)$$

Two events that have no outcomes in common are called *mutually exclusive events*. If two events are mutually exclusive, then $P(A \text{ and } B) = 0$. The *additive rule for mutually exclusive events* A and B is:

$$P(A \text{ or } B) = P(A) + P(B) - 0 = P(A) + P(B)$$

EXAMPLE 4 A card is selected at random from a deck consisting of 52 cards (see Figure 6.4). Event A is the event that a club is selected and event B is the event that a spade is selected. Elements in A are underlined and elements in event B are shaded gray. Events A and B are seen to be mutually exclusive and $P(A \text{ or } B) = P(A) + P(B) = \frac{13}{52} + \frac{13}{52}$ which equals $\frac{26}{52}$ or $\frac{1}{2}$ or 0.5.

If n events are mutually exclusive, the probability of any one of the events occurring is:

$$P(A_1 \text{ or } A_2 \text{ or } \cdots \text{ or } A_n) = P(A_1) + P(A_2) + \cdots + P(A_n)$$

A♣	2♣	3♣	4♣	5♣	6♣	7♣	8♣	9♣	10♣	J♣	Q♣	K♣
A♦	2♦	3♦	4♦	5♦	6♦	7♦	8♦	9♦	10♦	J♦	Q♦	K♦
A♥	2♥	3♥	4♥	5♥	6♥	7♥	8♥	9♥	10♥	J♥	Q♥	K♥
A♠	2♠	3♠	4♠	5♠	6♠	7♠	8♠	9♠	10♠	J♠	Q♠	K♠

Figure 6.4 Illustration of the additive rule for mutually exclusive events.

EXAMPLE 5 The probability of selecting an ace or a 10 or a queen or a king when selecting one card from a standard deck of 52 is $\frac{4}{52}+\frac{4}{52}+\frac{4}{52}+\frac{4}{52}=\frac{16}{52}$. Note that selecting an ace, selecting a 10, selecting a queen, or selecting a king are four mutually exclusive events. When we add the probabilities of the four mutually exclusive events, we obtain $\frac{16}{52}$.

A set of events are said to be *exhaustive* if the events use up the whole sample space. When a set of events are exhaustive and mutually exclusive, an interesting result occurs. Consider the following example.

EXAMPLE 6 In the experiment of rolling a die, the events $A_1 = \{a\ 1\ occurs\}$, $A_2 = \{a\ 2\ occurs\}$, ..., $A_6 = \{a\ 6\ occurs\}$ are both exhaustive and mutually exclusive. Note that $P(A_1\ or\ A_2\ or\ ...\ or\ A_6) = \frac{1}{6}+\frac{1}{6}+\frac{1}{6}+\frac{1}{6}+\frac{1}{6}+\frac{1}{6}=1$.

When a set of events are exhaustive and mutually exclusive their probabilities add to 1.

The Multiplicative Rule and Independent Events

When two events are connected by "**and**," the probability of **A and B** is written as $P(A\ and\ B)$. The formula for the probability of **A and B** is given next.

$$P(A\ and\ B) = P(A)P(B\mid A).$$

The probability $P(B\mid A)$ is read "the probability of event B given A is known to have occurred." The probability $P(B\mid A)$ is known as a *conditional probability*. It does not necessarily indicate a division of probabilities.

EXAMPLE 7 A card is selected at random from a deck consisting of 52 cards. Find the probability that the card is red and a queen. Let A be the event that the card is red and B be the event that the card is a queen. Using the formula for $P(A\ and\ B)$, we see that we need to find $P(A)$ and $P(B|A)$: $P(A) = \frac{26}{52}$ since 26 of the 52 cards are red. If we know the card was red, there are 26 red cards and 2 are queens. Therefore $P(B|A) = \frac{2}{26}$. Using the formula $P(A\ and\ B) = P(A)P(B|A) = \frac{26}{52}\frac{2}{26} = \frac{2}{52}$. We could have arrived at this result without using the formula. Two of the cards are red and a queen, namely the queen of hearts and the queen of diamonds. There are 52 outcomes all together and $P(red\ queen) = \frac{k}{n} = \frac{2}{52}$. There are times when the formula is the preferred way to work the problem.

EXAMPLE 8 There are 30 male rats and 10 female rats in a psychological experiment. Two of the 40 rats are selected at random. What is the probability that one is a male and the other is a female? The event that one is a male and the other is a female will occur if a male is selected first and then a female or if a female is selected first and then a male. We are looking for the probability of male on the first selection and a female on the second or female on the first selection and a male on the second. The probability of a male on the first selection and a female on the second is $\frac{30}{40}\frac{10}{39}$. The probability of a female on the first selection and a male on the second is $\frac{10}{40}\frac{30}{39}$. Because the two events—a male and then a female or a female then a male—are mutually exclusive we add the two $\frac{30}{40}\frac{10}{39}+\frac{30}{40}\frac{10}{39}=0.385$.

Two events, A and B, are *independent* if $P(B\mid A) = P(B)$. In this case $P(A\ and\ B) = P(A)P(B)$. In the above example, if the same rat can be selected twice, that is if we *select with replacement*, the answer would be $\frac{30}{40}\frac{10}{40}+\frac{30}{40}\frac{10}{40}=0.375$. Selecting with replacement gives independence.

If A and B are *independent events*, then

$$P(A\ and\ B) = P(A)P(B).$$

This can be extended to more than two events. If n events are independent, the probability of all the events occurring is

$$P(A_1\ and\ A_2\ and\ \cdots\ and\ A_n) = P(A_1) \times P(A_2) \times \cdots \times P(A_n)$$

EXAMPLE 9 A card is drawn from a well-shuffled deck of 52 cards. The card is replaced. This is repeated four more times. What is the probability that an ace occurred on all five draws? The probability of an ace on any draw is $\frac{4}{52}$. Because the card is replaced this probability does not change on each shuffle and draw. The event of an ace on any draw is independent of any other such event. The probability of an ace on all five draws is $\frac{4}{52}$ times itself five times or $\left(\frac{4}{52}\right)^5$ or 0.000002693. Don't look for it to happen often!

If A, B, and C are dependent events, then $P(\text{A and B and C}) = P(\text{A})P(\text{B} \mid \text{A})P(\text{C} \mid \text{A,B})$. This relationship is extendable to n events.

EXAMPLE 10 Four cards are drawn from a deck and the cards are not replaced. This is called *selection without replacement*. Find the probability that all four are aces. The probability is $\frac{4}{52} \times \frac{3}{51} \times \frac{2}{50} \times \frac{1}{49} = \frac{24}{6497400}$ or 0.000003694. Don't hold your breath while you wait for this event to occur.

Probability and the Binomial Distribution

The *binomial distribution* is widely used in statistics. It can be used when the following *binomial conditions* are present. The conditions are:

1. There is a sequence of n identical trials and, on each trial, one of two things can happen called *success* and *failure*.
2. The probabilities of success, p, and failure, q, remain constant from trial to trial and $(p + q = 1)$.
3. There is independence from trial to trial. The variable of interest is $X =$ the number of successes in the n trials. X is called a binomial variable. X can assume any of the values $0, 1, \ldots, n$.

EXAMPLE 11 A coin is tossed four times and $X =$ the number of heads to occur in the four tosses. X, is binomial and is based on four identical trials. Success is when a head appears; failure is when a tail appears on any trial. p and q are 0.5 each and remain the same trial to trial.

The probability $X = 0$ is the probability of 0 heads in 4 tosses or the probability of a tail on toss 1 and a tail on toss 2 and a tail on toss 3 and a tail on toss 4. Because of the extended multiplicative rule, the probability is $\frac{1}{2} \times \frac{1}{2} \times \frac{1}{2} \times \frac{1}{2} = \frac{1}{16}$.

The probability $X = 1$ is the probability of 1 head in 4 tosses of the coin. One head occurs if the following occurs: httt or thtt or ttht or ttth.: httt represents a head followed by a tail followed by a tail followed by a tail. The probability of htttt is $\frac{1}{2} \times \frac{1}{2} \times \frac{1}{2} \times \frac{1}{2} = \frac{1}{16}$. The four events htttt or thtt or ttht or ttth are mutually exclusive, so we add the probabilities of the four to get $\frac{1}{16} + \frac{1}{16} + \frac{1}{16} + \frac{1}{16} = \frac{4}{16} = 0.25$.

Similarly we get, using the *and/or rules*, that the probability $X = 2$ is 0.375, the probability that $X = 3$ is 0.25, and the probability that $X = 4$ is 0.0625.

EXCEL comes to our rescue once again. These probabilities can easily be computed using EXCEL without going through the excruciating mathematical details.

Figure 6.5 shows the five values that the variable may assume in A2:A6. The binomial probabilities are shown in column B. In B2 is shown the probability of 0 heads in four trials or tosses; in B3 the probability of 1 head in four trials; and so forth. In C2 through C6 is shown the binomial function that computes the binomial probabilities. The function is =BINOMIAL(x, n, p, 0 or 1). The first parameter is x, the number of heads for which the computation is being made. The second parameter, n, is the number of trials, which is 4. The third, p, is the probability of heads on any trial which is 0.5. The fourth parameter is 0 or 1. If a 0 is entered, the individual probabilities are computed. If 1 is entered, the probabilities are cumulative as you progress from 0 to 4. This will be illustrated in the next section.

	A	B	C	D
1	X	P(X = x)	EXCEL formula	
2	0	0.0625	BINOMDIST(A2,4,0.5,0)	
3	1	0.25	BINOMDIST(A3,4,0.5,0)	
4	2	0.375	BINOMDIST(A4,4,0.5,0)	
5	3	0.25	BINOMDIST(A5,4,0.5,0)	
6	4	0.0625	BINOMDIST(A6,4,0.5,0)	
7				

Figure 6.5 EXCEL computation of binomial probabilities for *X* heads in 4 tosses of a coin, where *X* = 0, 1, 2, 3, or 4.

Using Excel to Find Binomial Probabilities

In this section we will give some examples of using EXCEL to solve problems involving the binomial distribution.

EXAMPLE 12 A die is rolled five times. Give the probabilities associated with the events that the face 6 turns up 0 times, 1 time, 2 times, all the way up to all five tosses of the die results in a 6. There are five independent trials and on each trial only two things can occur: the face 6 occurs or some other face occurs. The probability $p = 1/6$ that the face 6 occurs and $q = 5/6$. q is the probability that the face 6 does not occur on any toss. Figure 6.6 shows the binomial probabilities of 0 through 5 occurrences of the face 6 on the five tosses.

The probability is 0.00012834 that the face 6 occurs on all five tosses as shown in Figure 6.7. That event can be expected to happen about 1 time out of 10,000.

	A	B	C
1	x	P(X = x)	
2	0	0.401894	
3	1	0.401874	
4	2	0.160742	
5	3	0.032147	
6	4	0.003215	
7	5	0.000129	
8			

Figure 6.6 EXCEL computation of 0 through 5 occurrences of the face 6.

Figure 6.7 The face 6 turns up on all five tosses (not very likely, but not impossible).

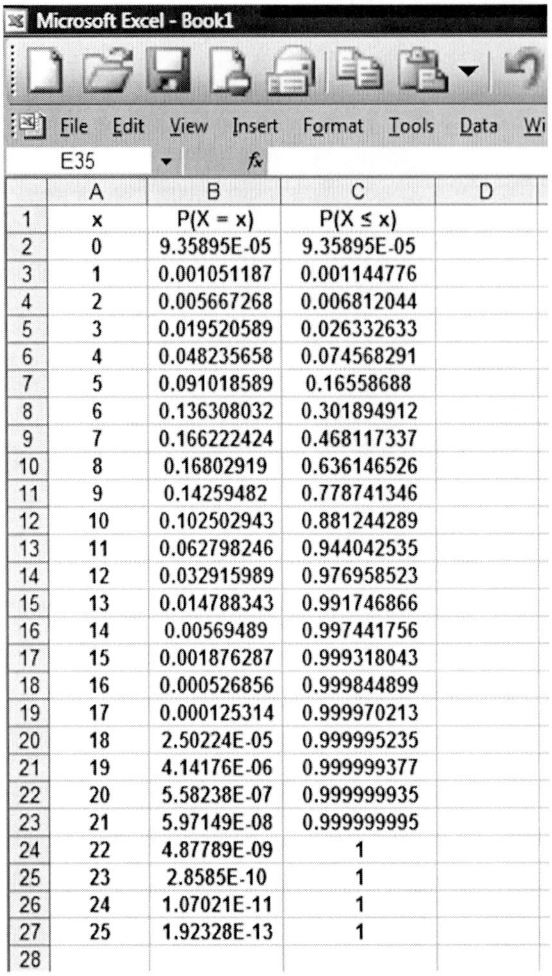

	A	B	C	D
1	x	P(X = x)	P(X ≤ x)	
2	0	9.35895E-05	9.35895E-05	
3	1	0.001051187	0.001144776	
4	2	0.005667268	0.006812044	
5	3	0.019520589	0.026332633	
6	4	0.048235658	0.074568291	
7	5	0.091018589	0.16558688	
8	6	0.136308032	0.301894912	
9	7	0.166222424	0.468117337	
10	8	0.16802919	0.636146526	
11	9	0.14259482	0.778741346	
12	10	0.102502943	0.881244289	
13	11	0.062798246	0.944042535	
14	12	0.032915989	0.976958523	
15	13	0.014788343	0.991746866	
16	14	0.00569489	0.997441756	
17	15	0.001876287	0.999318043	
18	16	0.000526856	0.999844899	
19	17	0.000125314	0.999970213	
20	18	2.50224E-05	0.999995235	
21	19	4.14176E-06	0.999999377	
22	20	5.58238E-07	0.999999935	
23	21	5.97149E-08	0.999999995	
24	22	4.87789E-09	1	
25	23	2.8585E-10	1	
26	24	1.07021E-11	1	
27	25	1.92328E-13	1	
28				

Figure 6.8 Binomial and cumulative binomial probabilities.

EXAMPLE 13 Currently 31 percent of adults have a body mass index of 30 or more and are classified as obese. A psychologist studying the psychological factors involved in obesity selects 25 adults at random. What is the probability that 10 or fewer in the sample are obese? This is a binomial probability. We are selecting 25 from the millions of adults. There is a 0.31 probability of success and a probability of 0.69 of failure on each trial. Because the numbers are so large, the probabilities of success and failure on each trial remain constant at 0.31 and 0.69. We have 25 trials and on each trial the success probability is $p = 0.31$ and the failure probability is $q = 0.69$. We want to find the probability of 10 or fewer successes in the 25 trials. To find the probability of 10 or fewer obese adults in the sample of 25, go opposite $X = 10$ under the cumulative probabilities and find 0.88124. There is a probability of 0.88124 of obtaining 10 or fewer obese adults in the sample of 25.

The possible outcomes are listed in A2:A27. That is, anywhere from none to all of the sample might be obese. The expression =BINOMDIST(A2,25,0.31,0) is entered into B2 and a click-and-drag is performed from B2 to B27. The individual binomial probabilities are generated from B2 to B27. We see that the most likely outcome is $X = 8$ with a probability equal to 0.16803. That is, you are most likely to find 8 obese adults in your sample. The cumulative probability in C12 is opposite the X value 10 in A12. The cumulative sum of the individual probabilities for 10 or fewer obese adults is the probability in C12.

Probability and the Normal Distribution Using EXCEL

The *normal probability model* for a variable centered at mean μ and having standard deviation σ is $Y = \frac{1}{\sqrt{2\pi}\sigma} e - \frac{(X-\mu)^2}{2\sigma^2}$. This is the equation of the bell-shaped curve known as the *normal curve*. If this

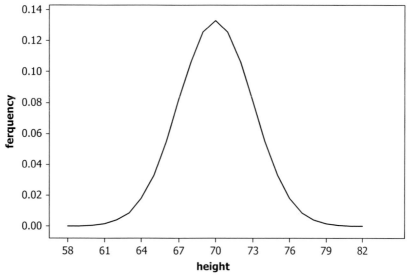

Figure 6.9 Normal curve for male heights.

model is used to describe the distribution of adult male heights, then $\mu = 70$ inches and $\sigma = 3$ inches. The curve is shown in Figure 6.9.

The percent of males with heights between 67 and 73 inches or the probability of a male height between 67 and 73 inches is represented by $(67 < X < 73)$, where X represents male height. EXCEL may be used to find the area between 67 and 73. The expression =NORMDIST(73,70,3,1) gives 0.8413, the area to the left of 73 under the curve in Figure 6.10. The expression =NORMDIST(67,70,3,1) gives the area under the normal curve in Figure 6.10 to the left of 67. The difference =NORMDIST(73,70,3,1) −NORMDIST(67,70,3,1) gives 0.6827, the area between 67 and 73 in Figure 6.10.

The event $(67 < X < 73)$ is equivalent to $\dfrac{67-70}{3} < \dfrac{X-70}{3} < \dfrac{73-70}{3}$ or $-1 < z < 1$. The expression has been converted to one involving the z-score. The probability of the event involving z is $P(-1 < z < 1)$. This probability may be found as =NORMSDIST(1) − NORMSDIST(−1) which equals 0.6827 also. Notice that

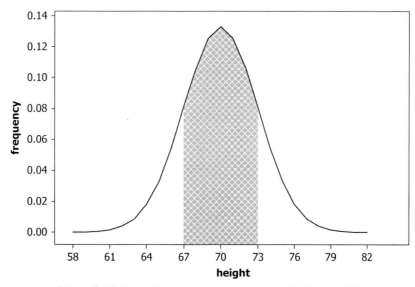

Figure 6.10 Normal curve representation of $(67 < X < 73)$.

the function NORMSDIST involves the normal with mean 0 and standard deviation equal to 1. This special normal distribution is called the *standard normal distribution*. Any normal probability may be found by converting the normal variable to a standard normal variable and then using the function NORMSDIST rather than NORMDIST. You may use either of the functions to find normal probabilities. Also, note that a 1 in the last position of the function =NORMDIST(x, μ, σ, 1) gives areas under the normal curve centered at μ to the left of x. The function =NORMDIST(x, μ, σ, 0) gives the height up to the normal curve at x and is used if you wish to plot the normal curve.

> **EXAMPLE 14** The scores for an IQ test are normally distributed with mean 100 and standard deviation 15. Find the percent below 85 and the percent above 130. We wish to find $P(X < 85)$ and $P(X > 130)$. Find the percents or probabilities using NORMDIST first and then find them using NORMSDIST of EXCEL. Figure 6.11 Shows $X < 85$ and $X > 130$. In Figure 6.12, the probability $P(X < 85)$ is found as =NORMDIST(85,100,15,1), the area to the left of 85. Also in Figure 6.12, the area to the right of 130 is =1–NORMDIST(130,100,15,1).

Because 85 is one standard deviation below the mean, and 130 is two standard deviations above the mean, we could express the probability we are seeking as $P(z < -1)$ and $P(z > 2)$. In Figure 6.12, this is found as $P(z < -1)$ = NORMSDIST(-1) and $P(z > 2) = 1 -$ NORMSDIST(2).

Remember, if you are using EXCEL to find normal probabilities, you can use either =NORMDIST (x, μ, σ, 1) or =NORMSDIST(z) where $Z = \dfrac{X - \mu}{\sigma}$. EXCEL may also be used to find percentiles for a normal distribution. The function =NORMINV(x, μ, σ, 1) or =NORMSINV(z) may be used.

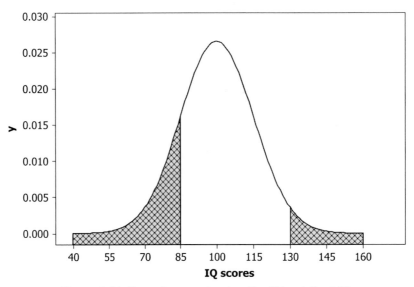

Figure 6.11 Normal curve showing $X < 85$ and $X > 130$.

	A	B	C
1	0.158655	NORMDIST(85,100,15,1)	
2	0.02275	1-NORMDIST(130,100,15,1)	
3			
4	0.158655	NORMSDIST(-1)	
5	0.02275	1-NORMSDIST(2)	
6			

Figure 6.12 Using NORMDIST and NORMSDIST to find normal probabilities.

EXAMPLE 15 The scores for an IQ test are normally distributed with mean 100 and standard deviation 15. Find the 90th percentile of the IQ scores. The expression =NORMINV(0.9,100,15) gives 119.2. This is the 90th percentile of the IQ scores. The 99th percentile would be given by =NORMINV(0.99,100,15) or 134.9. The 90th percentile of the z distribution is given by 1.2816. Note that if the 119.2 is converted to a z-score, you get

$$Z = \frac{119.2 - 100}{15} = 1.28,$$ as would be expected.

Using a Table of the Normal Distribution

Most text books in statistics still include a *table of the standard normal distribution* and include instructions on the use of such tables. We will build the table using EXCEL and include instructions on its use. We will build the following table of probabilities for the z distribution.

Our table will have four columns. The first gives the z value starting at 0.00 and going to 2.75. The second will give the proportion in the body. The third will give the proportion in the tail. The fourth will give the proportion between 0 and z. See Figures 6.13 (a), (b), and (c) for the EXCEL expression giving the shaded area.

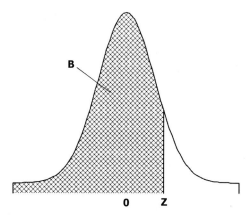

Figure 6.13 (a) B, Proportion in body, is given by =NORMSDIST(z).

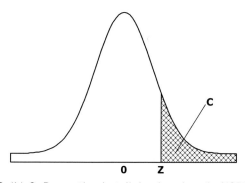

Figure 6.13 (b) C, Proportion in tail, is given by =1 –NORMSDIST(z).

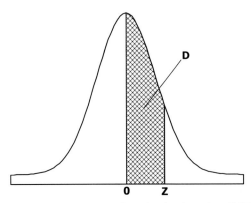

Figure 6.13 (c) D, Proportion between 0 and z, is given by =NORMSDIST(z) − 0.5.

TABLE 6.1 Standard Normal Table

z	B	C	D	z	B	C	D
0.00	0.5000	0.5000	0.0000	0.30	0.6179	0.3821	0.1179
0.01	0.5040	0.4960	0.0040	0.31	0.6217	0.3783	0.1217
0.02	0.5080	0.4920	0.0080	0.32	0.6255	0.3745	0.1255
0.03	0.5120	0.4880	0.0120	0.33	0.6293	0.3707	0.1293
0.04	0.5160	0.4840	0.0160	0.34	0.6331	0.3669	0.1331
0.05	0.5199	0.4801	0.0199	0.35	0.6368	0.3632	0.1368
0.06	0.5239	0.4761	0.0239	0.36	0.6406	0.3594	0.1406
0.07	0.5279	0.4721	0.0279	0.37	0.6443	0.3557	0.1443
0.08	0.5319	0.4681	0.0319	0.38	0.6480	0.3520	0.1480
0.09	0.5359	0.4641	0.0359	0.39	0.6517	0.3483	0.1517
0.10	0.5398	0.4602	0.0398	0.40	0.6554	0.3446	0.1554
0.11	0.5438	0.4562	0.0438	0.41	0.6591	0.3409	0.1591
0.12	0.5478	0.4522	0.0478	0.42	0.6628	0.3372	0.1628
0.13	0.5517	0.4483	0.0517	0.43	0.6664	0.3336	0.1664
0.14	0.5557	0.4443	0.0557	0.44	0.6700	0.3300	0.1700
0.15	0.5596	0.4404	0.0596	0.45	0.6736	0.3264	0.1736
0.16	0.5636	0.4364	0.0636	0.46	0.6772	0.3228	0.1772
0.17	0.5675	0.4325	0.0675	0.47	0.6808	0.3192	0.1808
0.18	0.5714	0.4286	0.0714	0.48	0.6844	0.3156	0.1844
0.19	0.5753	0.4247	0.0753	0.49	0.6879	0.3121	0.1879
0.20	0.5793	0.4207	0.0793	0.50	0.6915	0.3085	0.1915
0.21	0.5832	0.4168	0.0832	0.51	0.6950	0.3050	0.1950
0.22	0.5871	0.4129	0.0871	0.52	0.6985	0.3015	0.1985
0.23	0.5910	0.4090	0.0910	0.53	0.7019	0.2981	0.2019
0.24	0.5948	0.4052	0.0948	0.54	0.7054	0.2946	0.2054
0.25	0.5987	0.4013	0.0987	0.55	0.7088	0.2912	0.2088
0.26	0.6026	0.3974	0.1026	0.56	0.7123	0.2877	0.2123
0.27	0.6064	0.3936	0.1064	0.57	0.7157	0.2843	0.2157
0.28	0.6103	0.3897	0.1103	0.58	0.7190	0.2810	0.2190
0.29	0.6141	0.3859	0.1141	0.59	0.7224	0.2776	0.2224

(Continued)

TABLE **6.1** (***Continued***)

z	B	C	D	z	B	C	D
0.60	0.7257	0.2743	0.2257	1.14	0.8729	0.1271	0.3729
0.61	0.7291	0.2709	0.2291	1.15	0.8749	0.1251	0.3749
0.62	0.7324	0.2676	0.2324	1.16	0.8770	0.1230	0.3770
0.63	0.7357	0.2643	0.2357	1.17	0.8790	0.1210	0.3790
0.64	0.7389	0.2611	0.2389	1.18	0.8810	0.1190	0.3810
0.65	0.7422	0.2578	0.2422	1.19	0.8830	0.1170	0.3830
0.66	0.7454	0.2546	0.2454	1.20	0.8849	0.1151	0.3849
0.67	0.7486	0.2514	0.2486	1.21	0.8869	0.1131	0.3869
0.68	0.7517	0.2483	0.2517	1.22	0.8888	0.1112	0.3888
0.69	0.7549	0.2451	0.2549	1.23	0.8907	0.1093	0.3907
0.70	0.7580	0.2420	0.2580	1.24	0.8925	0.1075	0.3925
0.71	0.7611	0.2389	0.2611	1.25	0.8944	0.1056	0.3944
0.72	0.7642	0.2358	0.2642	1.26	0.8962	0.1038	0.3962
0.73	0.7673	0.2327	0.2673	1.27	0.8980	0.1020	0.3980
0.74	0.7704	0.2296	0.2704	1.28	0.8997	0.1003	0.3997
0.75	0.7734	0.2266	0.2734	1.29	0.9015	0.0985	0.4015
0.76	0.7764	0.2236	0.2764	1.30	0.9032	0.0968	0.4032
0.77	0.7794	0.2206	0.2794	1.31	0.9049	0.0951	0.4049
0.78	0.7823	0.2177	0.2823	1.32	0.9066	0.0934	0.4066
0.79	0.7852	0.2148	0.2852	1.33	0.9082	0.0918	0.4082
0.80	0.7881	0.2119	0.2881	1.34	0.9099	0.0901	0.4099
0.81	0.7910	0.2090	0.2910	1.35	0.9115	0.0885	0.4115
0.82	0.7939	0.2061	0.2939	1.36	0.9131	0.0869	0.4131
0.83	0.7967	0.2033	0.2967	1.37	0.9147	0.0853	0.4147
0.84	0.7995	0.2005	0.2995	1.38	0.9162	0.0838	0.4162
0.85	0.8023	0.1977	0.3023	1.39	0.9177	0.0823	0.4177
0.86	0.8051	0.1949	0.3051	1.40	0.9192	0.0808	0.4192
0.87	0.8078	0.1922	0.3078	1.41	0.9207	0.0793	0.4207
0.88	0.8106	0.1894	0.3106	1.42	0.9222	0.0778	0.4222
0.89	0.8133	0.1867	0.3133	1.43	0.9236	0.0764	0.4236
0.90	0.8159	0.1841	0.3159	1.44	0.9251	0.0749	0.4251
0.91	0.8186	0.1814	0.3186	1.45	0.9265	0.0735	0.4265
0.92	0.8212	0.1788	0.3212	1.46	0.9279	0.0721	0.4279
0.93	0.8238	0.1762	0.3238	1.47	0.9292	0.0708	0.4292
0.94	0.8264	0.1736	0.3264	1.48	0.9306	0.0694	0.4306
0.95	0.8289	0.1711	0.3289	1.49	0.9319	0.0681	0.4319
0.96	0.8315	0.1685	0.3315	1.50	0.9332	0.0668	0.4332
0.97	0.8340	0.1660	0.3340	1.51	0.9345	0.0655	0.4345
0.98	0.8365	0.1635	0.3365	1.52	0.9357	0.0643	0.4357
0.99	0.8389	0.1611	0.3389	1.53	0.9370	0.0630	0.4370
1.00	0.8413	0.1587	0.3413	1.54	0.9382	0.0618	0.4382
1.01	0.8438	0.1562	0.3438	1.55	0.9394	0.0606	0.4394
1.02	0.8461	0.1539	0.3461	1.56	0.9406	0.0594	0.4406
1.03	0.8485	0.1515	0.3485	1.57	0.9418	0.0582	0.4418
1.04	0.8508	0.1492	0.3508	1.58	0.9429	0.0571	0.4429
1.05	0.8531	0.1469	0.3531	1.59	0.9441	0.0559	0.4441
1.06	0.8554	0.1446	0.3554	1.60	0.9452	0.0548	0.4452
1.07	0.8577	0.1423	0.3577	1.61	0.9463	0.0537	0.4463
1.08	0.8599	0.1401	0.3599	1.62	0.9474	0.0526	0.4474
1.09	0.8621	0.1379	0.3621	1.63	0.9484	0.0516	0.4484
1.10	0.8643	0.1357	0.3643	1.64	0.9495	0.0505	0.4495
1.11	0.8665	0.1335	0.3665	1.65	0.9505	0.0495	0.4505
1.12	0.8686	0.1314	0.3686	1.66	0.9515	0.0485	0.4515
1.13	0.8708	0.1292	0.3708	1.67	0.9525	0.0475	0.4525

(*Continued*)

TABLE 6.1　(*Continued*)

z	B	C	D	z	B	C	D
1.68	0.9535	0.0465	0.4535	2.22	0.9868	0.0132	0.4868
1.69	0.9545	0.0455	0.4545	2.23	0.9871	0.0129	0.4871
1.70	0.9554	0.0446	0.4554	2.24	0.9875	0.0125	0.4875
1.71	0.9564	0.0436	0.4564	2.25	0.9878	0.0122	0.4878
1.72	0.9573	0.0427	0.4573	2.26	0.9881	0.0119	0.4881
1.73	0.9582	0.0418	0.4582	2.27	0.9884	0.0116	0.4884
1.74	0.9591	0.0409	0.4591	2.28	0.9887	0.0113	0.4887
1.75	0.9599	0.0401	0.4599	2.29	0.9890	0.0110	0.4890
1.76	0.9608	0.0392	0.4608	2.30	0.9893	0.0107	0.4893
1.77	0.9616	0.0384	0.4616	2.31	0.9896	0.0104	0.4896
1.78	0.9625	0.0375	0.4625	2.32	0.9898	0.0102	0.4898
1.79	0.9633	0.0367	0.4633	2.33	0.9901	0.0099	0.4901
1.80	0.9641	0.0359	0.4641	2.34	0.9904	0.0096	0.4904
1.81	0.9649	0.0351	0.4649	2.35	0.9906	0.0094	0.4906
1.82	0.9656	0.0344	0.4656	2.36	0.9909	0.0091	0.4909
1.83	0.9664	0.0336	0.4664	2.37	0.9911	0.0089	0.4911
1.84	0.9671	0.0329	0.4671	2.38	0.9913	0.0087	0.4913
1.85	0.9678	0.0322	0.4678	2.39	0.9916	0.0084	0.4916
1.86	0.9686	0.0314	0.4686	2.40	0.9918	0.0082	0.4918
1.87	0.9693	0.0307	0.4693	2.41	0.9920	0.0080	0.4920
1.88	0.9699	0.0301	0.4699	2.42	0.9922	0.0078	0.4922
1.89	0.9706	0.0294	0.4706	2.43	0.9925	0.0075	0.4925
1.90	0.9713	0.0287	0.4713	2.44	0.9927	0.0073	0.4927
1.91	0.9719	0.0281	0.4719	2.45	0.9929	0.0071	0.4929
1.92	0.9726	0.0274	0.4726	2.46	0.9931	0.0069	0.4931
1.93	0.9732	0.0268	0.4732	2.47	0.9932	0.0068	0.4932
1.94	0.9738	0.0262	0.4738	2.48	0.9934	0.0066	0.4934
1.95	0.9744	0.0256	0.4744	2.49	0.9936	0.0064	0.4936
1.96	0.9750	0.0250	0.4750	2.50	0.9938	0.0062	0.4938
1.97	0.9756	0.0244	0.4756	2.51	0.9940	0.0060	0.4940
1.98	0.9761	0.0239	0.4761	2.52	0.9941	0.0059	0.4941
1.99	0.9767	0.0233	0.4767	2.53	0.9943	0.0057	0.4943
2.00	0.9772	0.0228	0.4772	2.54	0.9945	0.0055	0.4945
2.01	0.9778	0.0222	0.4778	2.55	0.9946	0.0054	0.4946
2.02	0.9783	0.0217	0.4783	2.56	0.9948	0.0052	0.4948
2.03	0.9788	0.0212	0.4788	2.57	0.9949	0.0051	0.4949
2.04	0.9793	0.0207	0.4793	2.58	0.9951	0.0049	0.4951
2.05	0.9798	0.0202	0.4798	2.59	0.9952	0.0048	0.4952
2.06	0.9803	0.0197	0.4803	2.60	0.9953	0.0047	0.4953
2.07	0.9808	0.0192	0.4808	2.61	0.9955	0.0045	0.4955
2.08	0.9812	0.0188	0.4812	2.62	0.9956	0.0044	0.4956
2.09	0.9817	0.0183	0.4817	2.63	0.9957	0.0043	0.4957
2.10	0.9821	0.0179	0.4821	2.64	0.9959	0.0041	0.4959
2.11	0.9826	0.0174	0.4826	2.65	0.9960	0.0040	0.4960
2.12	0.9830	0.0170	0.4830	2.66	0.9961	0.0039	0.4961
2.13	0.9834	0.0166	0.4834	2.67	0.9962	0.0038	0.4962
2.14	0.9838	0.0162	0.4838	2.68	0.9963	0.0037	0.4963
2.15	0.9842	0.0158	0.4842	2.69	0.9964	0.0036	0.4964
2.16	0.9846	0.0154	0.4846	2.70	0.9965	0.0035	0.4965
2.17	0.9850	0.0150	0.4850	2.71	0.9966	0.0034	0.4966
2.18	0.9854	0.0146	0.4854	2.72	0.9967	0.0033	0.4967
2.19	0.9857	0.0143	0.4857	2.73	0.9968	0.0032	0.4968
2.20	0.9861	0.0139	0.4861	2.74	0.9969	0.0031	0.4969
2.21	0.9864	0.0136	0.4864	2.75	0.9970	0.0030	0.4970

Suppose we work the problems of the previous section using Table 6.1 rather than the built-in EXCEL functions.

EXAMPLE 16 The heights of adult males are normally distributed with mean equal to 70 inches and standard deviation equal to 3. Find the percentage of males who have heights between 67 and 73 inches using Table 6.1. The event $67 < X < 73$ is equivalent to $-1 < z < 1$. Suppose we use Table 6.1 to find $P(-1 < z < 1)$. From Figure 6.13(c) if $z = 1$, column D tells us that the area from 0 to 1.00 is 0.3413. By symmetry the area between -1 and 1 is $2(0.3413) = 0.6826$, the same area obtained using NORMDIST in the previous section.

EXAMPLE 17 IQ scores are normally distributed with a mean of 100 and a standard deviation of 15. Use Table 6.1 to find the percent below 85 and the percent above 130. The event $X < 85$ is equivalent to $z < -1$. Using column C of table 6.1 we see that the area to the right of 1 is the same as the area to the left of -1. Therefore we use the relationship $P(z < -1) = P(z > 1)$. From column C of Table 6.1 the answer is 0.1587. The event $X > 130$ is equivalent to $z > 2$. Using column C of Table 6.1, $P(z > 2) = 0.0228$ is the probability we are seeking.

SOLVED PROBLEMS

Experiment, Sample Space, Events, and Probability

1. A pair of dice is rolled. Give the sample space, the elements of the event that a sum of 7 is obtained, and the probability of the event that a sum of 7 is obtained.

   Solution

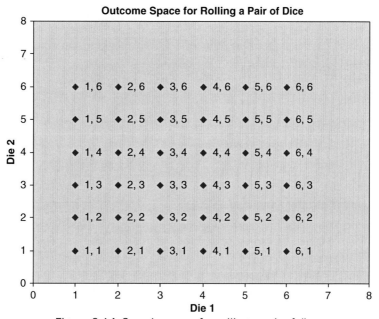

Figure 6.14 Sample space for rolling a pair of dice.

The outcome space for rolling a pair of dice is given in Figure 6.14. The elements of the event that a sum of seven is obtained are {(1,6), (2,5), (3,4), (4,3), (5,2), (6,1)}. The probability of getting a 7 when rolling a pair of dice is $6/36 = 1/6$.

2. An experiment looks at the sex distribution of the children of families having 3 children. Give the sample space of the experiment, the outcomes of the event that the family has more boys than girls, and the probability of this event.

Solution

The sample space is shown in Figure 6.15.

1	sex of first child	sex of second child	sex of third child	branch
2	male	male	male	m-m-m
3	male	male	female	m-m-f
4	male	female	male	m-f-m
5	male	female	female	m-f-f
6	female	male	male	f-m-m
7	female	male	female	f-m-f
8	female	female	male	f-f-m
9	female	female	female	f-f-f

Figure 6.15 Sample space for sex distribution of families with 3 children.

The event of more boys than girls is the event consisting of the following four outcomes {m-m-m, m-m-f, m-f-m, f-m-m}. The probability of the event is 4/8 = 0.5.

3. An experiment consists of randomly selecting people for a psychological experiment until a male is selected. Give the sample space for the experiment, the outcomes of the event that at most three are chosen before a male is chosen, and the probability of the event.

Solution

The sample space S = {male, female-male, female-female-male, female-female-female-male, ...} Note that this sample space is countably infinite. The event is A = { male, female-male, female-female-male}. The probability of the event A is $\frac{1}{2} + \frac{1}{2}\frac{1}{2} + \frac{1}{2}\frac{1}{2}\frac{1}{2} = \frac{7}{8}$. Apply the addition rule as well as the multiplication rule.

4. An experiment consists of flipping a coin and then rolling a die. Give the sample space for the experiment. Give the outcomes in the event A that a head was followed by an even number on the die. Find the probability of the event.

Solution

S = {H1, H2, H3, H4, H5, H6, T1, T2, T3, T4, T5, T6}

A = {H2, H4, H6}

P(A) = 3/12 = 1/4

The Addition Rule and Mutually Exclusive Events

5. Events M and N are defined on an experiment. The probability of M is 1/7, the probability of N is 1/9 and the probability of M and N is 8/63. Are M and N mutually exclusive? Find P(M or N).

Solution

M and N are not mutually exclusive because P(M and N) ≠ 0. The probability of M or N is given by P(M or N) = P(M) + P(N) − P(M and N) = 1/7 + 1/9 − 8/63 = (9 + 7 −8)/63 = 8/63.

6. Consider the experiment of selecting one card from a deck of 52. The event A is the event that a face card is selected, the event B is the event that an ace is selected, and the event C is the event that a 2 is selected. Are the events A, B, and C mutually exclusive? Are the events exhaustive? Find P(A or B or C).

Solution

The events are mutually exclusive. The events are not exhaustive. The probability of A or B or C occurring is 12/52 + 4/52 + 4/52 = 20/52.

7. A pair of dice are rolled once and the sample space is shown in Figure 6.14. Event A is that the same number is on both dice. Event B is the number on the second die is greater than the number on the

first die. Event C is the number on the first die is greater than the number on the second die. Are these events mutually exclusive as well as exhaustive?

Solution

A = {(1,1), (2,2), (3,3), (4,4), (5,5), (6,6)}

B = {(1,2), (1,3), (1,4), (1,5), (1,6), (2,3), (2,4), (2,5), (2,6), (3,4), (3,5), (3,6), (4,5), (4,6), (5,6)}

C = {(2,1), (3.1), (4,1), (5,1), (6,1), (3,2), (4,2), (5,2), (6,2), (4,3), (5,3), (6,3), (5,4), (6,4), (6,5)}

Yes, the events are mutually exclusive and exhaustive.

8. You are given that events A, B, C, and D have no common outcomes and $P(A) = 0.1$, $P(B) = 0.2$, $P(C) = 0.3$ and $P(C) = 0.4$. Are events A, B, C, and D mutually exclusive and exhaustive?

Solution

Yes, the events are mutually exclusive and exhaustive.

The Multiplicative Rule and Independent Events

9. A coin is flipped 5 times. What is the probability of 5 tails in the five flips?

Solution

The flips are independent of one another. The probability of a tail on each flip is ½. Because the events are independent, $P(\text{TTTTT}) = P(T)P(T)P(T)P(T)P(T) = (1/2)^5 = 1/32 = 0.03125$.

10. Five cards are selected without replacement. What is the probability of a face card on each of the 5 draws?

Solution

$$\frac{12}{52}\frac{11}{51}\frac{10}{50}\frac{9}{49}\frac{8}{48} = \frac{1188}{3898440} = 0.0003$$

11. Thirteen percent of adolescents suffer from anorexia. What is the probability that a psychologist selects five adolescents randomly and finds that none of them suffer from anorexia?

Solution

$(.87)^5 = 0.498$

12. In Problem 11, find the probability that exactly one of the five suffer from anorexia.

Solution

Exactly one suffers from anorexia if the first does and the other four do not, if the second does but none of the other four do, ..., if the last does but the other four do not. The event exactly one suffers from anorexia is equivalent to YNNNN or NYNNN or NNYNN or NNNYN or NNNNY, where Y means yes and N means no. There are 5 mutually excusive events connected by "or." Each sequence of Ns and Y's are independent. Therefore applying the and/or rules for events connected by "and's" and "or's," we have $(.13)(.87)(.87)(.87)$ $(.87) + (.87)(.13)(.87)(.87)(.87) + (.87)(.87)(.13)(.87)(.87) + (.87)(.87)(.87)(.13)(.87) + (.87)(.87)(.87)(.87)$ $(.13) = 5(.87)^4(.13) = 0.3724$.

Probability and the Binomial Distribution

13. Five marbles are selected from 25 without replacement. Ten of the marbles are white and fifteen are black. Variable X is the number of white marbles selected in the five. Why is X not binomial?

Solution

The probability of drawing a white marble (success) does not remain constant from trial to trial. In other words, there is not independence from trial to trial. The binomial conditions are not satisfied.

14. Five marbles are selected from 25 with replacement. Ten of the marbles are white and fifteen are black. Variable X is the number of white marbles selected in the five. Is X binomial?

Solution

The binomial conditions are satisfied. There are 5 trials. On each trial the probability of drawing a white marble is 0.4 and the probability that the marble is non-white is 0.6 and these remain constant from trial to trial. There is independence from trial to trial. X may be 0, 1, 2, 3, 4, or 5 when this experiment is performed. The binomial conditions are satisfied.

15. Seventeen percent of Americans have major depression. Let X = the number in a random sample size of 350 interviewed who suffer major depression. Why may X be treated as a binomial random variable?

Solution

Each individual who is interviewed either has major depression (success) or not (failure). The probability of success is $p = 0.17$ and the probability of failure is $q = 0.83$ on each interview (trial). Because of the large size of the population, the values of p and q do not change significantly as the sample is chosen. Because the sample is random, there is independence from trial to trial. X may assume any of the values 0 through 350 and the probabilities of different values of X are binomial probabilities.

16. As a coin is tossed, why are we able to assume independence from trial to trial?

Solution

The coin has no memory. The outcome on any trial is not influenced by outcomes on other trials. The probability is still 0.50 of a head and 0.50 of a tail on any toss.

Using EXCEL to Find Binomial Probabilities

17. Five percent of students, grades 9 through 12, drink alcohol on school property. As part of a psychology of teen drinking study, a sample of 500 teens, grades 9 through 12 was taken. Find the probability that in the 500, at most 30 will be found who drink on school property.

Solution

We have 500 binomial trials and the probability of success is 0.05 and the probability of failure is 0.95 on each trial. We are asked to find $P(X \le 30)$. We will use the cumulative binomial function of EXCEL to find the probability. The function =BINOMDIST(30,500,0.05,1) gives the probability and it is equal to 0.87. Note that this problem would be near impossible without EXCEL.

18. In a large psychology department, 70% of the students are females. What is the probability that in a random sample of 10, at least 8 would be female?

Solution

There are 10 binomial trials with $p = 0.7$ and q = 0.3 on each trial. We are asked to find $P(X \ge 8)$. The complement of the event $X \ge 8$ is $X \le 7$. We have: $P(X \ge 8) = 1 - P(X \le 7)$. The EXCEL expression =1−BINOMDIST(7,10,0.7,1) gives 0.383.

19. A coin is tossed 10 times. Find the probability of each of the 11 values that X may take on where X = the number of heads in the 10 tosses.

Solution

The numbers 0 through 10 are entered into A1:A11. The expression =BINOMDIST(A1,10,0.5,0) is entered into B1 and a click-and-drag is performed from B1 to B11. The probabilities are shown in Figure 6.16.

20. It was found that among a depressed population, 74% were introverts. If, in this population, 150 are selected, what is the probability that 100 or fewer are introverts?

Solution

The probability $P(X \le 100)$ is given by =BINOMDIST(100,150,0.74,1) which equals 0.027.

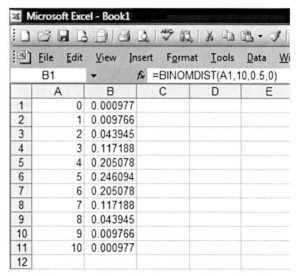

Figure 6.16 Binomial probabilities of 0 through 10 heads in 10 tosses of a coin.

Probability and the Normal Distribution Using EXCEL

21. The stress scores on a stress test are normally distributed with mean = 50 and standard deviation equal to 10. What percent score above 65 on the test?

Solution

The EXCEL answer is given by =1−NORMDIST(65,50,10,1). Two events such as $(X < 65)$ and $(X > 65)$ are called *complementary*. One or the other must happen. When two events are complementary, their probabilities add to one. That is $P(X < 65) + P(X > 65) = 1$. Or solving for $P(X > 65) = 1 − P(X < 65)$. Because $P(X < 65)$ is given by NORMDIST(65,50,10,1), $P(X > 65)$ is given by =1−NORMDIST(65,50,10,1). The answer is 0.0668.

22. A group has depression scores that are normally distributed with a mean equal to 75 and a standard deviation equal to 15. What percent score between 60 and 105?

Solution

The EXCEL answer is =NORMDIST(105,75,15,1) − NORMDIST(60,75,15,1) which equals 0.8186. That is, 81.86% score between 60 and 105.

23. A test for anxiety has scores that are normally distributed with a mean equal to 100 and a standard deviation equal to 15. What percent score below 70 on the test?

Solution

The EXCEL answer is =NORMDIST(70,100,15,1) which equals 0.0228. That is, 2.3% score below 70 on the test.

24. A psychological test designed to measure happiness has scores that are normally distributed with a mean equal to 80 and a standard deviation equal to 10. The higher the score the happier is the individual. What percent score above 75?

Solution

The EXCEL answer is =1−NORMDIST(75,80,10,1) which equals 0.6915. That is, 69.15% score above 75.

Using a Table of the Normal Distribution

25. Solve Problem 21, using a table of the standard normal distribution.

Solution

First the normal random variable must be transformed to a standard normal random variable by the transformation,

$Z = \dfrac{X - \mu}{\sigma}$. We are asked to find $P(X > 65)$ where X has $\mu = 50$ and $\sigma = 10$. This probability is equal to

$P(z > 1.5)$. Using column C of Table 6.1 and reading opposite $z = 1.50$, our answer is 0.0668, the same as obtained in Problem 21.

26. Solve Problem 22, using a table of the standard normal distribution.

Solution

First the normal random variable must be transformed to a standard normal random variable by the transformation, $Z = \dfrac{X - \mu}{\sigma}$. We are asked to find $P(60 < X < 110)$ where X has $\mu = 75$ and $\sigma = 15$. This probability is equal to $P(-1 < z < 2)$. Using Table 6.1 and column D, read opposite 1 to find $P(0 < z < 1)$ which, due to symmetry, is the same as $P(-1 < z < 0)$. The answer is 0.3413. Using Table 6.1 and column D, read opposite 2 to find $P(0 < z < 2)$ which is 0.4772. The answer is $0.3413 + 0.4772 = 0.8185$, the same answer obtained in problem 22.

27. Solve Problem 23, using a table of the standard normal distribution.

Solution

First the normal random variable must be transformed to a standard normal random variable by the transformation, $Z = \dfrac{X - \mu}{\sigma}$. We are asked to find $P(X < 70)$ where X has $\mu = 100$ and $\sigma = 15$. This probability is equal to $P(z < -2)$. Using column C of Table 6.1 and reading opposite $z = 2$, our answer is $P(z > 2) = 0.0228$, the same as $P(z < -2)$. The answer is 2.3%, the same as obtained in Problem 23.

28. Solve Problem 24, using a table of the standard normal distribution.

Solution

First the normal random variable must be transformed to a standard normal random variable by the transformation, $Z = \dfrac{X - \mu}{\sigma}$. We must find $P(z > -0.5)$. This is the same as $P(z < 0.5)$. Using column B and reading opposite $z = 0.5$, we see that $P(z < 0.5) = 0.6915$. This also equals $P(z > -0.5)$. That is 69.15% score above 75.

SUPPLEMENTARY PROBLEMS

Experiment, Sample Space, Events, and Probability

29. A die is rolled three times. How many outcomes are in the sample space? Give the outcomes in the event A that a sum equal to 17 is obtained. Find the probability of event A.

30. Four cards are dealt from a deck of 52 without replacement. How many outcomes are in the sample space? How many outcomes are in the event four aces are obtained. What is the probability of the event that four aces are obtained?

31. A psychology class consists of 10 freshmen, 15 sophomores, 3 juniors, and 2 seniors. A student is randomly selected from the class. How many outcomes are in the sample space? How many outcomes are in the event that a freshman was selected? What is the probability that a freshman was selected?

32. A die is rolled until a 6 is obtained. Give the sample space for this experiment. Find the probability of the event a 6 is obtained on or before the third roll of the die.

The Additive Rule and Mutually Exclusive Events

33. Three dice are tossed. Event A is the event that the sum of the dice is an odd number. Event B is the event that an even sum was obtained. Are A and B mutually exclusive and exhaustive?

34. The probability of event A is 0.35 and the probability of event B is 0.65. If the probability of A or B is 0.80, find $P(A \text{ and } B)$.

35. Thirty percent of a sample of patients are depressed. Fifty percent of the sample of patients are anxious. If fifteen percent are depressed and anxious, what is the probability of selecting a patient from the sample that is depressed or anxious?

36. In a psychological study, 40% of the participants are middle-aged, 67% are happy, and 85% are middle-aged or happy. What percent are both middle-aged and happy?

The Multiplicative Rule and Independent Events

37. A psychological researcher selects three from a group consisting of 10 introverts and 15 extroverts. What is the probability that all introverts are selected?

38. It is reported that 48% of state prisoners have relatives that have done time. "The numbers are amazing" says Oregon psychologist Mark Eddy, who is tracking 400 inmates. If 10 state prisoners are randomly selected, what is the probability that at least one will have relatives that have done time?

39. The Center for Addiction and Mental Heath reported that major depression impacts approximately 5 percent of people globally. If fifty people were selected globally, what is the probability that at least one would suffer from depression?

40. One in four hospital patients is admitted with a mental health or substance abuse disorder. A random sample of 10 hospital admissions is selected. What is the probability that none have a mental health or substance abuse disorder?

Probability and the Binomial Distribution

41. One in four hospital patients is admitted with a mental health or substance abuse disorder. A random sample of 10 hospital admissions is selected. Let X represent the number in the 10 who have a mental health or substance abuse disorder. Explain why X may be viewed as being binomial.

42. A die is rolled 5 times and X is defined to be the number of times the face 6 turns up. X is binomial. Find the number of trials, the probability of success on each trial, and give the values that X may equal.

43. The Center for Addiction and Mental Health reported that major depression impacts approximately 5 percent of people globally. If twenty-five people were selected globally, and X is defined to be the number in the 25 who suffer from depression, then find the number of trials, the probability of success on each trial, and give the values that X may equal.

44. A card is selected from a deck of 52. The card is replaced and another card is drawn. This is done 10 times. The variable X is defined to be the number of diamonds that are selected in the 10 selections. Find the number of trials, the probability of success on each trial, and give the values that X may equal.

Using EXCEL to Find Binomial Probabilities

45. One in four hospital patients is admitted with a mental health or substance abuse disorder. A random sample of 10 hospital admissions is selected. Let X represent the number in the 10 who have a mental health or substance abuse disorder. Find the probability that X is 3 or fewer.

46. A die is rolled 5 times and X is defined to be the number of times the face 6 turns up. X is binomial. Find the probability that $X = 1$.

47. The Center for Addiction and Mental Heath reported that major depression impacts approximately 5 percent of people globally. If twenty-five people were selected, and X is defined to be the number in the 25 who suffer from depression, then find the probability that X is 2 or less.

48. A card is selected from a deck of 52. The card is replaced and another card is drawn. This is done 10 times. The variable X is defined to be the number of diamonds that are selected. Find the probability that $X \leq 2$.

Probability and the Normal Distribution Using EXCEL

49. A psychological study of the causes of obesity is done. It is found that the body mass index (BMI) is normally distributed with a mean of 25 and a standard deviation equal to 5. Find the percent having a BMI of 27 or over.

50. Scores on a test for depression are normally distributed with a mean equal to 100 and a standard deviation equal to 20. Find the percent of the scores between 90 and 130.

51. Female heights are normally distributed with mean equal to 66 inches and standard deviation equal to 3 inches. Find the percent that are 64 inches or shorter.

52. The National Institute on Aging reports that the mean age for starting menopause is 51 years. If the age at which menopause begins is normally distributed with mean equal to 51 and standard deviation equal to 5 years, in what percent does menopause start at 45 or over?

Using a Table of The Normal Distribution

53. Use Table 6.1 to find the solution to Problem 49.

54. Use Table 6.1 to find the solution to Problem 50.

55. Use Table 6.1 to find the solution to Problem 51.

56. Use Table 6.1 to find the solution to Problem 52.

The Distribution of Sample Means

Population Distribution, Population Mean, Population Variance, and Population Standard Deviation

Let the population of interest be all online psychology majors. Suppose the variable of interest is the number of hours those majors are currently taking in psychology and define X as the number of credit hours being carried in psychology by the online psychology majors. Suppose there are 30,000 online majors, 10,000 of whom are taking 3 credit hours, 10,000 are taking 6 credit hours, and 10,000 are taking 9 credit hours. Note that 1/3 are taking 3 credit hours, 1/3 are taking 6 credit hours, and 1/3 are taking 9 credit hours. We may describe this population as shown in Table 7.1. The distribution in Table 7.1 is called the *population distribution*.

TABLE 7.1 Distribution of Credit Hours Taken by Online Psychology Majors

X	3	6	9
$P(x)$	1/3	1/3	1/3

The mean of this population is $\mu = \dfrac{3(10,000) + 6(10,000) + 9(10,000)}{30,000}$ credit hours. Note that this can be

written $\mu = 3x\dfrac{1}{3} + 6x\dfrac{1}{3} + 9x\dfrac{1}{3} = 1 + 2 + 3 = 6$. The mean credit hours taken on line in psychology is 6. The

population mean is $\mu = \Sigma xP(x)$. Similarly the *population variance* is $\sigma^2 = \Sigma x^2 P(x) - \mu^2$. For this population,

the variance is $\sigma^2 = 9\dfrac{1}{3} + 36\dfrac{1}{3} + 81\dfrac{1}{3} - 36 = 6$. The *population standard deviation* is the square root of the

variance or $\sigma = \sqrt{6} = 2.45$ credit hours. We say that the population described by Table 7.1 has mean equal to 6 and standard deviation equal to 2.45. The mean, μ, and the standard deviation, σ, are called *parameters of the population*.

EXAMPLE 1 Find the population mean and population standard deviation of the population whose distribution is given in Table 7.2. In this example, 20% are taking 3 credit hours, 60% are taking 6 credit hours, and 20% are taking 9 credit hours online.

TABLE 7.2 Distribution of Variable X in Example 1

x	3	6	9
$P(x)$	0.2	0.6	0.2

The population mean is $\mu = 3 \times 0.2 + 6 \times 0.6 + 9 \times 0.2 = 0.6 + 3.6 + 1.8 = 6$ credit hours. The population variance is $\sigma^2 = 9 \times 0.2 + 36 \times 0.6 + 81 \times 0.2 - 36 = 39.6 - 36 = 3.6$. The standard deviation is $\sigma = 1.90$. Note that the population distribution is more spread about the mean in Table 7.1 than in Table 7.2, and hence the standard deviation is larger for the population given in Table 7.1 than in Table 7.2.

EXAMPLE 2 Find the population mean and population standard deviation of the population whose population distribution is given in Table 7.3. In this example, 40% are taking 3 credit hours, 20% are taking 6 credit hours, and 40% are taking 9 credit hours.

TABLE 7.3 Distribution of Variable X in Example 2

X	3	6	9
$P(x)$	0.4	0.2	0.4

The population mean is $\mu = 3 \times 0.4 + 6 \times 0.2 + 9 \times 0.4 = 1.2 + 1.2 + 3.6 = 6$ credit hours. The population variance is $\sigma^2 = 9 \times 0.4 + 36 \times 0.2 + 81 \times 0.4 - 36 = 43.2 - 36 = 7.2$. The standard deviation is $\sigma = 2.68$. Note that the population distribution is more spread about the mean in Table 7.3 than in Table 7.1 or Table 7.2, and hence the standard deviation is larger for the population given in Table 7.3 than in Table 7.1 or Table 7.2.

The Distribution of Sample Means

Suppose we take samples of size $n = 2$ from the population described in Table 7.1. This population is of size $n = 30,000$. There are 9 different samples of size 2 that are possible and, because the population described in Table 7.1 is uniform, all 9 samples are equally likely of being selected, that is, have probability, 1/9. Because the population is large, sampling may be thought of as with replacement. The 9 samples are listed in Table 7.4 and their sample mean, M, and probability of being selected are given. Measures made on samples such as M and S are called *sample statistics*. We shall use sample statistics to obtain information about population parameters.

TABLE 7.4 All Possible Samples of Size 2 from the Population Described in Table 7.1

FIRST ITEM	SECOND ITEM	M	PROBABILITY
3	3	3.0	1/9
3	6	4.5	1/9
3	9	6.0	1/9
6	3	4.5	1/9
6	6	6.0	1/9
6	9	7.5	1/9
9	3	6.0	1/9
9	6	7.5	1/9
9	9	9.0	1/9

The *distribution of M*, the sample mean, is given in Table 7.5.

TABLE 7.5 Distribution of M for Sample Size $n = 2$

M	3.0	4.5	6.0	7.5	9.0
$P(M)$	1/9	2/9	3/9	2/9	1/9

For example, the sample mean equals 6.0 if sample (3, 9), or sample (6, 6), or sample (9, 3) is selected and, because of the OR rule, we add the probabilities of the three samples to get the probability that $M = 6.0$. Therefore, $P(M = 6.0) = 1/9 + 1/9 + 1/9 = 3/9$. The distribution of M is plotted in Figure 7.1. When the sample mean, M, is used to estimate the population mean, μ, the absolute difference between M and μ is called the *sampling error*. For example, if a sample of size $n = 2$ is taken and $M = 7.5$ is found and used as an estimate of μ, then the absolute difference between M and μ is 1.5 and the sampling error is 1.5.

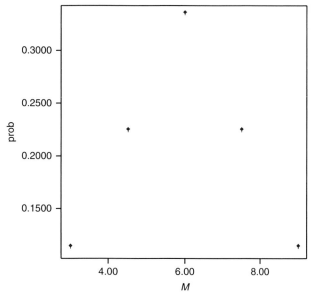

Figure 7.1 SPSS plot of the distribution of M for $n = 2$.

EXAMPLE 3 If all samples of size 3 are listed from the population described in Table 7.1, then Table 7.6 gives the 27 samples of size 3 that are possible and their sample mean, M, and probability of being selected. Each of the 27 samples has the same probability of being selected.

TABLE 7.6 All Possible Samples of Size 3 from the Population Described in Table 7.1

FIRST ITEM	SECOND ITEM	THIRD ITEM	M	PROBABILITY
3	3	3	3	1/27
3	3	6	4	1/27
3	3	9	5	1/27
3	6	3	4	1/27
3	6	6	5	1/27
3	6	9	6	1/27
3	9	3	5	1/27
3	9	6	6	1/27
3	9	9	7	1/27
6	3	3	4	1/27
6	3	6	5	1/27
6	3	9	6	1/27
6	6	3	5	1/27
6	6	6	6	1/27
6	6	9	7	1/27
6	9	3	6	1/27
6	9	6	7	1/27
6	9	9	8	1/27
9	3	3	5	1/27
9	3	6	6	1/27
9	3	9	7	1/27
9	6	3	6	1/27
9	6	6	7	1/27
9	6	9	8	1/27
9	9	3	7	1/27
9	9	6	8	1/27
9	9	9	9	1/27

Table 7.7 gives the sampling distribution of *M* obtained from Table 7.6.

TABLE 7.7 Distribution of *M* for Sample Size *n* = 3

M	3	4	5	6	7	8	9
P(M)	1/27	3/27	6/27	7/27	6/27	3/27	1/27

Figure 7.2 is an SPSS scatter plot of the distribution in Table 7.7.

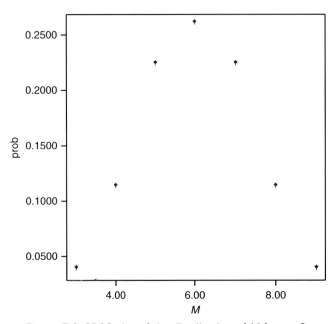

Figure 7.2 SPSS plot of the distribution of *M* for *n* = 3.

Note that as *n* gets larger, the distribution of *M* is approaching a normal curve (see Figures 7.1 and 7.2).

Sample Mean Distribution, Mean of the Sample Mean, and Variance of the Sample Mean

The sample mean, *M*, is a variable just as is *X*, the variable defined on the population. Recall that the mean of *X* is $\sum xP(x)$ and the variance of *X* is $\sum x^2P(x) - \mu^2$. The mean of *M* is $\sum mP(m)$ and the variance of *M* is $\sum m^2P(m) - (\text{mean of } M)^2$. The following relationships can be shown to be true:

$$\text{mean of } M = \text{mean of } X \quad \text{and} \quad \text{variance of } M = \frac{\text{Variance of } X}{n}.$$

EXAMPLE 4 Recall that variable *X*, with the distribution given in Table 7.1, had $\mu = 6$ credit hours and $\sigma^2 = 6$. The distribution of *M* for samples of size *n* = 2 was as follows.

M	3.0	4.5	6.0	7.5	9.0
P(M)	1/9	2/9	3/9	2/9	1/9

The mean of M is $3.0(1/9) + 4.5(2/9) + 6.0(3/9) + 7.5(2/9) + (1/9) = 54/9 = 6$ and the variance of M is $9(1/9) + 20.25(2/9) + 36(3/9) + 56.25(2/9) + 81(1/9) - 36 = 39 - 36 = 3$.

Note that from Example 4:

$$\text{mean of } M = \text{mean of } X \quad \text{and} \quad \text{variance of } M = \frac{\text{Variance of } X}{2}.$$

EXAMPLE 5 Recall that variable X, with the distribution given in Table 7.1, had $\mu = 6$ credit hours and $\sigma^2 = 6$. The distribution of M for samples of size $n = 3$ was as follows.

M	3	4	5	6	7	8	9
$P(M)$	1/27	3/27	6/27	7/27	6/27	3/27	1/27

The mean of M is

$$3(1/27) + 4(3/27) + 5(6/27) + 6(7/27) + 7(6/27) + 8(3/27) + 9(1/27) = 6$$

and the variance of M is:

$$9(1/27) + 16(3/27) + 25(6/27) + 36(7/27) + 49(6/27) + 64(3/27) + 81(1/27) - 36$$
$$= 38 - 36 = 2.$$

Note that: mean of M = mean of X and variance of $M = \dfrac{\text{Variance of } X}{3}$ for samples of size $n = 3$. We have also noticed in Figure 7.1 and Figure 7.2 that the shape of the sampling distribution of M approaches the normal distribution.

Standard Error of the Mean

When the standard deviation of M is obtained, it is found that the standard deviation of M is the standard deviation of X divided by the square root of n. The standard deviation of M is called the *standard error of the mean*.

EXAMPLE 6 Scores on a stress test have a mean equal to 100 and a standard deviation equal to 20. If a sample of 25 scores on the stress test is computed, what will the standard error of the mean equal? The standard error of the mean is $20/\sqrt{25} = 20/5 = 4$. Remember, the standard deviation gives the variation of the population characteristic. The standard error of the mean gives the variation of the sample mean based on sample size n taken from the population.

EXAMPLE 7 Give the standard error of the mean if a sample of size 36 is taken from a population with:
a. $\sigma = 1$ b. $\sigma = 10$ c. $\sigma = 100$

TABLE 7.8 The Standard Error Varies Directly as σ

σ	STANDARD ERROR
1	0.167
10	1.667
100	16.667

Table 7.8 shows how the standard error of the mean varies directly as the standard deviation of the population varies.

EXAMPLE 8 Give the standard error of the mean if $\sigma = 5$ and the sample size is a. $n = 4$ b. $n = 25$
c. $n = 100$.

TABLE 7.9 The Standard Error Varies Inversely as *n*

N	STANDARD ERROR
4	2.5
25	1
100	0.5

Table 7.9 shows how the standard error of the mean varies inversely as the sample size.

The Central Limit Theorem (Putting It All Together)

If all samples of size n (≥ 30) are to be taken from an infinite (large) population having mean μ and standard deviation σ, then the following are true regarding the means of these samples.

1. Their distribution is normal regardless of the distribution of the population from which the samples are taken.

2. The mean of the sample means is the population mean from which the samples are taken.

3. The standard deviation of the sample means, called the *standard error of the mean* is equal to the population standard deviation divided by the square root of n.

The above results are called the *central limit theorem*.

The distribution of the sample means are normal for all sample sizes (not just samples whose sample size is larger than 30) if the samples are taken from a population whose distribution is normal.

EXAMPLE 9 Consider the population of adult male heights, X, whose distribution is normal with $\mu = 70$ inches and whose standard deviation $\sigma = 3$ inches. The distribution of male heights is shown in Figure 7.3.

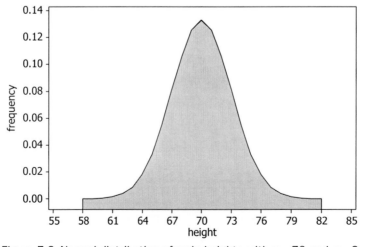

Figure 7.3 Normal distribution of male heights with $\mu = 70$ and $\sigma = 3$.

The distribution of means of male heights, based on samples of $n = 25$ from the population in Figure 7.3, is shown in Figure 7.4.

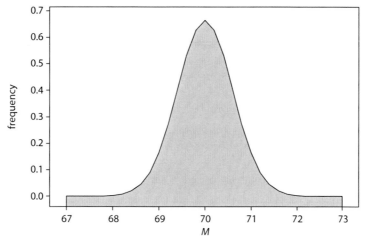

Figure 7.4 Distribution of M with $\mu_M = 70$ and $\sigma_M = 0.6$.

The percent of males that are over 6 foot tall is $P(X > 72)$, which is given by the EXCEL expression =1–NORMDIST(72, 70, 3, 1) or 25.25%. The probability that the mean of a sample, based on $n = 25$, is greater than 72 inches is given by $P(M > 72)$ or the EXCEL expression =1–NORMDIST(72, 70, 0.6, 1) or 0.000429. When the central limit theorem is first presented, students tend to confuse the distribution of X and the distribution of M. Note that 25.25% of the males are taller than 72 inches. The probability that M is greater than 72 inches is 0.000429. $P(X > 72)$ and $P(M > 72)$ are measuring different things.

SOLVED PROBLEMS

Population Distribution, Population Mean, Population Variance, and Population Standard Deviation

1. The variable of interest is the semester hours taken online by psychology majors at universities. Suppose the distribution of X, the number of semester hours taken online, is given in Table 7.10.

TABLE 7.10 **Distribution of Semester Hours Taken Online by Psychology Majors**

X	3	6	9	12
$P(x)$	0.25	0.25	0.25	0.25

Find the mean, variance, and standard deviation for this population.

Solution

$\mu = \Sigma xP(x) = 3(0.25) + 6(0.25) + 9(0.25) + 12(0.25) = 7.5$ credit hours.

$\sigma^2 = \Sigma x^2 P(x) - \mu^2 = 9(0.25) + 36(0.25) + 81(0.25) + 144(0.25) - (7.5)^2$

$= 67.5 - 56.25 = 11.25$ and $\sigma = 3.354$.

2. The variable of interest is the semester hours taken online by psychology majors at universities. Suppose the distribution of X, the number of semester hours taken online, is given in Table 7.11.

TABLE 7.11 **Distribution of Semester Hours Taken Online by Psychology Majors**

X	3	6	9	12
$P(x)$	0.1	0.4	0.4	0.1

Find the mean, variance, and standard deviation for this population.

Solution

$\mu = \Sigma xP(x) = 3(0.1) + 6(0.4) + 9(0.4) + 12(0.1) = 7.5$ credit hours.

$\sigma^2 = \Sigma x^2 P(x) - \mu^2 = 9(0.1) + 36(0.4) + 81(0.4) + 144(0.1) - (7.5)^2 = 62.1 - 56.25 = 5.85$ and $\sigma = 2.42$.

3. The variable of interest is the number semester hours taken online by psychology majors at universities. Suppose the distribution of X, the number of semester hours taken online, is given in Table 7.12.

TABLE 7.12 **Distribution of Semester Hours Taken Online by Psychology Majors**

X	3	6	9	12
$P(x)$	0.4	0.1	0.1	0.4

Find the mean, variance, and standard deviation for this population.

Solution

$\mu = \Sigma xP(x) = 3(0.4) + 6(0.1) + 9(0.1) + 12(0.4) = 7.5$ credit hours.

$\sigma^2 = \Sigma x^2 P(x) - \mu^2 = 9(0.4) + 36(0.1) + 81(0.1) + 144(0.4) - (7.5)^2 = 72.9 - 56.25 = 16.65$ and $\sigma = 4.08$.

4. A population has mean 9 and standard deviation equal to 6. Find the sum, $\Sigma x^2 P(x)$.

Solution

$\sigma^2 = \Sigma x^2 P(x) - \mu^2$ or $36 = \Sigma x^2 P(x) - 81$. Solving for $\Sigma x^2 P(x)$, we find 117.

The Distribution of Sample Means

5. Give the distribution of the sample mean for all samples of size $n = 2$ taken from the population described in problem 1.

Solution

Table 7.13 is used to build the distribution of M shown in Table 7.14.

TABLE **7.13** **All Possible Samples of Size 2 Taken from the Population in Table 7.10**

FIRST ITEM	SECOND ITEM	M	PROBABILITY
3	3	3	1/16
3	6	4.5	1/16
3	9	6	1/16
3	12	7.5	1/16
6	3	4.5	1/16
6	6	6	1/16
6	9	7.5	1/16
6	12	9	1/16
9	3	6	1/16
9	6	7.5	1/16
9	9	9	1/16
9	12	10.5	1/16
12	3	7.5	1/16
12	6	9	1/16
12	9	10.5	1/16
12	12	12	1/16

Table 7.14 uses Table 7.13 along with the and/or rules for probability to build the distribution of M for $n = 2$.

TABLE **7.14** **Distribution of M for Sample Size $n = 2$**

M	3.0	4.5	6.0	7.5	9.0	10.5	12.0
$P(M)$	0.0625	0.1252	0.1875	0.25	0.1875	0.1252	0.0625

6. Give the distribution of the sample mean for all samples of size $n = 3$ taken from the population described in Problem 1.

Solution

All samples of size $n = 3$ from the distribution given in Problem 1 is given in Table 7.15.

TABLE **7.15** **All Possible Samples of Size 3 from the Population in Table 7.10**

FIRST ITEM	SECOND ITEM	THIRD ITEM	M	PROBABILITY
3	3	3	3	1/64
3	3	6	4	1/64
3	3	9	5	1/64
3	3	12	6	1/64
3	6	3	4	1/64
3	6	6	5	1/64
3	6	9	6	1/64
3	6	12	7	1/64
3	9	3	5	1/64
3	9	6	6	1/64
3	9	9	7	1/64
3	9	12	8	1/64

(Continued)

TABLE 7.15 (*Continued*)

FIRST ITEM	SECOND ITEM	THIRD ITEM	M	PROBABILITY
3	12	3	6	1/64
3	12	6	7	1/64
3	12	9	8	1/64
3	12	12	9	1/64
6	3	3	4	1/64
6	3	6	5	1/64
6	3	9	6	1/64
6	3	12	7	1/64
6	6	3	5	1/64
6	6	6	6	1/64
6	6	9	7	1/64
6	6	12	8	1/64
6	9	3	6	1/64
6	9	6	7	1/64
6	9	9	8	1/64
6	9	12	9	1/64
6	12	3	7	1/64
6	12	6	8	1/64
6	12	9	9	1/64
6	12	12	10	1/64
9	3	3	5	1/64
9	3	6	6	1/64
9	3	9	7	1/64
9	3	12	8	1/64
9	6	3	6	1/64
9	6	6	7	1/64
9	6	9	8	1/64
9	6	12	9	1/64
9	9	3	7	1/64
9	9	6	8	1/64
9	9	9	9	1/64
9	9	12	10	1/64
9	12	3	8	1/64
9	12	6	9	1/64
9	12	9	10	1/64
9	12	12	11	1/64
12	3	3	6	1/64
12	3	6	7	1/64
12	3	9	8	1/64
12	3	12	9	1/64
12	6	3	7	1/64
12	6	6	8	1/64
12	6	9	9	1/64
12	6	12	10	1/64
12	9	3	8	1/64
12	9	6	9	1/64
12	9	9	10	1/64
12	9	12	11	1/64
12	12	3	9	1/64
12	12	6	10	1/64
12	12	9	11	1/64
12	12	12	12	1/64

The sample means in Table 7.15, as well as the and/or probability rules, are used to build the distribution of M for $n = 3$ shown in Table 7.16.

TABLE 7.16 Distribution of M for Sample Size $n = 3$

M	3	4	5	6	7
$P(M)$	0.015625	0.046875	0.09375	0.15625	0.1875
M	8	9	10	11	12
$P(M)$	0.1875	0.15625	0.09375	0.046875	0.015625

7. Give the distribution of M for all samples of size $n = 4$ taken from the population described in Problem 1.

Solution

Using the technique shown in Problems 5 and 6 and leaving out some of the steps, the distribution of M is given in Table 7.17.

TABLE 7.17 Distribution of M for Sample Size $n = 4$

M	3	3.75	4.5	5.25	6	6.75	7.5
$P(M)$	0.003906	0.015625	0.039063	0.078125	0.121094	0.15625	0.171875
M	8.25	9	9.75	10.5	11.25	12	
$P(M)$	0.15625	0.121094	0.078125	0.039063	0.015625	0.003906	

8. Plot the distributions of M derived in Problems 5, 6, and 7.

Solution

The distributions of M for $n = 2, 3,$ and 4 are shown in Figure 7.5. Notice that the distribution of M approaches a normal curve as n gets larger.

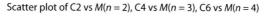

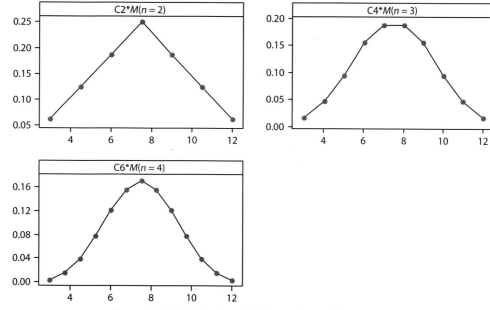

Figure 7.5 Distribution of M for $n = 2$, $n = 3$, and $n = 4$.

Sample Mean Distribution, Mean of the Sample Mean, and Variance of the Sample Mean

9. Use the distribution of M given in Table 7.14 to find the mean of M and the variance of M for the samples of size 2 from the population described in Problem 1.

Solution

The distribution of M for $n = 2$ is:

M	3.0	4.5	6.0	7.5	9.0	10.5	12.0
$P(M)$	0.0625	0.1252	0.1875	0.25	0.1875	0.1252	0.0625

The mean of M is $\Sigma mP(m) = (3.0)(0.0625) + (4.5)(0.1252) + (6)(0.1875) + (7.5)(0.25) + (9.0)(0.1875) + (10.5)(0.1252) + (12.0)(0.0625) = 7.5$ showing that the mean of M equals the mean of the population, μ.

The variance of M is $\Sigma mP(m) - (\text{mean of } M)^2$. Referring to the distribution above $(9)(0.0625) + (20.25)(0.1252) + (36)(0.1875) + (56.25)(0.25) + (81)(0.1875) + (110.25)(0.1252) + (144)(0.0625) - 7.5^2 = 5.625$ showing that the variance of M = population variance/2 = $\sigma^2/2$.

10. Use the distribution of M given in Table 7.15 to find the mean of M and the variance of M for the samples of size 3 from the population described in Problem 1.

Solution

The distribution of M for $n = 3$ is:

M	3	4	5	6	7
$P(M)$	0.015625	0.046875	0.09375	0.15625	0.1875
M	8	9	10	11	12
$P(M)$	0.1875	0.15625	0.09375	0.046875	0.015625

The mean of M is $\Sigma mP(m) = (3.0)(0.015625) + (4)(0.046875) + (5)(0.09375) + (6)(0.15625) + (7)(0.1875) + (8)(0.1875) + (9)(0.15625) + (10)(0.09375) + (11)(0.046875) + (12)(0.015625) = 7.5$ showing once again that the mean of M equals the mean of the population.

The variance of M is $\Sigma mP(m) - (\text{mean of } M)^2$. Referring to the distribution above, $(9)(0.015625) + (16)(0.046875) + (25)(0.09375) + (36)(0.15625) + (49)(0.1875) + (64)(0.1875) + (81)(0.15625) + (100)(0.09375) + (121)(0.046875) + (144)(0.015625) - 7.5^2 = 3.75$ showing that the variance of M = population variance/3 = $\sigma^2/3$.

11. Use the distribution of M given in Table 7.17 to find the mean of M and the variance of M for the samples of size 4 from the population described in problem 1.

Solution

The distribution of M for $n = 4$ is:

M	3	3.75	4.5	5.25	6	6.75	7.5
$P(M)$	0.003906	0.015625	0.039063	0.078125	0.121094	0.15625	0.171875
M	8.25	9	9.75	10.5	11.25	12	
$P(M)$	0.15625	0.121094	0.078125	0.039063	0.015625	0.003906	

The distribution of M for $n = 4$ is entered into Figure 7.6. The mean is found in C15 as =SUM(C2:C14) and =SUM(E2:E14) in E15 gives $\Sigma mP(m)$ and finally the variance of M is $59.06256 - 7.5^2 = 2.81$. The variance of $M = \sigma^2/4 = 11.25/4$.

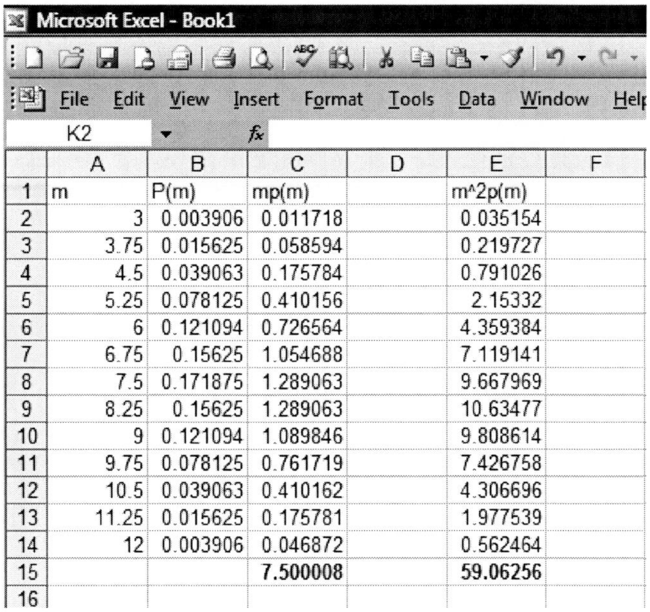

Microsoft Excel - Book1

File Edit View Insert Format Tools Data Window Help

K2

	A	B	C	D	E	F
1	m	P(m)	mp(m)		m^2p(m)	
2	3	0.003906	0.011718		0.035154	
3	3.75	0.015625	0.058594		0.219727	
4	4.5	0.039063	0.175784		0.791026	
5	5.25	0.078125	0.410156		2.15332	
6	6	0.121094	0.726564		4.359384	
7	6.75	0.15625	1.054688		7.119141	
8	7.5	0.171875	1.289063		9.667969	
9	8.25	0.15625	1.289063		10.63477	
10	9	0.121094	1.089846		9.808614	
11	9.75	0.078125	0.761719		7.426758	
12	10.5	0.039063	0.410162		4.306696	
13	11.25	0.015625	0.175781		1.977539	
14	12	0.003906	0.046872		0.562464	
15			**7.500008**		**59.06256**	
16						

Figure 7.6 Using EXCEL to work Problem 11.

12. In Problems 9, 10, and 11, find the probability that M will be within 1 of μ or $P(6.5 < M < 8.5)$.

Solution

In Problem 9, the distribution of $M(n = 2)$ is

M	3.0	4.5	6.0	7.5	9.0	10.5	12.0
$P(M)$	0.0625	0.1252	0.1875	0.25	0.1875	0.1252	0.0625

and the probability $P(6.5 < M < 8.5) = 0.25$).

In Problem 10, the distribution of $M(n = 3)$ is

M	3	4	5	6	7
$P(M)$	0.015625	0.046875	0.09375	0.15625	0.1875
M	8	9	10	11	12
$P(M)$	0.1875	0.15625	0.09375	0.046875	0.015625

and the probability $P(6.5 < M < 8.5) = 0.1875 + 0.1875 = 0.375$.

In Problem 11, the distribution of $M(n = 4)$ is

M	3	3.75	4.5	5.25	6	6.75	7.5
$P(M)$	0.003906	0.015625	0.039063	0.078125	0.121094	0.15625	0.171875
M	8.25	9	9.75	10.5	11.25	12	
$P(M)$	0.15625	0.121094	0.078125	0.039063	0.015625	0.003906	

and the probability $P(6.5 < M < 8.5) = 0.15625 + 0.171875 + 0.15625 = 0.484375$.

We see that as n increases, the probability that M is within 1 unit of the population mean increases.

Standard Error of the Mean

13. What is the standard error of the mean in Problem 9?

Solution

The variance of M is 5.625 and the standard error of M is the square root of the variance of M or 2.372. The standard error of M is also $\dfrac{\sigma}{\sqrt{n}} = \dfrac{3.354}{\sqrt{2}} = 2.372$.

14. What is the standard error of the mean in Problem 10?

Solution

The variance of M is 3.75 and the standard error of M is the square root of the variance of M or 1.936. The standard error of M is also $\dfrac{\sigma}{\sqrt{n}} = \dfrac{3.354}{\sqrt{3}} = 1.936$.

15. What is the standard error of the mean in Problem 11?

Solution

The variance of M is 2.813 and the standard error of M is the square root of the variance of M or 1.677. The standard error of M is also $\dfrac{\sigma}{\sqrt{n}} = \dfrac{3.354}{\sqrt{4}} = 1.677$.

16. A population has standard deviation equal 1.567 and the variance of the mean is equal 0.0818. Find n.

Solution

Variance of the mean $= \sigma^2/n$. Solving for n we get σ^2/variance of the mean $= 2.455/0.0818 = 30$.

The Central Limit Theorem (Putting it All Together)

17. The response time for rats when under the influence of a stimulant has a standard deviation of 2.5 seconds. A sample of size 36 is taken to estimate the population mean response time. What is the probability that the absolute difference between M and μ will be 3 seconds or less?

Solution

The mean of a sample of size 36 will be normally distributed with a standard error equal to $\dfrac{2.5}{\sqrt{36}} = 0.417$ and M will center at the population mean, μ. The probability we are seeking can be written as $P(-3 < M - \mu < 3)$. If all parts of the inequality is divided by the standard error, 0.417, the middle, $\dfrac{M-\mu}{0.417}$, becomes a standard normal variable. The equation becomes $P\left(-7.19 < \dfrac{M-\mu}{0.417} < 7.19\right)$ or $P(-7.19 < z < 7.19)$ which for all practical purposes is 1. We can be almost certain that the difference between M and μ will be less than 3 seconds. Recall that $P(-3 < z < 3) = 0.997$, so we know that $P(-7.19 < z < 7.19)$ is very close to 1.

18. The scores on a stress test are normally distributed with a standard deviation of 5.5. If the test is given to a sample of 20 individuals and it is desired to use the sample mean, M, as an estimate of the population mean, μ, what are the chances M overestimates μ by 2 or more points?

Solution

Because the scores on the test are normally distributed, M will have a normal distribution for any sample size. The problem is to find $P(M - \mu > 2)$. The standard error of M is $\dfrac{5.5}{\sqrt{20}} = 1.23$. Dividing $M - \mu$ by 1.23 will convert the normal to a standard normal. $P\left(\dfrac{M-\mu}{1.23} > \dfrac{2}{1.23}\right) = (z > 1.63)$. Using EXCEL, we find $= 1 - $ NORMSDIST $(1.63) = 0.0516$. Note that NORMSDIST is used when working with a **standard** normal distribution.

19. Sometimes it is necessary to use the sample variance, S^2 in place of the population variance and the sample standard deviation, S, in place of the population standard deviation. The following are 40 test scores.

Scores

64 84 93 60 94 88 87 65 58 74 66 58 66 61 98

82 64 77 61 85 59 59 57 74 87 64 71 98 60 65

67 93 56 62 80 72 96 57 57 56

The pull-down **Analyze → Descriptive Statistics → Descriptives** is given in SPSS. The following SPSS output for 40 test scores is given.

   Verify the variance and standard deviation (Std.) of the data.

Solution

The computing formula for the variance is $S^2 = \dfrac{\Sigma X^2 - \dfrac{(\Sigma X)^2}{n}}{(n-1)}$, where $\Sigma X = 2875$ and $\Sigma X^2 = 214085$, and $n = 40$. Using these values we find $S^2 = 190.881$. S is 13.816.

20. In problem 19, find the estimated standard error of the mean.

Solution

The standard error of the mean is $\dfrac{S}{\sqrt{n}} = \dfrac{13.816}{6.325} = 2.184$.

SUPPLEMENTARY PROBLEMS

Population Distribution, Population Mean, Population Variance, and Population Standard Deviation

21. A psychological study of families consisting of 4 children was undertaken. The variable of interest was the number of girls in the families. The number of girls could range from 0 to 4. The population had the following distribution.

X	0	1	2	3	4
$P(x)$	0.0625	0.25	0.375	0.25	0.0625

Find the population mean, the population variance, and the population standard deviation.

22. The number of dreams per night for a large class of people has the following distribution.

X	3	4	5	6	7
$P(x)$	0.2	0.2	0.2	0.2	0.2

Find the population mean, the population variance, and the population standard deviation.

23. The number of mood swings per week for a group of people has the following distribution.

X	5	10	15	20	25
$P(x)$	0.1	0.2	0.3	0.3	0.1

Find the population mean, the population variance, and the population standard deviation.

24. A smoking cessation study involved people who at the start of the study smoked the following number of cigarettes per day.

X	20	40	60
P(x)	0.2	0.6	0.2

Find the population mean, the population variance, and the population standard deviation.

The Distribution of Sample Means

25. Give the distribution of the sample mean for all samples of size $n = 2$ taken from the population described in Problem 21.

26. Give the distribution of the sample mean for all samples of size $n = 2$ taken from the population described in Problem 22.

27. Give the distribution of the sample mean for all samples of size $n = 2$ taken from the population described in Problem 23.

28. Give the distribution of the sample mean for all samples of size $n = 2$ taken from the population described in Problem 24.

Sample Mean Distribution, Mean of the Sample Mean, and Variance of the Sample Mean

29. Use SPSS to scatter plot the distribution of M in Problem 25, find the mean of M and the variance of M.

30. Use SPSS to scatter plot the distribution of M in Problem 26, find the mean of M and the variance of M.

31. Scatter plot the distribution of M in Problem 27, find the mean of M and the variance of M.

32. Scatter plot the distribution of M in Problem 28, find the mean of M and the variance of M.

Standard Error of the Mean

33. In Problem 29, show that $\sigma_M^2 = \dfrac{\sigma^2}{2}$ where σ^2 comes from Problem 21. Find σ_M.

34. In Problem 30, show that $\sigma_M^2 = \dfrac{\sigma^2}{2}$ where σ^2 comes from Problem 22. Find σ_M.

35. In Problem 31, show that $\sigma_M^2 = \dfrac{\sigma^2}{2}$ where σ^2 comes from Problem 23. Find σ_M.

36. In Problem 32, show that $\sigma_M^2 = \dfrac{\sigma^2}{2}$ where σ^2 comes from Problem 24. Find σ_M.

The Central Limit Theorem (Putting it All Together)

37. A sample of size $n > 30$ is taken from the population in Problem 21. What does the central limit theorem tell us about M?

38. A sample of size $n > 30$ is taken from the population in Problem 22. What does the central limit theorem tell us about M?

39. A sample of size $n > 30$ is taken from the population in Problem 23. What does the central limit theorem tell us about M?

40. A sample of size $n > 30$ is taken from the population in Problem 24. What does the central limit theorem tell us about M?

CHAPTER 8

Introduction to Hypothesis Testing and the z-Test Statistic

Research Problems in Psychology

We start this chapter by giving a few examples to see the nature of hypothesis testing. The sample sizes in the examples and problems will all be larger than 30. This will ensure that the sample mean, M, will have a normal distribution. We know from the previous chapter that M will have mean value, μ, and standard error $\frac{\sigma}{\sqrt{n}}$, where μ is the mean of the population from which the sample was taken and σ is the standard deviation of the population. It will also be assumed that σ is known. These assumptions will ensure that we may use the normal distribution in our tests of hypotheses. Small sample tests and the t-distribution will be introduced in Chapter 9.

1. Alcohol and Low Birth Weight   Let us investigate the relationship between birth weight and the use of alcohol during pregnancy. Suppose it is known that the average birth weight of a particular white rat is $\mu = 20$ grams with a standard deviation of $\sigma = 4$ grams. We have 50 rats available for an experiment. The females will be impregnated and given daily doses of alcohol and the birth weights of the baby rats will be recorded. The average birth weights for the sample are recorded and the average for the sample is found to be $M = 18$ grams. The average for the sample of 50, given daily doses of alcohol, is smaller than the average for all such rats ($M = 18 < \mu = 20$). Do we have research evidence that allows us to conclude that alcohol during pregnancy causes reduced birth weights?

2. Room Temperature and Food Consumption   A researcher knows that at room temperature (70 degrees), rats consume an average of $\mu = 12$ grams of food daily with a standard deviation of $\sigma = 4$ grams. Thirty-six such rats are maintained at room temperature 64 degrees. This sample averages $M = 13$ grams of food consumed per day. Is the sample average large enough to conclude that rats will consume more food if kept at 64 degrees rather than 70 degrees?

3. A New Drug for Stress and Response Time   The response time to an emergency situation is known to have an average time $\mu = 10$ seconds and a standard deviation $\sigma = 2$ seconds. A sample of 35 people take a particular drug and have their response time measured when they encounter an emergency situation. The objective is to determine if the average response time is different when a subject is taking the drug. When the researcher observes the average response time of the sample M, what can she conclude?

   In the sections that follow, we shall lay the framework for answering the above research problems. A large array of definitions will be needed to establish the theory of hypothesis testing.

Null Hypothesis (H₀) and Alternative Hypothesis (H₁)

In the above three example research problems, a *treatment* is applied to the members of a sample. In the first example, the treatment is a daily dose of alcohol given to pregnant rats. In the second, rats living in a cool environment is the treatment. In the third example, each person is given a drug for stress. These treatments are being tested to see if they affect the sample members. In the first example research problem, can we conclude that alcohol usage reduces the birth weight of the rats? In the second example, can we conclude that living in a cool environment will increase food consumption? In the third example, does the drug affect response time? In each of the examples the *null hypothesis* is that the treatment has a null or zero effect. We indicate this symbolically in the three examples as: H_0: $\mu = 20$ grams or the alcohol has no affect on birth weight; H_0: $\mu = 12$ grams or the cool temperature has no effect on the food consumption; and H_0: $\mu = 10$ seconds or the drug has no effect on response time. The *alternative hypotheses* are represented as H_1: $\mu < 20$ grams or the alcohol does reduce the average birth weight; H_1: $\mu > 12$ grams or the rats consume more food in the cooler environment; and H_1: $\mu \neq 10$ seconds or the drug affects response time. In each of these situations, μ represents the mean after the treatment has been applied.

Reaching a Decision

What is the probability of getting a sample of size $n = 50$ with a sample mean of $M = 18$ if the sample comes from a population with mean μ equal to 20? It is now that we turn to the results in Chapter 7 on the sampling distribution of the mean. We assume the null hypothesis to be true and calculate the probability of getting a sample mean of 18 or smaller from a population with $\mu = 20$. The distribution of M is normal with mean = 20 and standard error equal to $\sigma/\sqrt{n}$ or $4/\sqrt{50}$, which equals 0.57 as shown in Figure 8.1.

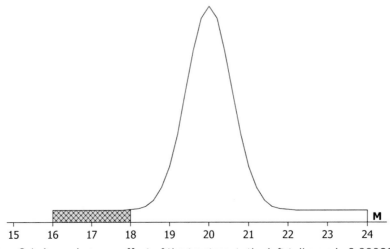

Figure 8.1 Assuming zero affect of the treatment, the left tail area is 0.0002251.

If MINITAB is used to calculate the area in the tail, we find 0.0002251. The MINITAB pull-down to give the area is **Calc → Probability distribution → Normal**. The output is:

```
Normal with mean=20 and standard deviation=0.57

x    P(X <=x)
18   0.0002251
```

If there is zero effect on the birth weight of baby rats of the treatment of daily doses of alcohol, the probability of getting a sample mean of 18 or smaller is 0.0002251. Our decision would be to reject the null hypothesis (because of the small probability) and conclude that daily doses of alcohol by the mother result in babies with a smaller average birth weight.

Rather than use the above technique, most users of statistics will convert the value of M above to a z-value first and then do the following equivalent test. The distribution of M is converted to a standard normal distribution by calculating the following *test statistic*.

$$Z = \frac{M - 20}{\frac{\sigma}{\sqrt{n}}} = \frac{18 - 20}{\frac{4}{\sqrt{50}}} = -3.54$$

This procedure is called the z-test. Locate the test statistic on the z-curve as in Figure 8.2.

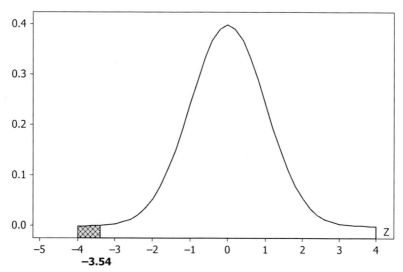

Figure 8.2 Standard normal curve with the p-value = 0.0002.

The probability of getting a test statistic as extreme as that shown in Figure 8.2 or beyond is called the *p-value*. Using EXCEL, the p-value is 0.0002, the same as obtained above. The usual rule is to reject the null hypothesis if the p-value <0.05. The value, 0.05, is called the α-*level* or *level of significance*. It is the level at which most researchers will reject the null hypothesis. It is possible that the null hypothesis is true even though the value of the test statistic has a probability less than 0.05, but it is the chance the researcher is willing to take.

Type 1 and Type 2 Errors

If the null hypothesis is rejected when it is true, a *type 1 error* is said to occur. If the null hypothesis is not rejected when it is false, a *type 2 error* is said to occur. These two errors are summarized in Table 8.1.

TABLE 8.1 Type 1 and Type 2 Errors

	THE NULL IS TRUE	THE NULL IS FALSE
Reject the Null	Type 1 error	No error made
Do Not Reject the Null	No error made	Type 2 error

EXAMPLE 1 The null hypothesis is that alcohol in the diet of female rats does not affect the birth weight of the baby rats; that is, H_0: $\mu = 20$ grams. A type 1 error occurs if this hypothesis is rejected but is true. If the average weight of the baby rats is <20, but we conclude that $\mu = 20$ grams, we commit a type 2 error.

The symbol α represents the probability of a type 1 error and the symbol β represents the probability of a type 2 error. As mentioned above, α is commonly set equal to 0.05.

One- and Two-Tailed Tests

The test illustrated in Figure 8.2 is called a *one-tailed test* because it uses only one tail of the standard normal distribution, namely the lower tail of the distribution. A test that uses both tails is called a *two-tailed test*. Consider a test that uses the other tail of the standard normal distribution.

EXAMPLE 2 A researcher knows that at room temperature (70 degrees), rats consume an average of $\mu = 12$ grams of food daily with a standard deviation of $\sigma = 4$ grams. Thirty-six such rats are maintained at a room temperature of 64 degrees. Let μ represent the average food consumption at room temperature 64 degrees. The null hypothesis is H_0: $\mu = 12$ grams; that is, the average food consumption is the same at room temperature 64 degrees as at room temperature 70 degrees. The alternative hypothesis is H_1: $\mu > 12$; that is, the average food consumption increases at the lower temperature. The sample average is 13 grams. The computed test statistic is

$$Z = \frac{M - 12}{\frac{\sigma}{\sqrt{n}}} = \frac{13 - 12}{\frac{4}{\sqrt{36}}} = 1.5.$$ The decision curve is shown in Figure 8.3.

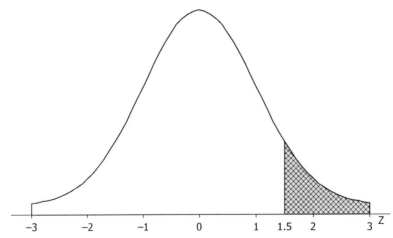

Figure 8.3 Standard normal curve with the p-value = 0.067.

The MINITAB computation of the p-value is as follows.

```
Normal with mean = 0 and standard deviation = 1

x       P(X <= x)
1.5     0.933193
```

The probability to the right of 1.5 is $1 - 0.933 = 0.067$. Taking $\alpha = 0.05$ and comparing the p-value with 0.05 we see that it is not smaller that 0.05 and we would conclude that our evidence is not strong enough to reject the null.

EXAMPLE 3 The response time to an emergency situation is known to have an average time $\mu = 20$ seconds and a standard deviation $\sigma = 6$ seconds. A sample of 36 people are given a drug and have their response time measured when they encounter an emergency situation. It is desired to test if the average response time is different when taking the drug. When the researcher observes the average response time of the sample, she finds that it equals 22 seconds. Test H_0: $\mu = 20$ versus H_a: $\mu \neq 20$ at $\alpha = 0.05$. When you find the p-value, compare it with $\alpha = 0.05$. If the p-value $< \alpha$, then reject the null hypothesis. Otherwise, do not reject the null. The computed value of

the test statistic is $Z = \dfrac{M - 20}{\dfrac{\sigma}{\sqrt{n}}} = \dfrac{22 - 20}{\dfrac{6}{\sqrt{36}}} = 2.00$. The decision curve is shown in Figure 8.4.

In this case, because we have a two-tailed alternative, we find the area to the right of 2 and add to it the area to the left of −2 to find the p-value. Because the p-value is smaller than 0.05, reject the null hypothesis. Conclude that the drug does affect the average response time.

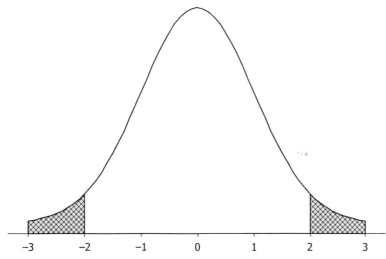

Figure 8.4 Standard normal curve with p-value = 0.0455.

Summarizing the z-Test for Testing Hypotheses

The z-test may be summarized as follows:

1. State the null hypothesis and the alternative hypothesis. The alternative hypothesis may be one-tailed or two-tailed. The research situation usually determines whether the test is one-tailed or two-tailed.

2. Set your level of significance or α-level. The α-level is usually set equal to 0.05, however any value between 0 and 1 is possible.

3. Conduct the experiment and gather the data.

4. Assuming the null hypothesis to be true, calculate the value of your test statistic. The test statistic is $Z = \dfrac{M - \mu_0}{\dfrac{\sigma}{\sqrt{n}}}$, where M is the value of the sample mean, μ_0 is the null hypothesis value of the population mean, σ is the assumed known value of the standard deviation, and n is the sample size.

5. Calculate the p-value. If it is less than α, reject the null hypothesis. If it is not less than α, do not reject the null hypothesis.

An Alternative Method of Testing an Hypothesis

EXAMPLE 4 Suppose we would like to investigate the relationship between birth weight and the use of alcohol during pregnancy. It is known that the average birth weight of a particular type rat is $\mu = 20$ grams with a standard deviation of $\sigma = 4$ grams. We have 50 rats available for an experiment. The females will be made pregnant and will be given daily doses of alcohol. The birth weights will be recorded for the offspring of the 50 rats. The average birth weights for the sample are recorded and the average for the sample is found to be $M = 18$. The null hypothesis is $H_0: \mu = 20$ and $H_1: \mu < 20$, where μ represents the average birth weight of the baby rats. The α-level is set equal to 0.05. Next a *critical value* is determined corresponding to the α-level. The critical value is illustrated in Figure 8.5. The critical value is determined so that area 0.05 is in the lower tail.

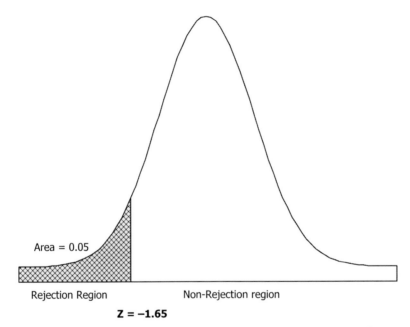

Area = 0.05

Rejection Region   Non-Rejection region

Z = –1.65

Figure 8.5 Critical value –1.65 is such that area = 0.05 is in the left tail.

In this *classical method of testing hypotheses*, the critical value divides the axis into a *rejection region* and a *non-rejection region*. The gray region corresponds to the rejection region and the remaining possible values of z are the non-rejection region. The test statistic is computed and, as before, found to be –3.54. Because the test statistics is in the rejection region, we reject the null hypothesis. **The same conclusion will always be reached by using the classical method of testing or the p-value method of testing.** Recall that the *p-value method of testing hypotheses* takes the computed test statistic, –3.54 and computes the p-value that goes with it and if p-value $< \alpha$, then reject the null hypothesis.

Using Software to Perform the z-Test

We now illustrate how to perform the tests using software.

EXAMPLE 5 Alcohol and Low Birth Weight. Test $H_0: \mu = 20$ versus $H_1: \mu < 20$ using MINITAB software. Using the pull-down menu **Stat → Basic Statistics → 1-sample Z** gives the dialog box, which is filled in as shown in Figure 8.6.

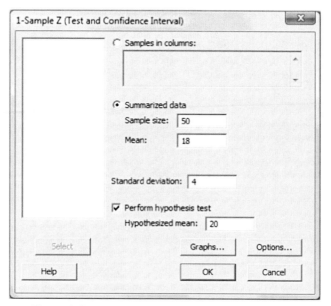

Figure 8.6 MINITAB dialog box for 1-sample z-Test.

The Options dialog box is filled in as shown in Figure 8.7.

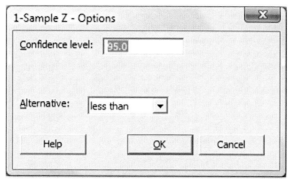

Figure 8.7 MINITAB Options dialog box where less than alternative is chosen.

The MINITAB output is

```
Test of mu = 20 vs < 20
The assumed standard deviation = 4
                        95% Upper
N    Mean    SE Mean    Bound      Z       P
50   18.000  0.566      18.930    -3.54   0.000
```

These are the same results arrived at previously in the section entitled "Reaching a Decision."

Note that in Example 5, the population standard deviation is entered ($\sigma = 4$) in Figure 8.6, the sample mean has already been found to be $M = 18$, the null hypothesized value of the population mean, 20, is also entered. In the Options box (Figure 8.7), the alternative that the population mean is less than 20 is also entered. The computed test statistic is found to be -3.54.

Software is most often used in situations where the data are *raw data* rather than *summarized data*. In other words, the sample mean has not been computed.

EXAMPLE 6 Alcohol and Low Birth Weight. Test H_0: $\mu = 20$ versus H_1: $\mu < 20$ using MINITAB software. Suppose the raw data are as shown in Table 8.2.

TABLE 8.2 Raw Birth Weight Data in Grams

12.2	17.9	18.9	23.8	23.2
7.8	24.9	16.3	21.5	22.0
16.1	19.0	11.9	19.3	18.9
22.4	18.8	17.5	14.6	26.6
22.2	16.0	12.5	14.8	22.4
19.5	16.3	8.5	10.5	26.6
14.7	31.1	13.5	21.3	13.6
22.0	15.3	20.2	13.0	15.3
21.4	12.9	22.5	17.9	17.4
12.1	17.1	25.7	19.3	22.5

The MINITAB solution is as follows. The data are entered into column C1. Column C1 is given the name birthweight, and the pull-down **Stat → Basic Statistics → 1-sample z** is given.

The dialog box is completed as shown in Figure 8.8. The population standard deviation ($\sigma = 4$) is entered and the software finds the mean of the data in column C1. Using the computed sample mean M, the supplied population standard deviation ($\sigma = 4$), and the null value of the population mean, the computed test statistic, -3.12 and the p-value $= 0.002$ are computed. The output for the routine, 1-sample z, is as follows.

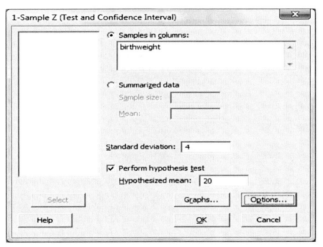

Figure 8.8 MINITAB dialog box for 1-sample z-test.

One-Sample Z: birthweight

```
Test of mu=20 vs not=20
The assumed standard deviation = 4

Variable      N    Mean   StDev  SE Mean   95% CI              Z      P
birthweight  50  18.234   4.950   0.566   (17.125,19.343)   -3.12  0.002
```

Because the p-value <0.05, the null hypothesis is rejected. The 1-sample z assumes the population standard deviation, σ, is known and σ is used in the test statistic rather than the standard deviation of the sample. The sample data are used to compute the mean of the sample, M. The null hypothesis defines the value to be used for the population mean. The test statistic is $Z = \dfrac{M - \mu_0}{\dfrac{\sigma}{\sqrt{n}}}$. This value is used to compute the p-value.

SOLVED PROBLEMS

Research Problems in Psychology

1. The general population scores an average of $\mu = 80$ with a standard deviation of $\sigma = 4.5$ on a memory test. A researcher conducts an experiment with 40 alcoholics. She believes the alcoholics will score lower on the average on the memory test. Is this test a one-sided or two-sided test?

   Solution

   This is a one-sided test.

2. A test to measure anxiety and depression has a mean score of $\mu = 55$ with a standard deviation equal to 3.5 for the general population. A group of 45 persons known to be suffering from anxiety and depression is given the test. It is of interest to know if the group will score differently than the general population on the test. Is this a one-sided or two-sided test?

   Solution

   This is a two-sided test.

3. Rats are known to take a mean of 10 minutes to find their way through a maze to reach a food source with a standard deviation equal to 2.5 minutes. A researcher wishes to determine if taking a certain drug will change the time it takes to run the maze. Fifty rats are given the drug and timed on their run times through the maze. Is this a one-sided or two-sided test?

   Solution

   This is a two-sided test.

4. A psychological researcher would like to evaluate a new approach to teaching statistics for the behavioral sciences. She knows that the average score that has been attained in this course over the past several years is 75 with $\sigma = 7$. She uses the new approach on a sample of 75 to see if they score differently. Should she conduct a one-side or two-sided test to find the answer?

   Solution

   She should conduct a two-sided test.

Null Hypothesis (H_0) and Alternative Hypothesis (H_1)

5. State the null hypothesis and the alternative hypothesis in Problem 1.

   Solution

   Let μ represent the average score on the memory test for alcoholics.

   $H_0: \mu = 80$ $H_1: \mu < 80$

6. State the null hypothesis and the alternative hypothesis in Problem 2.

   Solution

   Let μ represent the average score on the anxiety and depression test for the group known to be suffering from depression and anxiety.

   $H_0: \mu = 55$ $H_1: \mu \neq 55$

7. State the null hypothesis and the alternative hypothesis in Problem 3.

   Solution

   Let μ represent the average time to run the maze when under the influence of the drug.

   $H_0: \mu = 10$ $H_1: \mu \neq 10$

8. State the null hypothesis and the alternative hypothesis in Problem 4.

Solution

Let μ represent the average score in the behavioral statistics course using the new technique.

$H_0: \mu = 75 \qquad H_1: \mu \neq 75$

Reaching a Decision

9. Refer to Problems 1 and 5. Suppose the mean of the sample of 40 memory test scores for the 40 alcoholics is $M = 78.4$. Give the computed z-test statistic, compute the p-value, and give your conclusion for $\alpha = 0.05$.

Solution

$H_0: \mu = 80 \qquad H_1: \mu < 80 \qquad Z = \dfrac{M - 80}{\dfrac{\sigma}{\sqrt{n}}} = \dfrac{78.4 - 80}{\dfrac{4.5}{\sqrt{40}}} = -2.25$

The p-value is the area under the standard normal curve to the left of –2.25. Using EXCEL, we find =NORMSDIST(–2.25), which equals 0.0122. The p-value for this hypothesis test is 0.0122, which is less than $\alpha = 0.05$ and we therefore reject the null hypothesis.

10. Refer to Problems 2 and 6. Suppose the mean of the sample of 45 depression and anxiety test scores for the 45 known anxiety and depression sufferers is $M = 56.1$. Give the computed z-test statistic, compute the p-value, and give your conclusion for $\alpha = 0.05$.

Solution

$H_0: \mu = 55 \qquad H_1: \mu \neq 55 \qquad Z = \dfrac{M - 55}{\dfrac{\sigma}{\sqrt{n}}} = \dfrac{56.1 - 55}{\dfrac{3.5}{\sqrt{45}}} = 2.11.$

The p-value is the area under the standard normal curve to the left of –2.11 plus the area to the right of 2.11. We may find the area to the left of –2.11 and double it to find the p-value. Using EXCEL, the answer is =2*NORMSDIST(–2.11), which equals 0.0349. Remember, we find the area in two tails to find the p-value because it is a two-tailed test. The p-value for this hypothesis test is 0.0349, which is less than $\alpha = 0.05$, and we therefore reject the null hypothesis.

11. Refer to Problems 3 and 7. Suppose the mean of the sample of run times for the 50 rats taking the drug is $M = 10.5$ minutes. Give the computed z-test statistic, compute the p-value, and give your conclusion for $\alpha = 0.05$.

Solution

$H_0: \mu = 10 \qquad H_1: \mu \neq 10 \qquad Z = \dfrac{M - 10}{\dfrac{\sigma}{\sqrt{n}}} = \dfrac{10.5 - 10}{\dfrac{2.5}{\sqrt{50}}} = 1.41$

The p-value is the area to the left of –1.41 plus the area to the right of 1.41. Using EXCEL, we find the p-value to be 0.1585. Because the p-value is greater than 0.05 we do not have enough evidence to reject the null hypothesis.

12. Refer to Problems 4 and 8. Suppose the average score on the test in behavioral statistics for the sample is 77.5. Give the computed z-test statistic, compute the p-value, and give your conclusion for $\alpha = 0.05$.

Solution

$H_0: \mu = 75 \qquad H_1: \mu \neq 75 \qquad Z = \dfrac{M - 75}{\dfrac{\sigma}{\sqrt{n}}} = \dfrac{77.5 - 75}{\dfrac{7}{\sqrt{75}}} = 3.09$

The p-value is equal to area to the left of –3.09 plus the area to the right of 3.09. Using EXCEL, the area is given by the area to the left of –3.09 doubled. The area to the left of –3.09 is =NORMSDIST (–3.09) or 0.001. The p-value is 2(0.001) = 0.002. The new method gives better scores on the average.

Type 1 and Type 2 Errors

13. In Problem 9, describe a type 1 and a type 2 error.

> ### Solution
>
> A type 1 error occurs if it is concluded that $\mu < 80$ when $\mu = 80$.
>
> A type 2 error occurs if it is concluded that $\mu = 80$ when $\mu < 80$.

14. In Problem 10, describe a type 1 and a type 2 error.

> ### Solution
>
> A type 1 error occurs if the sample evidence leads us to conclude that $\mu \neq 55$ when $\mu = 55$.
>
> A type 2 error occurs if sample evidence does not lead to rejecting that $\mu = 55$ when $\mu \neq 55$.

15. In Problem 11, describe a type 1 and a type 2 error.

> ### Solution
>
> A type 1 error occurs if the sample evidence leads us to conclude that $\mu \neq 10$ when $\mu = 10$.
>
> A type 2 error occurs if sample evidence does not lead to rejecting that $\mu = 10$ when $\mu \neq 10$.

16. In Problem 12, describe a type 1 and a type 2 error.

> ### Solution
>
> A type 1 error occurs if the sample evidence leads us to conclude that $\mu \neq 75$ when $\mu = 75$.
>
> A type 2 error occurs if sample evidence does not lead to rejecting that $\mu = 75$ when $\mu \neq 75$.

Summarizing the z-Test for Testing Hypotheses

Problems 17–20. After working your way through Problems 1 to 16, put your z-test together as a complete test of hypotheses for Problems 1 through 4.

17. 1. Let μ represent the average score on the memory test for alcoholics.

$H_0: \mu = 80$ The average score on the memory test for alcoholics equals 80, the same as the general population.
$H_1: \mu < 80$ The average score on the memory test for alcoholics is less than 80, the average score for the general population.

2. α is set equal to 0.05.

3. Forty alcoholics are administered the memory test and the sample mean, M, is found to equal 78.4.

4. The value of the test statistic is $Z = \dfrac{M - \mu_0}{\dfrac{\sigma}{\sqrt{n}}} = \dfrac{78.4 - 80}{\dfrac{4.5}{\sqrt{40}}} = -2.25$

5. The p-value, the area under the standard normal curve to the left of –2.25, is 0.0122. Because the p-value is less than α, reject the null hypothesis and conclude that alcohol reduces the score made on the memory test.

18. 1. Let μ represent the average score on the anxiety and depression test for the group known to be suffering from depression and anxiety.

$H_0: \mu = 55$ The average made on the test given to the group known to be suffering from depression and anxiety is 55, the same as it is for the general population.
$H_1: \mu \neq 55$ The average made on the test given to the group known to be suffering from depression and anxiety is not 55, the value it is for the general population.

2. α is set equal to 0.05.

3. Forty-five subjects known to be suffering from anxiety and depression are administered the test for anxiety and depression and the sample mean for that group is $M = 56.1$.

4. The value of the test statistic is $Z = \dfrac{M - \mu_0}{\dfrac{\sigma}{\sqrt{n}}} = \dfrac{56.1 - 55}{\dfrac{3.5}{\sqrt{45}}} = 2.11$.

5. The p-value is the area under the standard normal curve to the left of -2.11 plus the area to the right of 2.11 or 0.0349. Because the p-value is less than α, we reject the null and conclude that the group suffering from anxiety and depression score higher on the test than the general population.

19. 1. Let μ represent the average time to run the maze when under the influence of the drug.

   H_0: $\mu = 10$ The average time to run the maze when under the influence of the drug is the 10 minutes, the same as when not under the influence of the drug.
   H_1: $\mu \neq 10$ The average time to run the maze when under the influence of the drug is not 10 minutes, which is the time when not under the influence of the drug.

   2. α is set equal to 0.05.

   3. Fifty rats are given the drug and timed when running the maze. The average time to run the maze when under the influence is 10.5 minutes.

   4. The value of the test statistic is $Z = \dfrac{M - \mu_0}{\dfrac{\sigma}{\sqrt{n}}} = \dfrac{10.5 - 10}{\dfrac{2.5}{\sqrt{50}}} = 1.41$.

   5. The p-value is the area under the standard normal curve to the left of -1.41 plus the area under the standard normal curve to the right of 1.41. The p-value is 0.1585. Because the p-value is greater than α, we do not reject the null.

20. 1. Let μ represent the average grade made when teaching statistics for the behavioral sciences using the new approach.

   H_0: $\mu = 75$ The new approach produces the same average results as the old technique.
   H_1: $\mu \neq 75$ The new approach produces the different average results as the old technique.

   2. α is set equal to 0.05.

   3. Seventy-five students are taught using the new approach. The average score made by this sample of 75 using the new approach is $M = 77.5$.

   4. The value of the test statistic is $Z = \dfrac{M - \mu_0}{\dfrac{\sigma}{\sqrt{n}}} = \dfrac{77.5 - 75}{\dfrac{7.0}{\sqrt{75}}} = 3.09$.

   5. The p-value is the area under the standard normal curve to the left of -3.09 plus the area under the standard normal curve to the right of 3.09. The p-value is 0.002. Because the p-value is less than α, we conclude the new approach produces different results than the old approach.

Using Minitab Software to Perform the z-Test

In Problems 21 through 24, the hypotheses in Problems 1 through 4 are tested when the data are in raw form rather than summarized form. This is the situation most often encountered in actual research studies.

21. Table 8.3 contains the test scores made on the memory test for 40 alcoholics. Test that the mean of these scores are less than 80, the average score for the general population.

   ### Solution

   The MINITAB output follows. The standard deviation is assumed to be 4.5, the value of M computed from the data is 74.8, the computed test statistic is $z = -7.31$, and the p-value is 0.000. The null hypothesis is rejected.

TABLE 8.3 Memory Test Scores for 40 Alcoholics

66	79	76	77
75	70	80	69
67	67	67	70
85	75	75	87
81	72	79	75
81	75	76	75
72	74	69	70
73	80	76	70
72	78	75	81
75	77	80	71

One-Sample Z: memory scores

```
Test of mu = 80 vs < 80
The assumed standard deviation = 4.5
                                  95% Upper
Variable          N     Mean    StDev   SE Mean   Bound     Z       P
memory scores    40   74.800    4.988    0.712    75.970   -7.31   0.000
```

22. Table 8.4 contains the test scores made on the anxiety and depression test given to 45 individuals suffering from anxiety and depression. Test that the average of these scores is not equal to 55, the average score for the general population.

TABLE 8.4 Test Scores for Anxiety and Depression Sufferers

55	55	55	60	50
50	54	57	51	62
57	59	57	60	59
59	49	63	50	58
58	54	56	56	54
61	57	58	52	54
60	55	55	59	60
50	57	54	61	51
59	55	56	59	54

Solution

The MINITAB output follows. The standard deviation is assumed to be 3.5, the value of M computed from the data is 56.111, the computed test statistic is $z = 2.13$, and the p-value is 0.033. The null hypothesis is rejected.

One-Sample Z: test scores

```
Test of mu = 55 vs not = 55
The assumed standard deviation = 3.5

Variable       N     Mean    StDev   SE Mean    95% CI              Z       P
test scores   45   56.111   3.563    0.522   (55.089, 57.134)    2.13   0.033
```

23. Table 8.5 contains the run times for 50 rats when under the influence of a drug. Test that the average run time is different than 10 minutes for the 50 rats.

TABLE 8.5 Times to Run the Maze when under the Influence of the Drug

16.2	13.6	10.6	9.2	6.8
6.1	9.9	8.8	12.0	11.0
6.8	9.5	9.1	11.6	12.7
11.8	15.6	10.9	8.7	10.7
9.4	14.2	14.7	9.0	13.2
8.3	9.9	11.5	8.5	9.5
15.3	11.3	9.9	9.2	2.3
3.6	11.1	11.4	10.0	14.5
8.8	10.1	12.9	11.1	7.7
12.1	10.1	14.4	9.4	10.3

Solution

The MINITAB output follows. The standard deviation is assumed to be 2.5, the value of M computed from the data is 10.506, the computed test statistic is $z = 1.43$, and the p-value is 0.152. The null hypothesis is not rejected.

One-Sample Z: run times

```
Test of mu = 10 vs not = 10
The assumed standard deviation = 2.5
```

Variable	N	Mean	StDev	SE Mean	95% CI	Z	P
run times	50	10.506	2.799	0.354	(9.813, 11.199)	1.43	0.152

24. Table 8.6 contains the test scores for 75 students in statistics for the behavioral sciences when taught using the new technique. Test that the average test score is different than 75, the average when the course is taught using the traditional method.

TABLE 8.6 Test Scores when Using the New Technique to Teach Statistics

67	74	67	77	76
73	72	80	77	73
67	73	73	75	85
77	79	80	79	74
75	79	72	78	82
74	72	80	64	69
84	72	70	79	81
75	81	79	68	79
71	71	75	70	65
68	62	69	85	77
74	82	84	77	71
72	63	73	75	71
82	61	66	69	85
61	79	68	85	65
67	75	73	72	73

Solution

The MINITAB output follows. The standard deviation is assumed to be 7, the value of M computed from the data is 73.96, the computed test statistic is $z = -1.29$, and the p-value is 0.198. The null hypothesis is not rejected.

One-Sample Z: test scores

```
Test of mu = 75 vs not = 75
The assumed standard deviation = 7

Variable       N    Mean    StDev    SE Mean    95% CI            Z       P
test scores    75   73.960  6.079    0.808      (72.376, 75.544)  -1.29   0.198
```

SUPPLEMENTARY PROBLEMS

Research Problems in Psychology

25. A psychological researcher believes that extra playtime with infants will result in a higher average weight at 2 years age. The average weight of humans at 2 years of age is 26 pounds with a standard deviation of 3.5 pounds for the general population. The researcher plans an experiment with 36 infants. She instructs the parents of the 36 infants to spend extra time playing with the infants and then determines their weights at 2 years of age. Would this be a one-sided or two-sided test?

26. A psychological researcher wishes to test whether a drug reduces appetite and, as a result, food consumption. Suppose rats are known to consume 12 grams of food per day with a standard deviation of 3 grams. Fifty of these rats are given the drug over a period of time and their average food consumption is determined. Would this be a one-sided or two-sided test?

27. An educational psychologist wishes to increase the usage of statistical software in her Statistics for Psychology course. She wants to determine if it will change the average performance of her students. The average previously on a final exam in the course has been 70 with a standard deviation of 5. Fifty students are taught the course with the increased use of statistical software. Would this be a one-sided or two-sided test?

28. Rats are known to reach an average weight at maturity of 930 grams with a standard deviation equal to 25 grams. Researchers believe that if the rats are fed a growth hormone, they will reach an average weight that exceeds 930 grams. Would this be a one-sided or two-sided test?

Null Hypothesis (H_0) and Alternative Hypothesis (H_1)

29. State the null hypothesis and the alternative hypothesis in Problem 25.

30. State the null hypothesis and the alternative hypothesis in Problem 26.

31. State the null hypothesis and the alternative hypothesis in Problem 27.

32. State the null hypothesis and the alternative hypothesis in Problem 28.

Reaching a Decision

33. Refer to Problems 25 and 29. Suppose the mean weight of the sample of 36 two-year-olds who had longer playtimes as infants is 27.1 pounds. Give the computed z-test statistic, compute the p-value, and give your conclusion for $\alpha = 0.05$.

34. Refer to Problems 26 and 30. The average weight of the sample of 50 rats when given the appetite suppressant is 11.2 grams. Give the computed z-test statistic, compute the p-value, and give your conclusion for $\alpha = 0.05$.

35. Refer to Problems 27 and 31. Suppose the average score on the test when computer software is used for a sample of 50 students is 69.3. Give the computed z-test statistic, compute the p-value, and give your conclusion for $\alpha = 0.05$.

36. Refer to Problems 28 and 32. Suppose the average weight of 50 rats, when given the growth hormone, is 945 grams. Give the computed z-test statistic, compute the p-value, and give your conclusion for $\alpha = 0.05$.

Type 1 and Type 2 Errors

37. In Problem 33, describe a type 1 and a type 2 error.

38. In Problem 34, describe a type 1 and a type 2 error.

39. In Problem 35, describe a type 1 and a type 2 error.

40. In Problem 36, describe a type 1 and a type 2 error.

Summarizing the z-Test for Testing Hypotheses

Problems 41–44. After working your way through Problems 25 to 40, put your z-test together as a complete test of hypotheses for Problems 41 through 44.

Using Minitab Software to Perform the z-Test

45. Table 8.7 gives the weights of $n = 36$ two-year-olds who received extra playtime as infants. Use MINITAB to test $H_0: \mu = 26$ $H_1: \mu > 26$ with $\alpha = 0.05$.

TABLE 8.7 **Weights of Two-Year-Old Children Receiving Extra Playtime**

28	32	30	31
30	27	30	24
26	23	30	33
26	23	25	23
23	25	22	28
25	29	22	20
30	28	28	27
25	25	26	21
26	20	29	23

46. Table 8.8 gives the food consumption of $n = 50$ rats given a appetite suppressant. Use MINITAB to test $H_0: \mu = 12$ $H_1: \mu < 12$ with $\alpha = 0.05$.

TABLE 8.8 **Food Consumption while Taking an Appetite Suppressant**

9	10	16	10	5
16	9	11	7	8
9	9	8	14	19
9	6	8	11	9
14	12	15	12	10
10	14	13	5	9
5	11	11	15	15
11	10	14	9	10
18	13	14	12	9
12	13	11	12	14

47. Table 8.9 gives the test scores from a sample of 50 students in a Statistics for Psychology course that uses statistical software on a weekly basis. Use MINITAB to test H_0: $\mu = 70$ H_1: $\mu \neq 70$ with $\alpha = 0.05$.

TABLE **8.9 Test Scores for Students Using Statistical Software**

75	66	76	72	78
68	70	78	71	74
75	82	67	69	74
69	65	74	75	77
73	73	70	83	68
67	74	73	75	69
74	65	69	70	72
64	74	74	65	72
67	74	76	72	74
74	73	75	61	73

48. Table 8.10 gives the weights of 50 rats taking a growth hormone. Use MINITAB to test H_0: $\mu = 930$ H_1: $\mu > 930$ with $\alpha = 0.05$.

TABLE **8.10 Weights of Rats Taking a Growth Hormone**

947	972	896	981	973
976	948	902	966	963
958	934	934	935	968
960	948	933	874	917
930	928	925	932	916
893	980	953	926	935
922	938	901	902	962
909	936	926	920	953
970	916	933	913	937
934	958	967	936	916

CHAPTER 9

The t-Test Statistic and the t-Test

Introduction to the t-Distribution

In Chapter 8, we were introduced to testing hypotheses. The techniques for testing hypotheses are easiest to develop in terms of the z-test. The z-test basically assumes that the population standard deviation is known and that the sample size exceeds 30. These conditions ensure that $Z = \dfrac{M - \mu_0}{\dfrac{\sigma}{\sqrt{n}}}$ will follow a standard normal distribution. Hence, the name z-test is appropriate, because z represents the standard normal distribution. Sometimes this is a very appropriate test. We may know the standard deviation and we may also know that it has not changed over time. For example the standard deviation of human adult male heights is known to equal $\sigma = 2.5$ inches. However, the population standard deviation is often not known. Also, many times sample units are expensive and we are forced to work with as small a sample as possible. In case σ is not known, the sample standard deviation, S, is substituted for σ. The statistic $T = \dfrac{M - \mu_0}{\dfrac{S}{\sqrt{n}}}$ has a *student t-distribution*, provided the sample comes from a normally distributed population. This is an extremely important assumption and is critical for small samples. There is a measure called the *degrees of freedom* associated with the t-distribution. The degrees of freedom is represented by (df) and we write df = $n - 1$, or degrees of freedom is one less than the sample size.

The Relationship between the z- and t-Distributions

There is a separate t-curve determined by each different degree of freedom. That is, for each df value, there is a separate t-curve. Figure 9.1 compares the t-curve with 3 df, the t-curve with 30 df, and the z-curve. Note that the z-curve is very similar to the t-curve with 30 df. When $n > 30$, the t-curve and the z-curve are practically the same curve. Following are some of the properties of the z- and the student t-curve with degrees of freedom.

Properties of the z-Distribution Curve

1. The total area under the z-curve is 1.

2. The z-curve is symmetrical about 0.

3. The mean of the z-distribution is 0.

4. The standard deviation of the z-distribution is 1.

5. Because of the symmetry of the z-distribution about 0, the area to the right of z = 0 is 0.5 and the area to the left of z = 0 is 0.5.

6. The z-curve is asymptotic to the horizontal axis in both directions, that is to the right and to the left.

Properties of the t-Distribution Curve with Degrees of Freedom

1. The total area under the t-curve with df degrees of freedom is 1.

2. The t-distribution curve with df degrees of freedom is symmetrical at about 0.

3. The mean of the t-distribution curve with df degrees of freedom distribution is symmetrical about 0.

4. The standard deviation of the t-distribution curve with df degrees of freedom is $\sqrt{\dfrac{df}{df-2}}$ for df > 2.

5. Because of the symmetry of the t-distribution curve with df degrees of freedom about 0, the area to the right of t = 0 is 0.5 and the area to the left of t = 0 is 0.5.

6. The t-distribution curve with df degrees of freedom is asymptotic to the horizontal axis in both directions, that is to the right and to the left.

These properties show how similar the z-distribution and the t-distribution curves with df degrees of freedom are. Most statistical practitioners accept the two distributions as being basically the same for samples greater than 30.

Figure 9.1 shows how the t-distribution approaches the z-distribution as *n* (or df) becomes larger. The curves are hard to differentiate when df > 30.

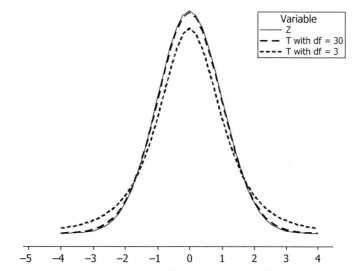

Figure 9.1 Comparing t-curves with the z-curve (MINITAB multiple plot).

EXAMPLE 1 Find the standard deviation for the t-distribution having degrees of freedom equal to 5, 10, 20, 30, and 100. We will evaluate $\sqrt{\dfrac{df}{df-2}}$ for degrees of freedom equal to each of the five values. For df = 5, $\sigma = 1.29$; for df = 10, $\sigma = 1.12$; for df = 20, $\sigma = 1.05$; for df = 30, $\sigma = 1.04$; and for df = 100, $\sigma = 1.01$. We see that the t-distribution's variability approaches that of the z-distribution's variability as *n* gets larger.

Areas under the t-Distribution

Table 9.1 gives the areas in the right tail of the t-distribution with df degrees of freedom. Many statistics books have tables such as this; it is included so that the reader will be familiar with its structure. It is recommended

TABLE **9.1** **Areas in the Right Tail of the t-Distribution**

			AREA IN THE RIGHT TAIL			
DF	0.25	0.1	0.05	0.025	0.01	0.005
1	1	3.078	6.314	12.710	31.820	63.660
2	0.816	1.886	2.920	4.303	6.965	9.925
3	0.765	1.638	2.353	3.182	4.541	5.841
4	0.741	1.533	2.132	2.776	3.747	4.604
5	0.727	1.476	2.015	2.571	3.365	4.032
6	0.718	1.440	1.943	2.447	3.143	3.707
7	0.711	1.415	1.895	2.365	2.998	3.499
8	0.706	1.397	1.860	2.306	2.896	3.355
9	0.703	1.383	1.833	2.262	2.821	3.250
10	0.700	1.372	1.812	2.228	2.764	3.169
11	0.697	1.363	1.796	2.201	2.718	3.106
12	0.695	1.356	1.782	2.179	2.681	3.055
13	0.694	1.350	1.771	2.160	2.650	3.012
14	0.692	1.345	1.761	2.145	2.624	2.977
15	0.691	1.341	1.753	2.131	2.602	2.947
16	0.690	1.337	1.746	2.120	2.583	2.921
17	0.689	1.333	1.740	2.110	2.567	2.898
18	0.688	1.330	1.734	2.101	2.552	2.878
19	0.688	1.328	1.729	2.093	2.539	2.861
20	0.687	1.325	1.725	2.086	2.528	2.845
21	0.686	1.323	1.721	2.080	2.518	2.831
22	0.686	1.321	1.717	2.074	2.508	2.819
23	0.685	1.319	1.714	2.069	2.500	2.807
24	0.685	1.318	1.711	2.064	2.492	2.797
25	0.684	1.316	1.708	2.060	2.485	2.787
26	0.684	1.315	1.706	2.056	2.479	2.779
27	0.684	1.314	1.703	2.052	2.473	2.771
28	0.683	1.313	1.701	2.048	2.467	2.763
29	0.683	1.311	1.699	2.045	2.462	2.756
30	0.683	1.310	1.697	2.042	2.457	2.750

that the z-distribution be used if the degrees of freedom exceed 30, because the two distributions are very similar when the degrees of freedom exceed 30.

The table is formed by using EXCEL. The numbers 1 through 30 are entered in A1:A30. The expression =TINV(0.5,A1) is entered into B1 and a click-and-drag is performed from B1 to B30. This produces the areas under the column labeled 0.25. Note that the number 0.5 is twice the column label. The expression =TINV(0.2,A1) is entered into C1 and a click-and-drag is performed from C1 to C30. This produces the areas under the column labeled 0.10. This is continued until the table is constructed. The reader is invited to construct a table to see how easy it is. This table is used to find critical values and to find p-values in hypothesis testing. However, when SPSS is used, this software finds the p-values assuming a two-tailed alternative. If a one-tailed alternative is used, take 1/2 of the SPSS value and give it as your p-value.

EXAMPLE 2 Find the area under the t-distribution curve having 13 df between -1.350 and 2.650 using Table 9.1. Using the table, locate 13 df. Then, locate 1.350. The area to the right of 1.350 is 0.1. Due to symmetry, the area to the left of -1.350 is 0.1 also. The area to the right of 2.650 is 0.01. Putting this all together, the area between -1.350 and 2.650 is $1 - 0.1 - 0.01$ or 0.89. This is written as $p(-1.350 < t < 2.650) = 0.89$. This is shown in Figure 9.2.

EXAMPLE 3 Use the MINITAB pull-down **Calc → Probability distribution → T distribution** to find the area in Example 2.

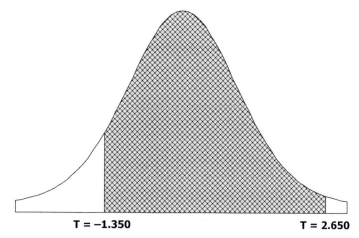

$$T = -1.350 \qquad\qquad T = 2.650$$

Figure 9.2 Area under t-distribution with df = 13 between t = −1.350 and t = 2.650.

Cumulative Distribution Function

Student's t distribution with 13 DF

x	P(X <= x)
2.65	0.989994

Cumulative Distribution Function

Student's t distribution with 13 DF

x	P(X <= x)
−1.35	0.100027

To find the area between −1.350 and 2.650, subtract 0.100027 from 0.989994 to get 0.889994 or 0.89 to 2 decimal places.

t-Test Using SPSS

EXAMPLE 4 A researcher believes that drinking alcohol during pregnancy gives below average birth weights of rats (normal birth weight of rats when alcohol is not used is 20 grams). A sample of pregnant rats are given alcohol to drink daily and the birth weights of the offspring are recorded. The weights in grams are as follows: 17, 17, 20, 19, 18, 19, 16, 21, 15, and 22. Test the hypothesis H_0: $\mu = 20$ versus H_1: $\mu < 20$ using SPSS. After entering the data in the SPSS data sheet, the pull-down **Analyze → Compare means → 1-sample t test** will allow you to perform the t-test.

One-Sample Statistics

	N	MEAN	STD. DEVIATION	STD. ERROR MEAN
Weights	10	18.4000	2.22111	0.70238

One-Sample Test

			TEST VALUE = 20			
				MEAN	95% CONFIDENCE INTERVAL	
	t	df	SIG. (2-TAILED)	DIFFERENCE	OF THE DIFFERENCE	
					LOWER	UPPER
Weights	−2.278	9	0.049	−1.60000	−3.1889	−0.0111

The SPSS output gives the following: the sample size $n = 10$; the mean of the sample, $M = 18.4$; the standard deviation of the sample $S = 2.22$; the standard error of the mean $= 0.70238$; the computed t-value $= -2.278$; $df = 9$; the two-tailed p-value $= 0.049$; and the mean difference $M - \mu_0 = -1.6$. The one-tailed p-value is $0.049/2 = 0.0245$. Because this p-value is less than 0.05, the null hypothesis would be rejected.

The part of the output called the **95% confidence interval of the difference** is an interval on $\mu - 20$, where μ represents the mean birth weight of rats whose mothers use alcohol. The interval is $-3.1889 < \mu - 20 < -0.0111$. If 20 is added to each part of the inequality, we get $20 - 3.1889 < \mu - 20 + 20 < 20 - 0.0111$ or $16.81 < \mu < 19.99$. This is an **estimation** of μ.

What Is the Meaning of a Confidence Interval?

Figure 9.3 shows ten 90% confidence intervals along with the value of μ. Note that nine of the ten intervals contain the true value of μ. Confidence interval 6 does not contain μ. Each interval is based on a different sample. The intervals move around. The fact that 90% of them would actually capture μ gives us 90% confidence in the one that we compute from our sample data. A *confidence interval* is an interval in which we have a measured amount of confidence that the population parameter will reside in that interval.

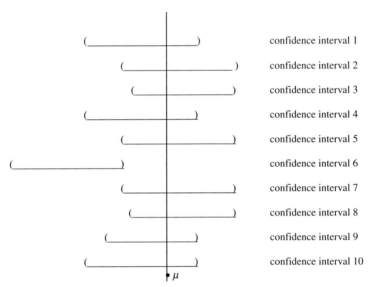

confidence interval 1
confidence interval 2
confidence interval 3
confidence interval 4
confidence interval 5
confidence interval 6
confidence interval 7
confidence interval 8
confidence interval 9
confidence interval 10

μ

Figure 9.3 Interpretation of a confidence interval.

SOLVED PROBLEMS

The Relationship between the t- and the z-Distributions

1. What is the basic difference between a z-test and a t-test?

   Solution

   The basic difference is whether the population standard deviation, σ, is known. If σ is known, then the z-test is appropriate. If S must be used because σ may not be assumed known, then a t-test is required.

2. Which of the two curves, the t-curve or the z-curve, has the more variability?

   Solution

   The t-curve has more variability than the z-curve. The variability is measured by variance or standard deviation. The variance of the t-curve, for more than 2 df, is $\dfrac{df}{df - 2}$. This is always greater than 1. One is the variability of the z-curve.

3. Find the area under the z-curve between z = −1 and z = 1 using EXCEL.

   ### Solution

   The area is given by =NORMSDIST(1)–NORMSDIST(−1), which is equal to 0.6829. This is the area within one standard deviation of the mean.

4. Find the area within one standard deviation of the mean for the t-curve having df = 4 using MINITAB.

   ### Solution

   The standard deviation for the t-curve with df = 4 is $\sqrt{\dfrac{df}{df-2}} = \sqrt{2} = 1.414$. The pull-down **Calc → Probability distribution → T** is used to obtain the following.

   Cumulative Distribution Function

   ```
   Student's t distribution with 4 DF

   x          P( X <= x )
   1.414      0.884871
   ```

   Cumulative Distribution Function

   ```
   Student's t distribution with 4 DF

   x          P( X <= x )
   -1.414     0.115129
   ```

   The area within one standard deviation is 0.884871 − 0.115129 = 0.769742.

Areas under the t-Distribution

5. Refer to Table 9.1 to find the area to the left of 2.015 under the t-distribution having df = 5.

   ### Solution

   From Table 2.1 the area to the right of 2.015 is 0.05 and the area to the left of 2.015 is 1 – 0.05 = 0.95.

6. Refer to Table 9.1 to find the area to the right of −2.764 under the t-distribution having df = 10.

   ### Solution

   The area to the left of −2.764 is the same as the area to the right of 2.764 because of symmetry, which is 0.01. The area to the right of −2.764 is 1 – 0.01 = 0.99.

7. Refer to Table 9.1 to find the area between −0.687 and 2.528, under the t-distribution having df = 20.

   ### Solution

   The area to the left of −0.687 is 0.25. The area to the right of 2.528 is 0.01. Therefore the area between −0.687 and 2.528 is 1 – 0.25 – 0.01 = 0.74.

8. Refer to Table 9.1 to find the area shown in Figure 9.4. The curve is a t-curve with df = 25.

   ### Solution

   The area is 1 – 0.025 = 0.975.

t-Test using SPSS

9. A psychological researcher believes that daily alcohol drinking results in memory loss. It is known that the general population scores an average of 50 on a test of memory. A low score indicates memory loss. She tests a group that drinks daily. They make the scores given in Table 9.2 on the memory test.

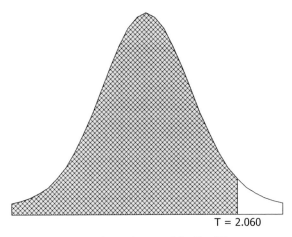

T = 2.060

Figure 9.4 t-Curve with df = 25.

TABLE 9.2 Scores on a Memory Test

44	42	44
40	43	46
51	46	42
46	50	44
52	48	39

Use SPSS and the data in Table 9.2 to test H_0: $\mu = 50$ versus H_1: $\mu < 50$ where μ is the average score of daily drinkers.

Solution

The SPSS solution is as follows.

One-Sample Statistics

	N	MEAN	STD. DEVIATION	STD. ERROR MEAN
Testscores	15	45.1333	3.85202	0.99459

One-Sample Test

			TEST VALUE = 50			
	t	df	SIG. (2-TAILED)	MEAN DIFFERENCE	95% CONFIDENCE INTERVAL OF THE DIFFERENCE	
					LOWER	UPPER
Testscores	−4.893	14	0.000	−4.86667	−6.9998	−2.7335

The SPSS output for the one sample t-test gives the following: the sample size $n = 15$, the mean of the sample $M = 45.1333$, the standard deviation of the sample $S = 3.85202$, the standard error of the mean = 0.99459, the computed t-value = −4.893, df = 14, the two-tailed p-value = 0.000, the mean difference $M - \mu_0 = -4.8667$, and the one-tailed p-value is 0.000/2 = 0.000. Because this p-value is less than 0.05, the null hypothesis would be rejected.

10. Rats are known to take a mean of 10 minutes to find their way through a maze to reach a food source. A researcher wishes to determine if taking a certain drug will change the time it takes to run the maze. The researcher wishes to test H_0: $\mu = 10$ versus H_1: $\mu \neq 10$, where μ is the average time required to run the maze while taking the drug. Twenty rats are timed while under the influence of the drug and the times are given in Table 9.3.

TABLE 9.3 Times Required to Run the Maze

10.5	9.9	10.8	11.5
10.2	8.9	10.5	12.3
9.6	11.3	10.8	10.0
9.8	11.5	10.4	11.7
10.5	12.1	12.5	10.0

Use SPSS and the data in Table 9.3 to test H_0: $\mu = 10$ versus H_1: $\mu \neq 10$.

Solution

The SPSS solution is as follows.

One-Sample Statistics

	N	MEAN	STD. DEVIATION	STD. ERROR MEAN
Time	20	10.7400	0.96595	0.21599

One-Sample Test

			TEST VALUE = 10			
	t	**df**	**SIG. (2-TAILED)**	**MEAN DIFFERENCE**	**95% CONFIDENCE INTERVAL OF THE DIFFERENCE**	
					LOWER	**UPPER**
Time	3.426	19	0.003	0.74000	0.2879	1.1921

The SPSS output for the one sample t-test gives the following: the sample size $n = 20$, the mean of the sample $M = 10.7400$, the standard deviation of the sample $S = 0.96595$, the standard error of the mean $= 0.21599$, the computed t-value $= 3.426$, df $= 19$, the mean difference $M - \mu_0 = 0.7400$, the two-tailed p-value $= 0.003$, and the one-tailed p-value is 0.003/2. Because this p-value is less than 0.05, the null hypothesis would be rejected.

11. A test to measure anxiety and depression has a mean score of $\mu = 55$ for the general population. A group of 20 people, known to be suffering from anxiety and depression, is given the test and it is of interest to know if the group will score higher on the test. The researcher wishes to test H_0: $\mu = 55$ versus H_1: $\mu > 55$ where μ is the average score made by individuals suffering from anxiety and depression. The 20 scores made on the test are given in Table 9.4.

TABLE 9.4 Scores Made on the Anxiety/Depression Test

58	65	53	57
56	49	56	58
55	52	50	59
56	56	54	60
54	54	57	52

Use SPSS and the data in Table 9.4 to test H_0: $\mu = 55$ versus H_1: $\mu > 55$ where μ is the average score made by anxiety and depression sufferers.

Solution

The SPSS solution is as follows.

One-Sample Statistics

	N	MEAN	STD. DEVIATION	STD. ERROR MEAN
Score	20	55.5500	3.63427	0.81265

One-Sample Test

					95% CONFIDENCE INTERVAL OF THE DIFFERENCE	
					TEST VALUE = 55	
	t	df	SIG. (2-TAILED)	MEAN DIFFERENCE	LOWER	UPPER
Score	0.677	19	0.507	0.55000	−1.1509	2.2509

The SPSS output for the one sample t-test gives the following: the sample size $n = 20$, the mean of the sample $M = 55.5500$, the standard deviation of the sample $S = 3.63427$, the standard error of the mean = 0.81265, the computed t-value = 0.677, df = 19, the mean difference $M - \mu_0 = 0.5500$, the two-tailed p-value = 0.507, and the one tailed p-value = 0.507/2 = 0.254. Because this p-value is not less than 0.05, the null hypothesis is not rejected.

12. A developmental psychologist wishes to test her new training program that she believes will increase problem-solving ability. A particular age group has scored 75 on a test of problem-solving ability. She uses the new training program on a sample of 20 from this age group. Let μ represent the average score that this new training program produces.

TABLE 9.5 Scores Made on the Test of Problem-Solving Ability

76	79	78	79
77	76	78	69
81	85	74	86
71	78	76	81
81	84	78	78

Use SPSS and the data in Table 9.5 to test H_0: $\mu = 75$ versus H_1: $\mu > 75$ where μ is the average score made by using the new training program.

Solution

The SPSS solution is as follows.

One-Sample Statistics

	N	MEAN	STD. DEVIATION	STD. ERROR MEAN
Scores	20	78.2500	4.20370	.93997

One-Sample Test

				TEST VALUE = 75		
					95% CONFIDENCE INTERVAL	
				MEAN	OF THE DIFFERENCE	
	t	df	SIG. (2-TAILED)	DIFFERENCE	LOWER	UPPER
Scores	3.458	19	.003	3.25000	1.2826	5.2174

The SPSS output for the one sample T test gives the following: the sample size $n = 20$, the mean of the sample $M = 78.2500$, the standard deviation of the sample $S = 4.2037$, the standard error of the mean $= 0.9399$ the computed t-value $= 3.458$, df $= 19$, the two-tailed p-value $= 0.003$, the mean difference $M - \mu_0 = 3.25$. The one tailed p-value $= 0.003/2 = 0.0015$. Since this p-value is less than 0.05, the null hypothesis is rejected.

Confidence Intervals for μ

13. In Problem 9, use the SPSS output to find a 95% confidence interval for μ, the average score of daily drinkers.

Solution

A 95% confidence interval for the difference is -6.9998 to -2.7735. This means that $-6.9998 < \mu - 50 < -2.7735$. If 50 is added to each part of the inequality, we obtain $43.0002 < \mu < 47.2265$, a 95% confidence interval on μ, where μ is the average score of daily drinkers.

14. In Problem 10, use the SPSS output to find a 95% confidence interval for μ, where μ is the average time required to run the maze while taking the drug.

Solution

A 95% confidence interval for the difference $(\mu - 10)$ is 0.2879 to 1.1921. This means that $0.2879 < \mu - 10 < 1.1921$. If 10 is added to each part of the inequality, we obtain $10.2879 < \mu < 11.1921$, a 95% confidence interval on μ, where μ is the average time taken to run the maze while taking the drug.

15. In Problem 11, use the SPSS output to find a 95% confidence interval for μ, where μ is the average score made by anxiety and depression sufferers.

Solution

A 95% confidence interval for the difference $\mu - 55$ is -1.1509 to 2.2509. This means that $-1.1509 < \mu - 55 < 2.2509$. If 55 is added to each part of the inequality, we obtain $55 - 1.1509 < \mu < 55 + 2.2509$ or $53.8491 < \mu < 57.2509$, where μ is the average made on the test by those suffering from anxiety and depression.

16. In Problem 12, find a 95% confidence interval for μ, where μ represents the average score that this new training program produces.

Solution

A 95% confidence interval for the difference $\mu - 75$ is 1.2826 to 5.2174. This means that $1.2826 < \mu - 75 < 5.2174$. If 75 is added to each part of the inequality, we obtain $75 + 1.2826 < \mu < 75 + 5.2174$ or $76.2826 < \mu < 80.2174$ where μ represents the average score that this new training program produces.

Kolmogorov-Smirnov Test of the Normality Assumption

17. Use the Kolmogorov-Smirnov test of normality from MINITAB to test the assumption that the data from Table 9.2 came from a normal distribution. This assumption is needed for the t-test to be valid. The data are reproduced below.

44	42	44
40	43	46
51	46	42
46	50	44
52	48	39

Solution

The data are entered into column C1. The pull-down menu **Stat → Basic Statistics → Normality Test** may be used to perform the test: H_0: the data come from a normal distribution versus H_1: the data do not come from a normal distribution. The output is given in Figure 9.5.

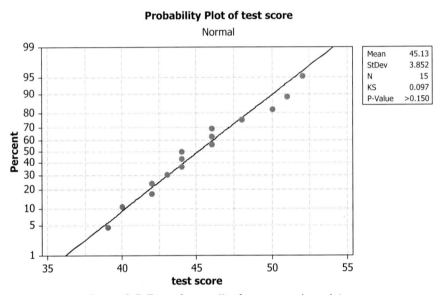

Figure 9.5 Test of normality for memory loss data.

The p-value for the test is given in the upper right corner of the graphic. Because the p-value >0.150, it is not less than 0.05. The null hypothesis is not rejected and the **normality assumption** is accepted. The normality assumption is made when the t-test is used to test a mean.

18. Use the Kolmogorov-Smirnov test of normality from MINITAB to test the assumption that the data from Table 9.3 came from a normal distribution. This assumption is needed for the t-test to be valid. The data are reproduced below.

10.5	9.9	10.8	11.5
10.2	8.9	10.5	12.3
9.6	11.3	10.8	10.0
9.8	11.5	10.4	11.7
10.5	12.1	12.5	10.0

Solution

The data are entered into column C1. The pull-down menu **Stat → Basic Statistics → Normality Test** may be used to perform the test: H_0: the data come from a normal distribution versus H_1: the data do not come from a normal distribution. The output is given in Figure 9.6.

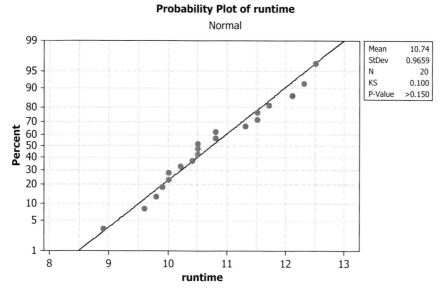

Figure 9.6 Test of normality for run times.

The p-value for the test is given in the upper right corner of the graphic. Because the p-value >0.150, it is not less than 0.05. The null hypothesis is not rejected and the **normality assumption** is accepted.

19. Use the Kolmogorov-Smirnov test of normality from MINITAB to test the assumption that the data from Table 9.4 came from a normal distribution. This assumption is needed for the t-test to be valid. The data are reproduced below.

58	65	53	57
56	49	56	58
55	52	50	59
56	56	54	60
54	54	57	52

Solution

The data are entered into column C1. The pull-down menu **Stat → Basic Statistics → Normality Test** may be used to perform the test: H_0: the data comefrom a normal distribution versus H_1: the data do not come from a normal distribution. The output is given in Figure 9.7.

The p-value for the test is given in the upper right corner of the graphic. Because the p-value >0.150, it is not less than 0.05. The null hypothesis is not rejected and the **normality assumption** is accepted.

20. Use the Kolmogorov-Smirnov test of normality from MINITAB to test the assumption that the data from Table 9.5 came from a normal distribution. This assumption is needed for the t-test to be valid. The data are reproduced below.

76	79	78	79
77	76	78	69
81	85	74	86
71	78	76	81
81	84	78	78

Solution

The data are entered into column C1. The pull-down menu **Stat → Basic Statistics → Normality Test** may be used to perform the test: H_0: the data come from a normal distribution versus H_1: the data do not come from a normal distribution. The output is given in Figure 9.8.

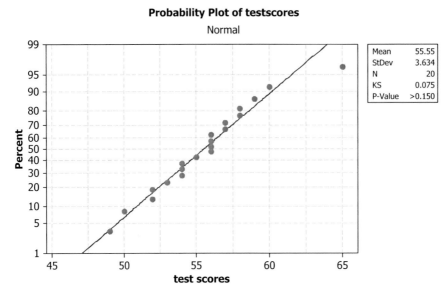

Figure 9.7 Test of normality for depression/anxiety data.

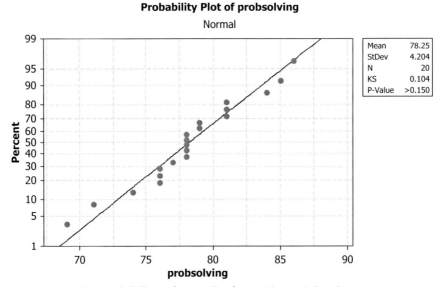

Figure 9.8 Test of normality for problem-solving data.

The p-value for the test is given in the upper right corner of the graphic. Because the p-value > 0.150, it is not less than 0.05. The null hypothesis is not rejected and the **normality assumption** is accepted.

SUPPLEMENTARY PROBLEMS

The Relationship between the t- and the z-Distributions

21. (*True or False*) The t-curves are all similar to the z- curve in that both are symmetrical about zero and both have half the area under their graphs to the right of zero and half to the left of zero.

22. (*True or False*) Areas under the t-curve or the z-curve may be found using EXCEL, MINITAB, or by using Tables 6.1 and 9.1.

23. Find the area under the z-curve between z = −2 and z = 2 using EXCEL.

24. Find the area within two standard deviations of the mean for the t-curve having df = 30 using MINITAB.

Areas under the t-Distribution

25. Refer to Table 9.1 to find the area to the left of 2.160 under the t-distribution having df = 13.

26. Refer to Table 9.1 to find the area to the right of −2.567 under the t-distribution having df = 17.

27. Refer to Table 9.1 to find the area between −1.714 and 2.500 under the t-distribution having df = 23.

28. Refer to Table 9.1 to find the area between −2.771 and 2.771 under the t-distribution having df = 27.

t-Test using SPSS

29. A mood questionnaire has a mean equal to 45. A psychologist would like to investigate how a person's environment affects mood. A sample of size 20 is given the test in a room that is darkly painted with no windows as well as other factors that tend to have a negative affect on mood. The null hypothesis is H_0: $\mu = 45$ and the research hypothesis is H_1: $\mu < 45$, where μ is the test score when in a setting that has a very negative environmental effect. The data for the experiment are shown in Table 9.6.

TABLE 9.6 Scores on a Mood Questionnaire Given in a Negative Environment

40	38	46	45
41	37	42	45
42	42	39	40
39	44	48	42
44	42	35	45

Use SPSS and the data in Table 9.6 to test H_0: $\mu = 45$ versus H_1: $\mu < 45$ where μ is the average test score when in a setting that has a very negative environmental effect.

30. A psychologist makes use of a test instrument for measuring depression. The instrument is known to have an average score of 70 for normal individuals. A group of individuals who have been described as severely depressed by a therapist takes the tests and scores as shown in Table 9.7.

TABLE 9.7 Scores Made by Severely Depressed Individuals

75	77	78	80
65	78	77	69
77	72	75	74
78	76	69	70
69	66	65	75

Use SPSS and the data in Table 9.7 to test H_0: $\mu = 70$ versus H_1: $\mu > 70$, where μ is the average test score made by severely depressed individuals.

31. A large group of army personnel score 90 on the average on a test designed to measure their memory. A group of 20 who have been in combat for the past 6 months are given the test. The results are shown in Table 9.8.

TABLE 9.8 Scores Made by Combat Veterans

85	88	87	85
87	88	86	85
90	86	89	94
79	92	93	92
93	93	88	90

Use SPSS and the data in Table 9.8 to test H_0: $\mu = 90$ versus H_1: $\mu < 90$, where μ is the average score made by combat veterans.

32. A psychologist has developed a test for measuring the vocabulary skills of 6 year olds. They score 60 on the average. She administers the test to a sample of single children (i.e., only child). The scores of the single children are given in Table 9.9.

TABLE 9.9 Scores Made by Single Children

60	64	57	63
58	57	56	57
62	62	66	62
59	58	63	58
61	60	60	60

Use SPSS and the data in Table 9.9 to test H_0: $\mu = 60$ versus H_1: $\mu \neq 60$, where μ is the average score made by single children.

Confidence Intervals for μ

33. Set a 95% confidence interval on μ in Problem 29.

34. Set a 95% confidence interval on μ in Problem 30.

35. Set a 95% confidence interval on μ in Problem 31.

36. Set a 95% confidence interval on μ in Problem 32.

Shapiro-Wilk Test of the Normality Assumption

Problems 37 through 40. Test the data in Problems 29 through 32 for normality using the statistical package STATISTIX and the Shapiro-Wilk test of normality.

CHAPTER 10

The t-Test for Two Independent Samples

Introduction

The past two chapters discussed using one sample to make inferences about one population. Although these tests are used in psychological research, it is more common to use two or more samples and make inferences about two or more populations. This chapter will introduce you to techniques where two samples are used. Although the statistical theory and mathematical equations will be discussed, our primary goal will be the use of SPSS and other computer software to perform these tests. We will consider how the data must be entered for the software to perform the tests. Then we will consider the output and its interpretation.

Independent Samples Versus Related Samples

A psychology student was investigating why females live on the average ten more years than males. Are there psychological factors involved or are they simply all physiological in nature? If the lifetimes of a large group of males and a large group of females are recorded by simply examining the obituary pages, we are using *independent samples*. The males and females whose deaths are listed (or lifetimes are determinable) constitute two independent samples.

	A	B	C	D	E
1	**Female**	**Male**	*Female*		
2	21	19			
3	41	30	Mean	78.34286	
4	54	41	Standard Error	2.82395	
5	60	43	Median	81	
6	62	52	Mode	93	
7	64	53	Standard Deviation	16.70671	
8	66	63	Sample Variance	279.1143	
9	70	64	Kurtosis	3.192021	
10	72	64	Skewness	-1.46427	
11	73	65	Range	82	
12	74	66	Minimum	21	
13	75	68	Maximum	103	
14	76	68	Sum	2742	
15	77	68	Count	35	
16	78	68			
17	79	69	*Male*		
18	80	70			
19	81	71	Mean	70.15789	
20	82	71	Standard Error	2.616429	
21	83	72	Median	71.5	
22	84	75	Mode	68	
23	86	76	Standard Deviation	16.12875	
24	87	76	Sample Variance	260.1366	
25	88	78	Kurtosis	2.196881	
26	88	78	Skewness	-1.43597	
27	89	80	Range	71	
28	90	80	Minimum	19	
29	92	82	Maximum	90	
30	92	82	Sum	2666	
31	93	82	Count	38	
32	93	85			
33	93	85			
34	94	85			
35	102	86			
36	103	86			
37		87			
38		88			
39		90			
40					

Figure 10.1 Independent samples of female and male lifetimes.

Figure 10.1 gives two independent samples of female and male lifetimes recorded from the *Omaha World Herald*. Also shown in the figure are descriptive statistics for the two samples. The difference in mean lifetimes is 78.3 – 70.2 or 8.1 years. The difference in median lifetimes is 81.0 – 71.5 or 9.5 years. We also see that the variability in lifetimes is equal for all practical purposes. The standard deviation of female lifetimes is 16.7 years and the standard deviation of male lifetimes is 16.1 years.

Figure 10.2 gives two *related samples*. The pairs contain the groom's age, followed by the bride's age, followed by the difference in ages. These data were collected by a psychology student performing a study of ages at the time of marriage. The data were collected from the *Omaha World Herald*. The differences are of interest. The mean difference was 0.8 year and the median difference was 1 year. The grooms are on the average about 1 year older than the brides. The couples form pairs and their ages form paired sets of data. One of the hypotheses that may be tested from such paired data is that, on the average, grooms are older than brides at the time of marriage or the difference is positive.

EXAMPLE 1 A social psychologist wishes to compare men and women with respect to their attitudes toward abortion. She selects two independent samples and compares their responses. An educational psychologist wishes to compare two methods of teaching mathematics. One method involves traditional techniques and the other method incorporates the Internet in the teaching of the course. The average scores made by the students in the courses are compared.

EXAMPLE 2 A study makes measurements for a sample of depressed patients. Six months after therapy for depression has been initiated, the level of depression is again measured for each of the patients. The data are paired. The score before therapy is compared with the score after therapy for each patient. The samples here are related.

Examples and problems are worked in this chapter with and without using SPSS. When working the problems without the use of software, either EXCEL or a hand-held calculator is used. This helps the student understand how the paired t-test works and how to do the calculations. It also increases the confidence of the student to see both approaches; thus, many of the problems are solved twice. First the problem is solved "by hand" and then the problem is solved using SPSS.

The t-Test for Independent Samples Worked by Hand

The null hypothesis is $H_0: \mu_1 - \mu_2 = 0$ and the alternative hypothesis is one of three: $H_1: \mu_1 - \mu_2 \neq 0$, or $H_1: \mu_1 - \mu_2 < 0$, or $H_1: \mu_1 - \mu_2 > 0$. The *sum of squares*, SS, is defined to be $\sum X^2 - (\sum X)^2/n$ or $(n-1)S^2$. There are two sums of squares, SS_1 and SS_2, for two independent samples. For the female and male lifetimes in Figure 10.1, SS_1 is the sum of squares for females and SS_2 is the sum of squares for males: $SS_1 = (n_1 - 1)S_1^2 = (35 - 1)$ $16.70671^2 = 9489.8814$ and $SS_2 = (n_2 - 1)S_2^2 = (38 - 1)16.12875^2 = 9625.0533$. The means are $M_1 = 78.34286$

	A	B	C	D	E	F
				Microsoft Excel - book1		
				File Edit View Insert Format Tools Data Window Help		
		J5		f_x		
1	Groom	Bride	Groom - Bride	Groom - Bride		
2	23	21	2			
3	20	25	-5	Mean	0.787879	
4	34	33	1	Standard Error	0.744624	
5	35	30	5	Median	1	
6	44	50	-6	Mode	1	
7	26	26	0	Standard Deviation	4.27754	
8	27	30	-3	Sample Variance	18.29735	
9	29	31	-2	Kurtosis	0.324844	
10	25	24	1	Skewness	-0.54067	
11	32	33	-1	Range	19	
12	22	23	-1	Minimum	-10	
13	31	25	6	Maximum	9	
14	20	19	1	Sum	26	
15	28	27	1	Count	33	
16	30	24	6			
17	39	49	-10			
18	31	24	7			
19	31	27	4			
20	26	27	-1			
21	26	24	2			
22	27	28	-1			
23	22	21	1			
24	25	20	5			
25	28	29	-1			
26	27	23	4			
27	29	26	3			
28	27	23	4			
29	24	21	3			
30	23	31	-8			
31	23	19	4			
32	25	25	0			
33	39	43	-4			
34	29	20	9			
35						

Figure 10.2 Related samples of bride and groom ages.

and $M_2 = 70.15789$. The *pooled variance* is defined to be $S_p^2 = \dfrac{SS_1 + SS_2}{df_1 + df_2} = \dfrac{9489.8814 + 9625.0533}{34 + 37} = 269.2245$.

The *two-sample standard error* or the *standard error of the difference* in sample means is

$$S_{(M_1 - M_2)} = \sqrt{\frac{S_p^2}{n_1} + \frac{S_p^2}{n_2}} = \sqrt{\frac{269.2245}{35} + \frac{269.2245}{38}} = 3.8441.$$

Finally, putting it all together, the t-statistic for testing $H_0: \mu_1 - \mu_2 = 0$ is

$$T = \frac{M_1 - M_2 - 0}{S_{(M_1 - M_2)}} \text{ with } df_1 + df_2 \text{ degrees of freedom.}$$

The t-statistic for testing $H_0: \mu_1 - \mu_2 = 0$ versus $H_1: \mu_1 - \mu_2 > 0$ is

$$T = \frac{M_1 - M_2 - 0}{S_{(M_1 - M_2)}} = \frac{8.18497}{3.8441} = 2.13 \text{ with 71 degrees of freedom.}$$

SPSS and the t-Test for Independent Samples

The data must be entered into the SPSS data editor in a *stacked form data file*. The lifetimes for both males and females are entered into one column. In another column, a 1 or 2 is entered to indicate whether the lifetime is for a female (1) or a male (2). Part of the stacked data file is shown in Figure 10.3.

	age	sex	var
1	21.00	1.00	
2	41.00	1.00	
3	54.00	1.00	
4	60.00	1.00	
5	62.00	1.00	
6	64.00	1.00	
7	66.00	1.00	
8	70.00	1.00	
9	72.00	1.00	
10	73.00	1.00	
11	74.00	1.00	
12	75.00	1.00	
13	76.00	1.00	
14	77.00	1.00	
15	78.00	1.00	
16	79.00	1.00	
17	80.00	1.00	
18	81.00	1.00	
19	82.00	1.00	
20	83.00	1.00	
21	84.00	1.00	
22	86.00	1.00	
23	87.00	1.00	
24	88.00	1.00	
25	88.00	1.00	
26	89.00	1.00	
27	90.00	1.00	
28	92.00	1.00	
29	92.00	1.00	
30	93.00	1.00	
31	93.00	1.00	
32	93.00	1.00	
33	94.00	1.00	
34	102.00	1.00	
35	103.00	1.00	
36	19.00	2.00	
37	30.00	2.00	

Figure 10.3 Partial display of the SPSS stacked data file.

The pull-down menu **Analyze → Compare means → Independent samples t-test** is given to perform the analysis.

The output is as follows. The group statistics are shown first. Under Sex, a 1 or a 2 is shown, with 1 representing a female and 2 representing a male. There are 35 females and 38 males. The mean lifetime for females is 78.3429 and for males 70.1579. The standard deviations and standard errors for males and females are also given.

Group Statistics

	SEX	N	MEAN	STD. DEVIATION	STD. ERROR MEAN
Age	1.00	35	78.3429	16.70671	2.82395
	2.00	38	70.1579	16.12875	2.61643

The modified independent samples output (**the SPSS output has been modified**) is:

Independent Samples Test

t	df	SIG(2-TAILED)	MEAN DIFFERENCE	STD. ERROR DIFFERENCE	LOWER LIMITS	UPPER LIMITS
2.129	71	0.037	8.1849	3.8440	0.5201	15.8498

The SPSS output entitled **independent samples test** has been modified. We shall discuss only the equal variances output. This means we are assuming equal variances of lifetimes for males and females. The t-value is equal to 2.129, the df is 71, the two-tailed p-value is 0.037. Because we have a one-tailed alternative, the p-value is one half of that, or 0.019. The mean difference is $78.3429 - 70.1579 = 8.185$. The standard error of the difference in sample means is 3.844. The student should be convinced that the **by-hand** solution and the SPSS solution are the same. We will emphasize the SPSS solution. Summarizing, we have

$$M_1 - M_2 = 8.185$$

$$S_{(M_1-M_2)} = \sqrt{\frac{S_p^2}{n_1} + \frac{S_p^2}{n_2}} = \sqrt{\frac{269.2245}{35} + \frac{269.2245}{38}} = 3.844$$

$$T = \frac{M_1 - M_2 - 0}{S_{(M_1-M_2)}} = \frac{8.18497}{3.8441} = 2.13$$

Remember, SPSS saves a tremendous amount of arithmetic in calculating the parts that make up the test, but it is imperative that we know what SPSS is doing!

Assumptions Underlying the Independent Samples t-Test

1. The two samples are random and independent.

2. The two populations from which the samples are selected have a normal distribution.

3. The two populations from which the samples are selected have equal variances.

SOLVED PROBLEMS

The t-Test for Independent Samples Worked by Hand

1. The two samples have $n_1 = 6$, $SS_1 = 50$ and $n_2 = 6$, $SS_2 = 55$. Find the variance for each sample and the pooled variance for the two samples.

Solution

The variance for the first sample is $S_1^2 = \dfrac{SS_1}{n_1 - 1} = \dfrac{50}{6 - 1} = 10$. The variance for the second sample is

$S_2^2 = \dfrac{SS_2}{n_2 - 1} = \dfrac{55}{6 - 1} = 11$. The pooled variance is $S_p^2 = \dfrac{SS_1 + SS_2}{df_1 + df_2} = \dfrac{50 + 55}{5 + 5} = 10.5$. **Whenever the sample**

sizes are the same, the pooled variance will equal the average of the two sample variances.

2. The two samples have $n_1 = 10$, $SS_1 = 150$ and $n_2 = 8$, $SS_2 = 200$. Find the variance for each sample and the pooled variance for the two samples.

Solution

The variance for the first sample is $S_1^2 = \dfrac{SS_1}{n_1 - 1} = \dfrac{150}{10 - 1} = 16.6667$. The variance for the second sample is

$S_2^2 = \dfrac{SS_2}{n_2 - 1} = \dfrac{200}{8 - 1} = 28.5714$. The pooled variance is $S_p^2 = \dfrac{SS_1 + SS_2}{df_1 + df_2} = \dfrac{150 + 200}{9 + 7} = 21.875$.

3. The two samples have $n_1 = 5$, $SS_1 = 225$ and $n_2 = 10$, and $SS_2 = 275$. Find the variance for each sample and the pooled variance for the two samples.

Solution

The variance for the first sample is $S_1^2 = \dfrac{SS_1}{n_1 - 1} = \dfrac{225}{5 - 1} = 56.25$. The variance for the second sample is

$S_2^2 = \dfrac{SS_2}{n_2 - 1} = \dfrac{275}{10 - 1} = 30.5555$. The pooled variance is $S_p^2 = \dfrac{SS_1 + SS_2}{df_1 + df_2} = \dfrac{225 + 275}{4 + 9} = 38.4615$.

4. The two samples have $n_1 = 5$, $SS_1 = 200$ and $n_2 = 10$, and $SS_2 = 200$. Find the variance for each sample and the pooled variance for the two samples.

Solution

The variance for the first sample is $S_1^2 = \dfrac{SS_1}{n_1 - 1} = \dfrac{200}{5 - 1} = 50$. The variance for the second sample is

$S_2^2 = \dfrac{SS_2}{n_2 - 1} = \dfrac{200}{10 - 1} = 22.2222$. The pooled variance is $S_p^2 = \dfrac{SS_1 + SS_2}{df_1 + df_2} = \dfrac{200 + 200}{4 + 9} = 30.7692$.

5. The two sample sizes are $n_1 = 13$ and $n_2 = 15$ and the pooled variance for the two samples is $S_p^2 = 25$. Calculate the two sample standard error.

Solution

$$S_{(M_1 - M_2)} = \sqrt{\dfrac{S_p^2}{n_1} + \dfrac{S_p^2}{n_2}} = \sqrt{\dfrac{25}{13} + \dfrac{25}{15}} = \sqrt{3.5897} = 1.8947$$

6. The two sample sizes are $n_1 = 15$ and $n_2 = 15$ and the pooled variance for the two samples is $S_p^2 = 97.8$. Calculate the two sample standard error.

Solution

$$S_{(M_1 - M_2)} = \sqrt{\dfrac{S_p^2}{n_1} + \dfrac{S_p^2}{n_2}} = \sqrt{\dfrac{97.8}{15} + \dfrac{97.8}{15}} = \sqrt{13.04} = 3.6111$$

7. The two sample sizes are $n_1 = 20$ and $n_2 = 15$ and the pooled variance for the two samples is $S_p^2 = 77.2$. Calculate the two sample standard error.

Solution

$$S_{(M_1 - M_2)} = \sqrt{\dfrac{S_p^2}{n_1} + \dfrac{S_p^2}{n_2}} = \sqrt{\dfrac{77.2}{20} + \dfrac{77.2}{15}} = \sqrt{9.0067} = 3.0011$$

8. The difference in the means in two independent samples of sizes 5 and 7 is 2.3 and the two sample standard error is 3.5. Find the value of the t-statistic and find the degrees of freedom for the t-statistic.

Solution

$$T = \frac{M_1 - M_2 - 0}{S_{(M_1 - M_2)}} = \frac{2.3}{3.5} = 0.6571 \text{ with 10 df.}$$

9. Two samples of rats are timed for their maze running time. One group is taking a drug and the other is not. The times are given in Figure 10.4. Identify M_1, M_2, S_1, and S_2.

	A	B	C	D	E	F	G
	Drug sample	No drug sample	Drug sample		No drug sample		
1							
2	15	11					
3	12	13	Mean	12.17	Mean	10	
4	13	9	Standard Error	0.703	Standard Error	1.18	
5	12	6	Median	12	Median	11	
6	10	11	Mode	12	Mode	11	
7	11		Standard Deviation	1.722	Standard Deviation	2.65	
8			Sample Variance	2.967	Sample Variance	7	
9			Kurtosis	0.814	Kurtosis	0.67	
10			Skewness	0.678	Skewness	-0.81	
11			Range	5	Range	7	
12			Minimum	10	Minimum	6	
13			Maximum	15	Maximum	13	
14			Sum	73	Sum	50	
15			Count	6	Count	5	
16							
17							

Figure 10.4 EXCEL comparison of maze-running times of two groups of rats.

Solution

$$M_1 = 12.17 \qquad M_2 = 10.00 \qquad S_1 = 1.722 \qquad S_2 = 2.65$$

10. In Problem 9, find SS_1, SS_2, S_p^2, $S_{(M_1 - M_2)}$, and the value of the t-statistic. How many degrees of freedom does the t-statistic have?

Solution

$$SS_1 = (n_1 - 1) S_1^2 = 5(1.722)^2 = 14.8264 \qquad SS_2 = (n_2 - 1) S_2^2 = 4(2.65)^2 = 28.09$$

$$S_p^2 = \frac{SS_1 + SS_2}{df_1 + df_2} = \frac{14.8264 + 28.09}{5 + 4} = 4.7685$$

$$S_{(M_1 - M_2)} = \sqrt{\frac{S_p^2}{n_1} + \frac{S_p^2}{n_2}} = \sqrt{\frac{4.7685}{6} + \frac{4.7685}{5}} = 1.3222$$

$$T = \frac{M_1 - M_2 - 0}{S_{(M_1 - M_2)}} = \frac{2.17}{1.3222} = 1.64 \text{ with 9 df.}$$

11. An educational psychologist wishes to compare two methods of teaching statistics. Ten students are taught in the traditional way with very little computer involvement. The other group of 8 students integrates computer software in the same course. Their total points on similar tests are converted to percents. The results are shown in an SPSS descriptive statistics output given next.

Statistics

		TRADITIONAL	SOFTWARE
N	Valid	10	8
	Missing	0	2
Mean		76.9000	74.3750
Std. Error of Mean		4.08371	3.59035
Median		76.0000	72.5000
Mode		68.00[a]	70.00
Std. Deviation		12.91382	10.15505
Variance		166.767	103.125
Skewness		−0.832	0.224
Std. Error of Skewness		0.687	0.752
Kurtosis		0.710	−0.886
Std. Error of Kurtosis		1.334	1.481
Range		42.00	30.00
Minimum		50.00	60.00
Maximum		92.00	90.00
Sum		769.00	595.00

[a]Multiple modes exist. The smallest value is shown.

By looking at the SPSS Descriptive Statistics output for the study comparing a traditional section to a section that utilizes statistical software, find: M_1, M_2, S_1, and S_2. (Note that 1 corresponds to the traditional section and 2 to the software section.)

Solution

$$M_1 = 76.900 \quad M_2 = 74.375 \qquad S_1 = 12.91382 \qquad S_2 = 10.15505$$

12. In Problem 11, find SS_1, SS_2, S_p^2, $S_{(M_1-M_2)}$, and the value of the t-statistic. How many degrees of freedom does the t-statistic have?

Solution

$$SS_1 = (n_1 - 1)S_1^2 = 9(12.91382)^2 = 1500.9007$$

$$SS_2 = (n_2 - 1)S_2^2 = 7(10.15505)^2 = 721.87528$$

$$S_p^2 = \frac{SS_1 + SS_2}{df_1 + df_2} = \frac{1500.9007 + 721.87528}{9 + 7} = 138.9235$$

$$S_{(M_1-M_2)} = \sqrt{\frac{S_p^2}{n_1} + \frac{S_p^2}{n_2}} = \sqrt{\frac{138.9235}{10} + \frac{138.9235}{8}} = 5.5909$$

$$T = \frac{M_1 - M_2 - 0}{S_{(M_1-M_2)}} = \frac{2.525}{5.5909} = 0.452 \quad \text{with 16 df.}$$

SPSS and the t-Test for Independent Samples

13. Create the stacked data file worksheet for the SPSS analysis of the data given in Figure 10.4.

Solution

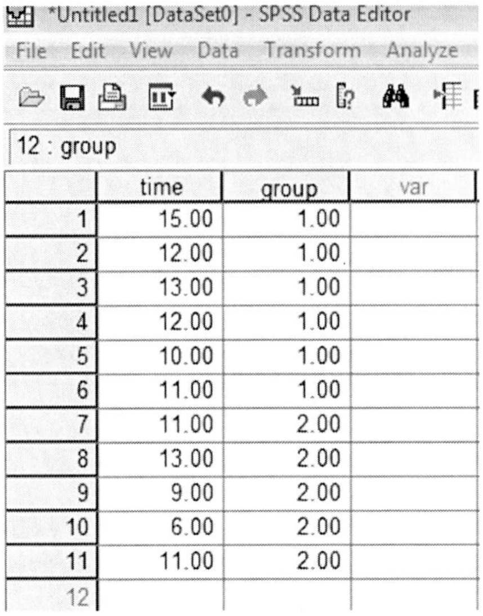

	time	group	var
1	15.00	1.00	
2	12.00	1.00	
3	13.00	1.00	
4	12.00	1.00	
5	10.00	1.00	
6	11.00	1.00	
7	11.00	2.00	
8	13.00	2.00	
9	9.00	2.00	
10	6.00	2.00	
11	11.00	2.00	
12			

Figure 10.5 SPSS stacked data file for the data in Figure 10.4.

14. Give the SPSS analysis of the data in Figure 10.4. Compare the results with the by-hand solution in Problem 10.

Solution

The pull-down menu **Analyze → Compare means → Independent samples t-test** is given to perform the analysis. The output is as follows.

Group Statistics

	GROUP	N	MEAN	STD. DEVIATION	STD. ERROR MEAN
Time	1.00	6	12.1667	1.72240	0.70317
	2.00	5	10.0000	2.64575	1.18322

The group statistics portion of the SPSS output gives the two groups as 1 = drug group sample and 2 = non-drug group sample. The two sample sizes are 6 and 5; the two means are 12.1667 and 10.0000; and the two standard deviation are 1.7224 and 2.64575.

The following output is modified SPSS output.

Independent Samples Test

t	df	SIG(2-TAILED)	MEAN DIFFERENCE	STD. ERROR DIFFERENCE	LOWER LIMITS	UPPER LIMITS
1.640	9	0.135	2.1667	1.3210	−0.8216	5.1550

The independent samples analysis assuming equal variances is: t-statistic = 1.64, df = 9, two-tailed p-value = 0.135, mean difference is 2.16667, and standard error of the difference of two sample means is 1.32101.

15. Create the stacked data file worksheet for the SPSS analysis of the data given in Problem 11.

Solution

The stacked file is shown in Figure 10.6.

	testpercent	group	var
1	75.00	1	
2	77.00	1	
3	89.00	1	
4	68.00	1	
5	75.00	1	
6	90.00	1	
7	50.00	1	
8	68.00	1	
9	85.00	1	
10	92.00	1	
11	60.00	2	
12	80.00	2	
13	85.00	2	
14	65.00	2	
15	70.00	2	
16	90.00	2	
17	70.00	2	
18	75.00	2	
19			

Figure 10.6 SPSS Stacked file for data in Problem 11.

16. Give the SPSS analysis of the data in Problem 11 and Figure 10.6. Compare the results with the by-hand solution in Problem 12.

Solution

The pull-down menu **Analyze → Compare means → Independent samples t-test** is given to perform the analysis. The output is as follows.

Group Statistics

	GROUP	N	MEAN	STD. DEVIATION	STD. ERROR MEAN
Test percent	1	10	76.9000	12.91382	4.08371
	2	8	74.3750	10.15505	3.59035

The group statistics portion of the SPSS output gives the two groups as 1 = traditional group sample and 2 = computer software sample. The two sample sizes are 10 and 8, the two means are 76.9 and 74.375, and the two standard deviations are 12.91382 and 10.15505.

Modified Independent Samples Test

t	df	SIG(2-TAILED)	MEAN DIFFERENCE	STD. ERROR DIFFERENCE	LOWER LIMITS	UPPER LIMITS
0.452	16	0.658	2.5250	5.5908	−9.3271	14.3771

NOTE: The SPSS output has been modified.

The modified independent samples analysis assuming equal variances is: t-statistic = 0.452, df = 16, two-tailed p-value = 0.658, mean difference is 2.525, and standard error of the difference of two sample means is 5.59087.

SUPPLEMENTARY PROBLEMS

The t-Test for Independent Samples Worked by Hand

17. Two samples of depressed patients are treated with anti-depressants. Drug A is given to patients in sample 1 and Drug B is given to patients in sample 2. After taking the drugs for 3 months, the two groups are given a test to measure depression. The scores for the two samples are shown in Figure 10.7. Use *sum of squares*, SS, defined as $\sum X^2 - (\sum X)^2/n$ to find SS_1 and SS_2.

	A	B	C
	DrugA, X	DrugB, Y	
1	DrugA, X	DrugB, Y	
2	67	70	
3	65	72	
4	70	73	
5	59	77	
6	67	71	
7		69	
8		75	
9			

Figure 10.7 Depression scores for the two sample groups.

18. Using the SS_1 and SS_2 found in Problem 17, find the value of the t-statistic.

19. Suppose you are given the results described in Problem 17 and the descriptive statistics as shown in Figure 10.8. Find SS_1 and SS_2.

	A	B	C	D	E	F	G
1	Drug A	Drug B	Drug A		Drug B		
2	67	70					
3	65	72	Mean	65.6	Mean	72.42857	
4	70	73	Standard Error	1.83303	Standard Error	1.065859	
5	59	77	Median	67	Median	72	
6	67	71	Mode	67	Mode	#N/A	
7		69	Standard Deviation	4.09878	Standard Deviation	2.819997	
8		75	Sample Variance	16.8	Sample Variance	7.952381	
9			Kurtosis	2.098214	Kurtosis	-0.54652	
10			Skewness	-1.19228	Skewness	0.573322	
11			Range	11	Range	8	
12			Minimum	59	Minimum	69	
13			Maximum	70	Maximum	77	
14			Sum	328	Sum	507	
15			Count	5	Count	7	
16							

Figure 10.8 Descriptive statistics for Drug A and Drug B.

20. Describe the use of MINITAB to find SS_1 and SS_2.

21. Suppose you are given the results described in Problem 17 as shown in Figure 10.9. The functions =VAR(A2:A6) and =VAR(B2:B8) are used in C1 and C2. Find SS_1 and SS_2.

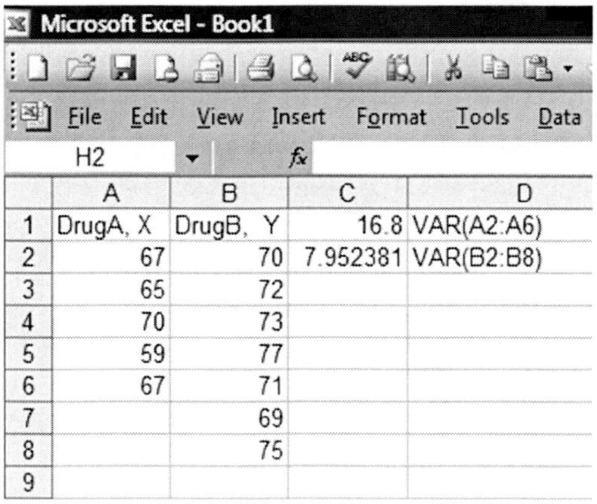

	A	B	C	D
1	DrugA, X	DrugB, Y	16.8	VAR(A2:A6)
2	67	70	7.952381	VAR(B2:B8)
3	65	72		
4	70	73		
5	59	77		
6	67	71		
7		69		
8		75		
9				

Figure 10.9 The EXCEL variance function used for Drug A and Drug B.

22. An educational psychologist compared two groups of high school ninth graders. One group had a TV in their bedrooms and the other group did not. The cumulative grade point averages of the two groups of students are shown in the EXCEL worksheet in Figure 10.10. Use *sum of squares*, SS, defined as $\Sigma X^2 - (\Sigma X)^2/n$ to find SS_1 and SS_2.

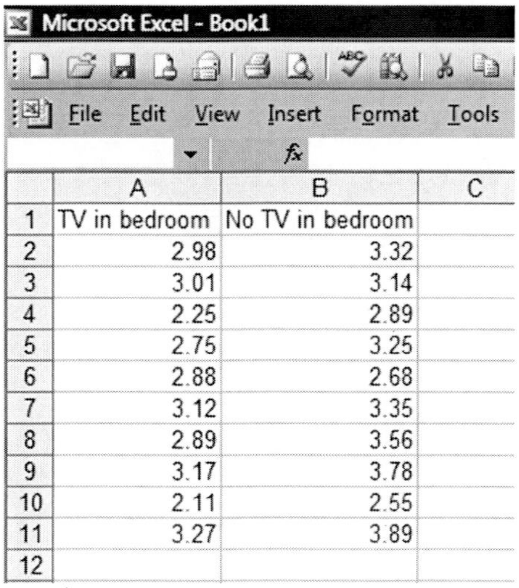

	A	B	C
1	TV in bedroom	No TV in bedroom	
2	2.98	3.32	
3	3.01	3.14	
4	2.25	2.89	
5	2.75	3.25	
6	2.88	2.68	
7	3.12	3.35	
8	2.89	3.56	
9	3.17	3.78	
10	2.11	2.55	
11	3.27	3.89	
12			

Figure 10.10 Cumulative grade point averages for two groups.

23. Using SS_1 and SS_2 found in Problem 22, find the value of the t-statistic.

24. Suppose you are given the results described in Problem 22 and the descriptive statistics as shown in Figure 10.11. Find SS_1 and SS_2.

Microsoft Excel - Book1

	A	B	C	D	E	F	G
1	TV in bedroom	No TV in bedroom	X		Y		
2	X	Y					
3	2.98	3.32	Mean	2.843	Mean	3.241	
4	3.01	3.14	Standard Error	0.1208217	Standard Error	0.139733	
5	2.25	2.89	Median	2.935	Median	3.285	
6	2.75	3.25	Mode	#N/A	Mode	#N/A	
7	2.88	2.68	Standard Deviation	0.3820718	Standard Deviation	0.441876	
8	3.12	3.35	Sample Variance	0.1459789	Sample Variance	0.195254	
9	2.89	3.56	Kurtosis	0.4141311	Kurtosis	-0.82043	
10	3.17	3.78	Skewness	-1.149739	Skewness	-0.13936	
11	2.11	2.55	Range	1.16	Range	1.34	
12	3.27	3.89	Minimum	2.11	Minimum	2.55	
13			Maximum	3.27	Maximum	3.89	
14			Sum	28.43	Sum	32.41	
15			Count	10	Count	10	
16							
17							

Figure 10.11 Descriptive statistics for educational psychology study.

25. Describe the use of MINITAB to find SS_1 and SS_2.

26. Suppose you are given the results described in Problem 22 as shown in Figure 10.12. The functions =VAR(A2:A6) and =VAR(B2:B8) are used in A13 and A14. Find SS_1 and SS_2.

Microsoft Excel - BookWorksh...

	A	B	C
1	TV in bedroom	No TV in bedroom	
2	X	Y	
3	2.98	3.32	
4	3.01	3.14	
5	2.25	2.89	
6	2.75	3.25	
7	2.88	2.68	
8	3.12	3.35	
9	2.89	3.56	
10	3.17	3.78	
11	2.11	2.55	
12	3.27	3.89	
13	0.145978889	VAR(A3:A12)	
14	0.195254444	VAR(B3:B12)	
15			
16			

Figure 10.12 The variance function used for educational psychology study.

SPSS and the t-Test for Independent Samples

27. Create the stacked data file worksheet for the SPSS analysis of the data given in Figure 10.7.

28. Give the SPSS analysis of the data in Figure 10.7. Compare the results with the by-hand solution in Problem 18.

29. Create the stacked data file worksheet for the SPSS analysis of the data given in Figure 10.10.

30. Give the SPSS analysis of the data in Figure 10.10. Compare the results with the by-hand solution in Problem 23.

CHAPTER 11

The t-Test for Two Related Samples

Two Related Samples

Rather than selecting two independent samples as in Chapter 10, often it is desirable to select two samples that are dependent. The samples are chosen so that the two observations are paired. This is accomplished in two steps. Two observations are made on the same person, animal, etc.: one observation **before** the treatment and another **after** the treatment on the same experimental unit. This design is called a *repeated-measures design*. The design may be looked at as consisting of one sample with two measurements per unit.

EXAMPLE 1 A psychologist records the time it takes 10 rats to make their way through a maze to a reward. The rats are then given a drug; the experiment is repeated and the time to run the maze to the reward is recorded again. The times and their differences are recorded and a set of data such as in Table 11.1 is recorded. The psychologist would like to know if the drug effects the time to run the maze. She will be able to answer this question by studying the differences.

TABLE 11.1 Times Required to Run a Maze by 10 Rats

BEFORE DRUG	AFTER DRUG	DIFFERENCE
10	13	3
8	10	2
11	10	−1
13	15	2
14	15	1
10	15	5
8	10	2
14	12	−2
11	15	4
16	18	2

Another design similar to the repeated measures design is the *matched-subjects design*. In this design, subjects are matched according to certain salient characteristics and a treatment is applied to one subject but not the other; it is then determined if the treatment makes a difference in some response variable. This is a *matched-subjects design*.

EXAMPLE 2 An educational psychologist wishes to compare two approaches to teaching second year algebra. She matches the students according to their scores on a standardized algebra test given at the beginning of the course. She teaches one group using Method I and the other group using Method II. At the end of the course both samples are given the same comprehensive algebra exam. Table 11.2 gives the results of the experiment. The standardized scores are used to pair the participants. The first row of Table 11.2 is 775, 777, 80, and 82. The two individuals who scored 775 and 777 on the standardized test form the first matched pair. The one taught second year algebra, by Method I, scored 80 and the one taught by Method II, scored 82. Similarly the other 9 pairs are listed, along with their standardized scores and their scores when taught by either Method I or Method II. This is a matched-subjects design.

TABLE 11.2 Matched-Subjects Design

STANDARDIZED TEST SCORE		ALGEBRA SCORE		DIFFERENCE
		METHOD I	**METHOD II**	**D**
775	777	80	82	2
850	860	85	83	−2
771	775	77	80	3
910	905	92	89	−3
830	820	88	85	−3
925	915	90	92	2
690	698	70	65	−5
759	744	75	77	2
880	885	85	81	−4
960	950	94	92	−2

Examples and problems are worked in this chapter with and without using SPSS. When working the problems without the use of software, either EXCEL or a hand-held calculator is used. This helps the student understand how the paired t-test works and how to do the calculations, increasing the student's confidence when both approaches are used. This is why many of the solutions of the problems are done twice. First the problem is solved "by hand" and then the problem is solved using SPSS.

The t-Test for the Repeated Measures Design Worked by Hand

We will take Example 1 and test the hypothesis that the difference in time required to run the maze is 0. Let D = the difference in time required to run the maze before taking the drug and after taking the drug. The null hypothesis is H_0: $\mu_D = 0$; that is, the mean difference is 0. The alternative hypothesis is H_1: $\mu_D \neq 0$; that is, the mean difference is not 0. This hypothesis is tested using the test statistic $T = \dfrac{M_D - \mu_D}{\dfrac{S_D}{\sqrt{n}}}$, where

$M_D = \dfrac{\Sigma D}{n}$, and $S_D = \sqrt{\dfrac{\Sigma D^2 - \dfrac{(\Sigma D)^2}{n}}{n-1}}$. M_D is the sample mean difference and S_D is the *sample standard deviation of differences*.

The t-test statistic has a student t-distribution with $(n-1)$ degrees of freedom (df). Figure 11.1 shows the EXCEL computation of the t-statistic by hand. The differences from Table 11.1 are entered in A2:A11 and the differences squared are entered in B2:B11. The expression =A2^2 is entered into B2 and a click-and-drag is performed from B2 to B11. The *sum of the differences* are given by =SUM(A2:A11) and is computed in A13, the *sum of the squares of the differences* are given by =SUM(B2:B11) and is in B13. The *variance of differences* is given by =(B13–A13^2/10)/9 and is in A15, the *standard deviation of differences* is given by =SQRT(A15) and is in A16. The standard error of differences, $\dfrac{S_D}{\sqrt{n}}$, is given by =A16/SQRT(10) and is in A17. The t-value is computed in A18 as =(1.8–0)/A17 and is equal to 2.714. This t-value has 9 df.

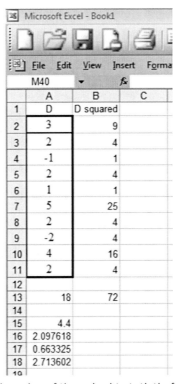

Figure 11.1 Calculating the value of the paired t-statistic for the repeated measures.

SPSS and the Paired t-Test for Repeated Measures

The SPSS solution to Example 1 (solved by hand in the previous section) will be described in this section. The SPSS routine to solve problems involving related samples is called the *paired t-test*. Figure 11.2 shows the data from the repeated-measure design discussed in Example 1. The following pull-down menu is given in SPSS: **Analyze → Compare means → Paired samples T Test**. The SPSS output is shown in Figure 11.3.

*Untitled1 [DataSet0] - SPSS Data Editor

File Edit View Data Transform Analyze

1 :

	Before	After	var
1	10.00	13.00	
2	8.00	10.00	
3	11.00	10.00	
4	13.00	15.00	
5	14.00	15.00	
6	10.00	15.00	
7	8.00	10.00	
8	14.00	12.00	
9	11.00	15.00	
10	16.00	18.00	
11			

Figure 11.2 SPSS data file for the paired t-test.

Paired Samples Statistics

		Mean	N	Std. Deviation	Std. Error Mean
Pair 1	Before	11.5000	10	2.67706	.84656
	After	13.3000	10	2.75076	.86987

	Paired Differences					
Pair	Mean	S_D	$\frac{S_D}{\sqrt{n}}$	T	df	Sig(2-tailed)
After - Before	1.8000	2.0976	0.6633	2.714	9	0.024

Figure 11.3 Paired t-test output from SPSS.

In Figure 11.3 the SPSS output is given in modified form. In the top part of the table called paired samples statistics, the mean time to run the maze before the drug is administered is 11.5, and the mean time to run the maze after the drug is 13.3, the standard deviation of **before run times** is 2.67706, and the standard deviation of **after run times** is 2.75076. In the bottom half of the table is given $M_D = \frac{\Sigma D}{n} = 1.8000$, $S_D = 2.0976$, $\frac{S_D}{\sqrt{n}} = 0.6633$, and $T = \frac{M_D - \mu_D}{\frac{S_D}{\sqrt{n}}} = 2.714$ with 9 df. The two-tailed p-value is 0.024 and because the p-value is <0.05, the null hypothesis is rejected.

The t-Test for the Matched Pairs Design Worked by Hand

The t-test for matched pairs is computed in the same manner as repeated measures. The solution for Example 2 is given in Figure 11.4. The null hypothesis is H_0: $\mu_D = 0$; that is, the mean difference is 0. The alternative hypothesis is H_1: $\mu_D \neq 0$; that is, the mean difference is not 0. This hypothesis is tested by using

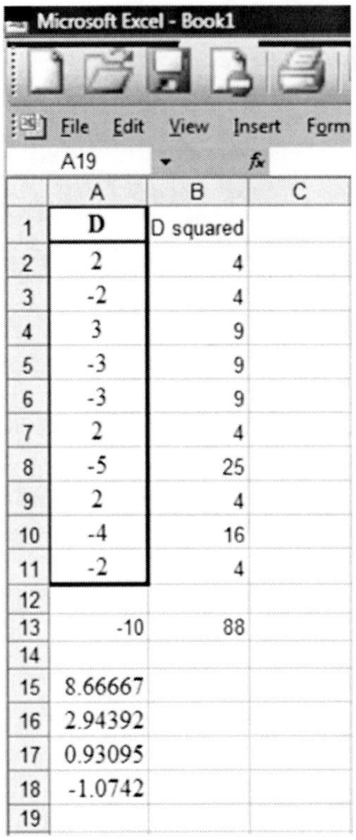

	A	B	C
1	D	D squared	
2	2	4	
3	-2	4	
4	3	9	
5	-3	9	
6	-3	9	
7	2	4	
8	-5	25	
9	2	4	
10	-4	16	
11	-2	4	
12			
13	-10	88	
14			
15	8.66667		
16	2.94392		
17	0.93095		
18	-1.0742		
19			

Figure 11.4 Calculating the value of the paired t-test for a matched pair.

$\mathrm{T} = \dfrac{M_D - \mu_D}{\dfrac{S_D}{\sqrt{n}}}$, where $M_D = \dfrac{\Sigma D}{n}$, and $S_D = \sqrt{\dfrac{\Sigma D^2 - \dfrac{(\Sigma D)^2}{n}}{n-1}}$. M_D is the sample mean difference and S_D is the *sample standard deviation of differences*. T has a t-distribution with $(n - 1)$ degrees of freedom. Figure 11.4 shows the computation of the t-value by hand. The differences are entered in A2:A11 and the differences squared are entered in B2:B11. The *sum of the differences* is given by =SUM (A2:A11) and is in A13, the *sum of the squares of the differences* is given by =SUM(B2:B11) and is in B13. The *variances of differences* is given by =(B13–A13^2/10)/9 and is in A15, the *standard deviation of differences* is given by =SQRT(A15) and is in A16. $\dfrac{S_D}{\sqrt{n}}$ is given by =A16/SQRT(10) and is in A17. The t-value is computed in A18 and is equal to −1.0742.

SPSS and the t-Test for Matched Pairs

The SPSS solution to Example 2 (solved by hand in the previous section) will be described in this section. The SPSS routine to solve problems involving matched pairs is called the *paired t test.* Figure 11.5 shows the data in the SPSS data window from the matched pair design discussed in Example 2.

The following pull-down menu is given in SPSS: **Analyze → Compare means → Paired samples T Test**. The output shown in Figure 11.6 is given for Example 2.

The mean difference is −1, the standard deviation of difference is 2.94392, the standard error of differences is 0.93095, the t-value is −1.0742, the degrees of freedom is 9, and the p-value is 0.311.

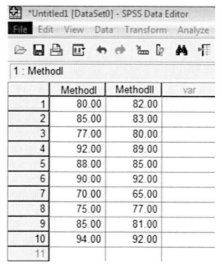

Figure 11.5 SPSS data file for the paired t-test.

Paired Samples Statistics

		Mean	N	Std. Deviation	Std. Error Mean
Pair 1	methodI	83.6000	10	7.87683	2.49087
	MethodII	82.6000	10	7.98888	2.52631

	Paired Differences					
Pair	Mean	S_D	$\dfrac{S_D}{\sqrt{n}}$	T	df	Sig(2-tailed)
Method II – Method I	−1.0000	2.94392	0.93095	−1.0742	9	0.311

Figure 11.6 Paired t-test output from SPSS.

Assumptions for the Related-Samples t-Test

1. The pairs of samples are independent.
2. The differences are normally distributed.

SOLVED PROBLEMS

The t-Test for the Repeated Measures Design Without Using SPSS

1. In a psychology of weight loss program, a therapist instructs overweight people on how to lose weight and how to keep the weight off. Table 11.3 gives the beginning weight and the weight six months later of five patients in such a program.

TABLE **11.3 Beginning, Ending, and Difference in Weight**

BEGINNING WEIGHT	ENDING WEIGHT	DIFFERENCE
235	222	13
220	225	−5
276	252	24
315	298	17
255	248	7

Find the following: M_D, S_D, and $T = \dfrac{M_D - \mu_D}{\dfrac{S_D}{\sqrt{n}}}$ when testing H_0: $\mu_D = 0$.

Solution

The sum of the differences is $13 - 5 + 24 + 17 + 7 = 56$ and the sum of the squares is $169 + 25 + 576 + 289 + 49 = 1108$. $M_D = 56/5 = 11.2$,

$$S_D = \sqrt{\dfrac{\Sigma D^2 - \dfrac{(\Sigma D)^2}{n}}{n-1}} = \sqrt{\dfrac{1108 - 627.2}{4}} = 10.9636 \quad \text{and} \quad T = \dfrac{M_D - \mu_D}{\dfrac{S_D}{\sqrt{n}}} = \dfrac{11.2 - 0}{\dfrac{10.9636}{\sqrt{5}}} = \dfrac{11.2}{4.90} = 2.286.$$

2. A psychological treatment for sleep apnea is used on 10 sleep apnea patients. The patients are evaluated and given a score that is reflective of their condition. After the treatment has been applied for a fixed amount of time, they are evaluated again and given another score. The lower the score, the less severe is the sleep apnea condition. The scores are shown in Table 11.4.

TABLE 11.4 Sleep Apnea Scores

BEGINNING SCORE	ENDING SCORE	DIFFERENCE
78	75	3
70	67	3
75	65	10
77	79	−2
80	75	5
65	70	−5
78	72	6
68	70	−2
79	72	7
74	77	−3

Use an EXCEL worksheet to find the following: M_D, S_D, and $T = \dfrac{M_D - \mu_D}{\dfrac{S_D}{\sqrt{n}}}$ when testing H_0: $\mu_D = 0$.

Solution

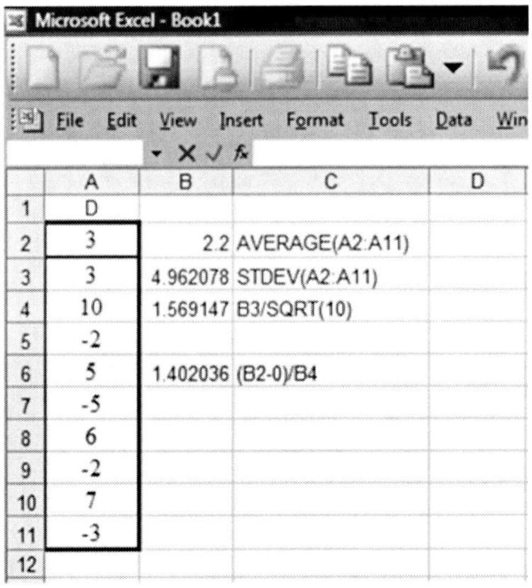

Figure 11.7 Computation of the paired t-statistic.

M_D is shown in B2, S_D in B3, the standard error of the difference in B4, and the computed T in B6 of Figure 11.7. The EXCEL commands are shown in column C.

SPSS and the Paired t-Test for Repeated Measures

3. Solve Problem 1 by using SPSS software. Interpret the output.

Solution

The data are entered into the worksheet and the pull-down **Analyze → Compare Means → Paired Samples T Test** is given. The following output is produced.

				PAIRED SAMPLES STATISTICS	
		MEAN	N	STD. DEVIATION	STD. ERROR MEAN
Pair	Beginwt	260.2000	5	37.18467	16.62949
1	Endwt	249.0000	5	30.47950	13.63085

			PAIRED DIFFERENCES			
PAIR	MEAN	S_D	$\dfrac{S_D}{\sqrt{n}}$	T	df	SIG(2-TAILED)
Beginwt–Endwt	11.2000	10.9636	4.9031	2.284	4	0.084

$M_D = 11.2000$ pounds, $S_D = 10.9636$, and T = 2.284. The two-tailed p-value is given as Sig(2-tailed). These are the same values given in Problem 1.

4. Solve Problem 2 by using SPSS software. Interpret the output.

Solution

The data are entered into the worksheet and the pull-down **Analyze → Compare Means → Paired Samples T Test** is given. The following output is produced.

				PAIRED SAMPLES STATISTICS	
		MEAN	N	STD. DEVIATION	STD. ERROR MEAN
Pair	Beginscore	74.4000	10	5.10338	1.61383
1	Endscore	72.2000	10	4.39191	1.38884

			PAIRED DIFFERENCES			
PAIR	MEAN	S_D	$\dfrac{S_D}{\sqrt{n}}$	T	df	SIG(2-TAILED)
Beginscore–Endscore	2.2000	4.9621	1.5692	1.402	9	0.194

$M_D = 2.2000$, $S_D = 4.9621$, and T = 1.402. The two-tailed p-value is given as Sig(2-tailed). These are the same values given in problem 2.

The t-Test for the Matched Pairs Design Worked Without Using SPSS

5. A psychological researcher assigns 10 pairs of diabetics to one of two groups. Each member of the pair is either assigned to a yoga group or a transcendental mediation (TM) group. They are paired according to their hemoglobin A1C values. After 6 months, their hemoglobin A1C values were determined. The results are given in Table 11.5.

TABLE 11.5 Diabetes Matched Pairs Study

PAIR	YOGA GROUP	TM GROUP	DIFFERENCE
1	6.4	6.2	0.2
2	6.6	6.5	0.1
3	6.8	6.9	−0.1
4	7.0	6.8	0.2
5	7.3	7.4	−0.1
6	6.6	6.3	0.3
7	7.0	7.2	−0.2
8	7.5	7.3	0.2
9	7.9	7.2	0.7
10	6.8	6.9	−0.1

Find the following: M_D, S_D, and $T = \dfrac{M_D - \mu_D}{\dfrac{S_D}{\sqrt{n}}}$ when testing H_0: $\mu_D = 0$.

Solution

The sum of the differences is $.2 + .1 - .1 + .2 - .1 + .3 - .2 + .2 + .7 - .1 = 1.2$ and the sum of the squares is $04 + .01 + .01 + .04 + .01 + .09 + .04 + .04 + .49 + .01 = 0.78$. $M_D = 1.2/10 = 0.12$,

$$S_D = \sqrt{\frac{\sum D^2 - \dfrac{(\sum D)^2}{n}}{n-1}} = \sqrt{\frac{0.78 - 0.144}{9}} = 0.2658$$

$$T = \frac{M_D - \mu_D}{\dfrac{S_D}{\sqrt{n}}} = \frac{0.12 - 0}{\dfrac{0.2658}{\sqrt{10}}} = \frac{0.12}{0.084} = 1.429.$$

6. A group of army veterans suffering from post-traumatic stress disorder (PTSD) were paired according to the severity of their condition. There were pairs ranging from mild to severe. One member of the pair was treated using **virtual reality computer modeling** and the other member was treated using **eye movement desensitization reprocessing** (EMDR). Their condition was evaluated after the treatments on a scale from 1 to 10. The results are shown in Table 11.6.

TABLE 11.6 PTSD Matched Pairs Study

PAIR	COMPUTER GROUP	EMDR GROUP	DIFFERENCE
1	9	7	2
2	5	6	−1
3	3	4	−1
4	5	7	−2
5	7	8	−1
6	3	5	−2
7	4	6	−2
8	7	5	2
9	9	8	1
10	7	9	−2

Use an EXCEL worksheet to find the following: M_D, S_D, and $T = \dfrac{M_D - \mu_D}{\dfrac{S_D}{\sqrt{n}}}$ when testing H_0: $\mu_D = 0$.

Solution

M_D is shown in B2, S_D in B3, the standard error of the difference in B4, and the computed T in B6 of Figure 11.8. The EXCEL commands are shown in column C.

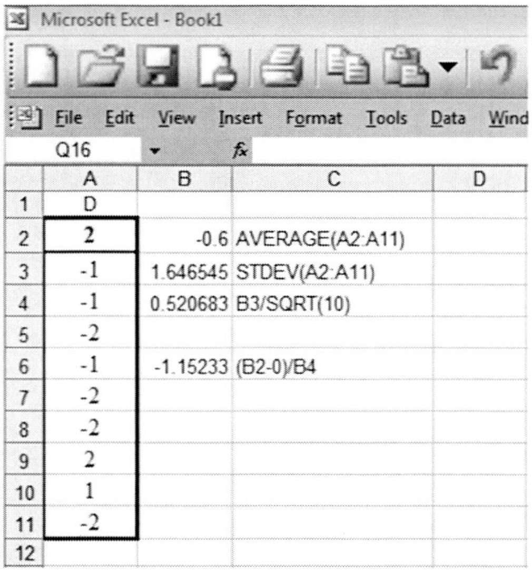

	A	B	C	D
1	D			
2	2	-0.6	AVERAGE(A2:A11)	
3	-1	1.646545	STDEV(A2:A11)	
4	-1	0.520683	B3/SQRT(10)	
5	-2			
6	-1	-1.15233	(B2-0)/B4	
7	-2			
8	-2			
9	2			
10	1			
11	-2			
12				

Figure 11.8 Computation of the paired t-statistic.

SPSS and the t-Test for Matched Pairs

7. Solve Problem 5 by using SPSS software. Interpret the output.

Solution

The data are entered into the worksheet and the pull-down **Analyze → Compare Means → Paired Samples T Test** is given. The following output is produced.

		PAIRED SAMPLES STATISTICS			
		MEAN	**N**	**STD. DEVIATION**	**STD. ERROR MEAN**
Pair	Yoga	6.9900	10	0.46056	0.14564
1	TM	6.8700	10	0.42177	0.13337

			PAIRED DIFFERENCES			
PAIR	**MEAN**	S_D	$\dfrac{S_D}{\sqrt{n}}$	**T**	**df**	**SIG(2-TAILED)**
Yoga–TM	0.1200	0.2658	0.0840	1.428	9	0.187

$M_D = 0.1200$, $S_D = 0.2658$, and $T = 1.428$. The two-tailed p-value is given as Sig(2-tailed) $= 0.187$. We are unable to reject the null hypothesis. These are the same values given in Problem 5.

8. Solve Problem 6 by using SPSS software. Interpret the output.

Solution

The data are entered into the worksheet and the pull-down **Analyze → Compare Means → Paired Samples T Test** is given. The following output is produced.

$M_D = -0.6000$, $S_D = 1.6466$, and $T = -1.152$. The two-tailed p-value is given as Sig(2-tailed) = 0.279. We are unable to reject the null hypothesis. These are the same values given in Problem 6.

		PAIRED SAMPLES STATISTICS			
		MEAN	N	STD. DEVIATION	STD. ERROR MEAN
Pair	Computer	5.9000	10	2.23358	0.70632
1	EMDR	6.5000	10	1.58114	0.50000

			PAIRED DIFFERENCES			
PAIR	MEAN	S_D	$\dfrac{S_D}{\sqrt{n}}$	T	df	SIG(2-TAILED)
Computer–EMDR	−0.6000	1.6466	0.5207	−1.152	9	0.279

SUPPLEMENTARY PROBLEMS

The t-Test for the Repeated Measures Design Worked Without Using SPSS

9. A psychologist conducts a repeated-measures design experiment in which the patients have the number of anxiety attacks measured for a month. Then they eat pumpkin seeds daily for a month and again measure the number of anxiety attacks they suffer. Pumpkin seed contain a large amount of L-tryptophan, which is believed to be a preventive for the onset of anxiety attacks. The data are given in Table 11.7. Find the following: M_D, S_D, and

$$T = \frac{M_D - \mu_D}{\dfrac{S_D}{\sqrt{n}}} \quad \text{when testing } H_0: \mu_D = 0.$$

TABLE 11.7 Number of Anxiety Attacks

BEFORE	AFTER	DIFFERENCE
25	20	5
16	12	4
20	19	1
11	8	3
13	11	2
7	6	1
10	9	1
23	24	−1
16	11	5
12	10	2

10. A sample of diabetics have their fasting blood sugar determined. They supplement their diets with brewers yeast daily for a month and then have their fasting blood sugar determined again. It is believed that brewers yeast increases the body's sensitivity to insulin. The data are given in Table 11.8.

TABLE **11.8** **Fasting Blood Sugar Values**

BEFORE	AFTER	DIFFERENCE
120	115	−5
125	123	−2
115	120	5
135	130	−5
140	125	−15
132	123	−9
150	137	−13
128	130	2
115	125	10
126	140	14

Use an EXCEL worksheet to find the following: M_D, S_D, and $T = \dfrac{M_D - \mu_D}{\dfrac{S_D}{\sqrt{n}}}$ when testing H_0: $\mu_D = 0$.

SPSS and the Paired t-Test for Repeated Measures

11. Solve Problem 9 by using SPSS software. Interpret the output.

12. Solve Problem 10 by using SPSS software. Interpret the output.

The t-Test for the Matched Pairs Design Worked Without Using SPSS

13. Ten pairs of patients being treated for stress have been paired by similar blood pressures. One member of each pair is given a placebo for stress and the other member practices meditation. After one month their blood pressures are taken again. The results are shown in Table 11.9.

TABLE **11.9** **Blood Pressure After Treatment for Stress**

PLACEBO	MEDITATION	DIFFERENCE
95	80	−15
90	85	−5
85	90	5
100	95	−5
85	80	−5
105	90	−15
92	85	−7
110	95	−15
90	80	−10
105	90	−15

Find the following: M_D, S_D, and $T = \dfrac{M_D - \mu_D}{\dfrac{S_D}{\sqrt{n}}}$ when testing H_0: $\mu_D = 0$.

14. Ten pairs of individuals suffering from bipolar disorder are matched. The individuals in each pair have the same number of episodes per year. One member of the pair is treated with GEODON and the other member is treated with psychotherapy. The number of episodes per year is the data recorded. The results are shown in Table 11.10.

TABLE **11.10 Number of Episodes for the Two Treatments**

GEODON	PSYCHOTHERAPY	DIFFERENCE
5	7	2
4	3	−1
7	4	−3
5	6	1
7	4	−3
9	8	−1
6	7	1
7	5	−2
5	7	2
3	2	−1

Use an EXCEL worksheet to find the following: M_D, S_D, and $T = \dfrac{M_D - \mu_D}{\dfrac{S_D}{\sqrt{n}}}$ when testing $H_0: \mu_D = 0$.

SPSS and the t-Test for Matched Pairs

15. Solve Problem 13 by using SPSS software. Interpret the output.

16. Solve Problem 14 by using SPSS software. Interpret the output.

Answers to Supplementary Problems

CHAPTER 1

23. The sample is the 2,900 men and women in the study. The population is all men and women in the United States.

24. The sample is the 1,500 schizophrenia patients and the population is all schizophrenia patients in the United States.

25. The sample is the 313 male Vietnam veterans and the population is all Vietnam veterans.

26. The 2 percent of the children aged 8 to 17 years old who are affected by restless legs syndrome (RLS).

27. 50 percent make more than $47,000 and 50 percent make less than $47,000.

28. Minimum is the smallest value, maximum is the largest value, median divides the data in half, mode is the most frequently occurring value, and range is the maximum minus the minimum.

29. The median height of women is 66 inches and the median height of men is 70 inches. The statement that men are taller than women means that the median height for men is greater than the median height for women.

30. Seventy percent of the population would show no decline in cognitive function over a similar 10-year period.

31. In this problem, 9.4 percent of the population aged 18 to 25 years is equal to 3 million. This can be expressed $0.094 X = 3$ million where X is the number in the population aged 18 to 25. Solving for X gives $X = \dfrac{3\,\text{million}}{0.094} = 31.9$ million.

32. Ordinal level.

33. Ratio level.

34. Interval level.

35. Nominal level.

36.

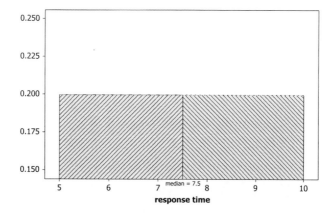

37. a. The answer is 500 have more than 24.5 tics and 500 have less than 24.5 tics. Such a value is called the median.
b. The answer is 200 of the 1000 have 25 tics. 25 tics occur more often than any other number. It is called the mode.

38. a. $\sum X^3$ b. $(\sum X)^3$ c. $\sum X^3 Y^3$

39. a. 353   b. 6561   c. 5.146

40. Linear correlation coefficient = 0.570.

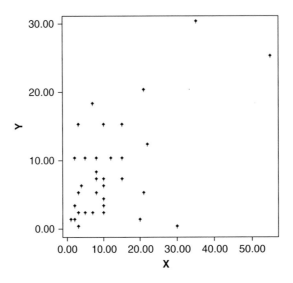

CHAPTER 2

21.

CLASS	FREQUENCY
68.5 to 72.5	16
72.5 to 76.5	32
76.5 to 80.5	27
80.5 to 84.5	22
84.5 to 88.5	19
88.5 to 92.5	14
92.5 to 96.5	7
96.5 to 100.5	7
100.5 to 104.5	4
104.5 to 108.5	2

22.

AGE	FREQUENCY	PERCENT
70	7	4.67
71	4	2.67
72	5	3.33
73	9	6.00
74	7	4.67
75	8	5.33
76	8	5.33
77	9	6.00
78	8	5.33
79	7	4.67

(*Continued*)

AGE	FREQUENCY	PERCENT
80	3	2.00
81	4	2.67
82	9	6.00
83	6	4.00
84	3	2.00
85	3	2.00
86	6	4.00
87	6	4.00
88	4	2.67
89	8	5.33
90	4	2.67
91	2	1.33
93	2	1.33
94	3	2.00
95	2	1.33
97	4	2.67
98	3	2.00
101	1	0.67
102	1	0.67
103	2	1.33
105	1	0.67
108	1	0.67

23.

AGE	FREQUENCY
66.5	0
70.5	16
74.5	32
78.5	27
82.5	22
86.5	19
90.5	14
94.5	7
98.5	7
102.5	4
106.5	2
110.5	0

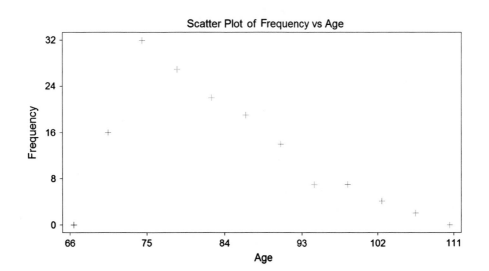

24.

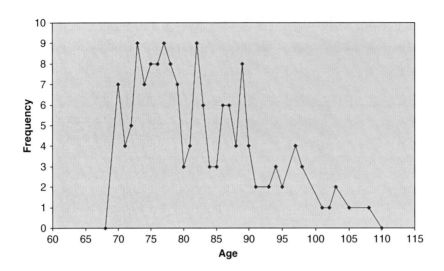

25. Both are skewed to the right.

26. The graph in Problem 24 shows more detail than the graph in Problem 23.

27. $P_{10} = 72$, $Q_3 = 88$, $P_{83} = 90$, and $P_{99} = 106.47$.

28. $P_{10} = 72$, $Q_3 = 88$, $P_{83} = 90$, and $P_{99} = 106.47$.

Statistics

Age		
N	Valid	150
	Missing	1
Percentiles	10	72.00
	75	88.00
	83	90.00
	99	106.47

29. $P_{10} = 72$, $Q_3 = 87.75$, $P_{83} = 89.67$, and $P_{99} = 104.02$.

30. $P_{10} = 72$, $Q_3 = 88$, $P_{83} = 90$, and $P_{99} = 106.47$.

31.

32. Considering the above dot plot, 6 or $(6/150) = 0.04$ or 4% are older than 100.

33. Age Stem-and-Leaf Plot

```
Frequency      Stem &  Leaf
   11.00        7 .  00000001111
   14.00        7 .  22222333333333
   15.00        7 .  444444455555555
   17.00        7 .  66666666777777777
   15.00        7 .  888888889999999
    7.00        8 .  0001111
   15.00        8 .  222222222333333
    6.00        8 .  444555
```

```
12.00       8 .  666666777777
12.00       8 .  888899999999
 6.00       9 .  000011
 2.00       9 .  33
 5.00       9 .  44455
 4.00       9 .  7777
 3.00       9 .  888
 1.00      10 .  1
 3.00      10 .  233
 1.00      10 .  5
 1.00 Extremes   (>=108)
Stem width:        10
Each leaf:     1 case(s)
```

The 17 means there are 17 numbers in that row. The numbers are 76, 76, 76, 76, 76, 76, 76, 76, 77, 77, 77, 77, 77, 77, 77, 77, and 77.

34. a. 110,000

b. 1,350,000

c. 710,000

d. 1,350,000 – 110,000 = 1,240,000

35.

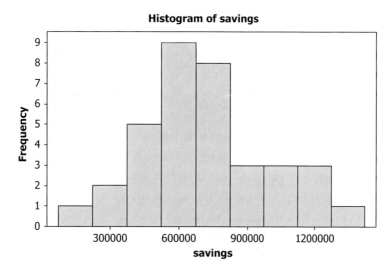

36.

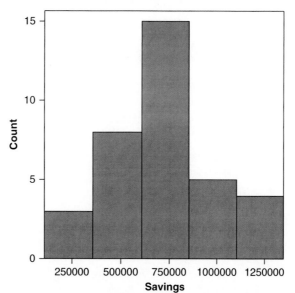

37.

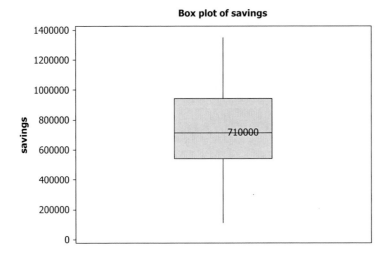

Box plot of savings

The median is the line shown in the center of the box. It is located at 710,000 dollars. Half of the accounts have more than the median savings and half have less than the median savings.

38. The median is the line in the center of the box. It is above 710,000. The box extends from just above Q_1 to just above Q_3.

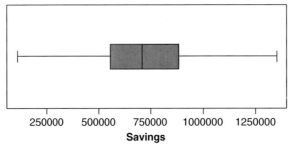

Savings

39. a. Freshman $(0.15)(300) = 45$ Sophomore $(0.20)(300) = 60$
Junior $(0.30)(300) = 90$ Senior $(0.35)(300) = 105$

b. Freshman $(0.15)(360°) = 54°$ Sophomore $(0.20)(360°) = 72°$
Junior $(0.30)(360°) = 108°$ Senior $(0.35)(360°) = 126°$

40. Islam $(25/150) = 0.167$, Judaism $(20/150) = 0.133$, Buddhism $(30/150) = 0.200$, Animism $(10/150) = 0.067$, Christianity $(40/150) = 0.267$, and Hinduism $(25/150) = 0.167$.

CHAPTER 3

18. a. The answer is median, because a few actors/actresses have huge incomes but most are not astronomical. This gives the distribution a skew to the right.

b. The answer is mean or median, because the heights of adult females have a symmetrical distribution with a center at 5 foot 6 inches.

c. These data would consist of categories and the most appropriate measure would be the mode. You would find that the typical student taking Beginning Psychology would be a freshman or sophomore.

19. Minimum = 6.4
Maximum = 7.6
Sum = 278.3
Mean = 6.9575

20. 6.4 6.5 6.6 6.6 6.6 6.7 6.7 6.8 6.8 6.8 6.8 6.8 6.8
6.9 6.9 6.9 6.9 6.9 6.9 **6.9** **6.9** 7.0 7.0 7.0 7.0 7.0
7.0 7.0 7.0 7.1 7.1 7.1 7.2 7.3 7.3 7.3 7.4 7.4 7.4
7.6

20th value in the sorted array = 6.9
21st value in the sorted array = 6.9
Median = (6.9 + 6.9)/2 = 6.9

21.

Value	Frequency
6.4	1
6.5	1
6.6	3
6.7	2
6.8	6
6.9	8
7.0	8
7.1	3
7.2	1
7.3	3
7.4	3
7.6	1

The data set is bi-modal. The modes are 6.9 and 7.0.

22. Minimum = 126

Maximum = 168

Sum = 10918

Mean = 149.56

23.

126	131	133	134	136	138	138	139	139	139	140	140	142
143	143	143	144	144	144	144	145	145	145	145	145	145
146	147	147	147	148	148	148	148	149	149	149	149	150
150	151	152	152	152	152	153	153	153	153	153	154	154
155	155	155	158	158	158	158	158	159	159	160	160	160
161	161	161	163	164	164	166	168					

37th value in the sorted array = 149
Median = 149

24. Mode = 145

Frequency = 6

25. Mean = $1,257,520

Median = $423,000

Median is the more typical salary.

26. a. Modal symptom is thirst.

b. Mode

27. The few high scores would cause the mean to be greater than most of the stress test scores. The median would divide the stress test scores in half, such that roughly 50% would be greater and 50% would be smaller than the median. The mean would be the least representative of the stress scores.

28. You know that the distribution is symmetrical. Furthermore, it is likely bell-shaped if a mode is mentioned. The uniform distribution is symmetrical but it does not have a mode.

29. True. The statements are all true for a normal distribution.

30. Because the distribution is skewed to the left, the median, 44, would be more representative than the mean, 39.1.

31. The scores are fairly symmetrical about 34. The median, 34, the mean, 33.9, or mode 34 would each be representative of the data.

32. Because the distribution is skewed to the right, the median, 26.5, would be more representative than the mean, 30.8.

33. Descriptive Statistics: Time

Variable	Total Count N	N	N*	CumN	Percent	CumPct	Mean	SE Mean	TrMean	StDev
time	54	54	0	54	100	100	4.9683	0.0784	4.9846	0.5760

Variable	Variance	CoefVar	Sum	Sum of Squares	Minimum	Q1	Median
time	0.3318	11.59	268.2900	1350.5397	3.4000	4.4700	5.0950

Variable	Q3	Maximum	Range	IQR	Mode	N for Mode
time	5.3525	5.8800	2.4800	0.8825	4.42, 5.08, 5.11, 5.14	2

Variable	Skewness	Kurtosis	MSSD
time	−0.36	−0.40	0.3284

The data contain at least five mode values. Only the smallest four are shown.

We are familiar with about half of these descriptive measures at this point in the book.

34. The measures of central tendency given by SPSS are found as follows: Use the pull-down **Analyze → Descriptive Statistics → Frequencies**. This gives the frequencies dialog box. Choose options and choose central tendency. There are four measures of central tendency: Mean, Median, Mode, and Sum. They are checked and the following output results.

Statistics

TIME

N	Valid	54
	Missing	0
Mean		4.9683
Median		5.0950
Mode		4.42[a]
Sum		268.29

[a]Multiple modes exist. The smallest value is shown.

The output for these four measures are the same, as shown under descriptive statistics for MINITAB in Problem 33.

35. The student who has an understanding of the material in the book up to this point will likely know the following terms: n, missing, sum, mean, minimum, 1st quartile, median, 3rd quartile, maximum, skew, and kurtosis. Many of the remaining terms will also be covered.

```
Statistix 8.1
Descriptive Statistics:
          Time
N                54
Missing          0
Sum              268.29
Lo 95% CI        4.8111
Mean             4.9683
Up 95% CI        5.1256
SD               0.5760
Variance         0.3318
SE Mean          0.0784
C.V.             11.594
Minimum          3.4000
1st Quarti       4.4700
```

```
Median              5.0950
3rd Quarti          5.3525
Maximum             5.8800
MAD                 0.4400
Biased Var          0.3257
Skew               -0.3457
Kurtosis           -0.4760
```

36. The EXCEL output for the data in Table 3.6 is as follows. The student should know all terms except standard deviation, variance, and standard error at this point in the book. This assumes that the student is reading the book sequentially from page 1.

TIME	
Mean	4.968333
Standard Error	0.078387
Median	5.095
Mode	5.26
Standard Deviation	0.576023
Sample Variance	0.331803
Kurtosis	−0.4033
Skewness	−0.3557
Range	2.48
Minimum	3.4
Maximum	5.88
Sum	268.29
Count	54

37. For a normal distribution, mean = median = mode. Furthermore, skewness = kurtosis = 0. For this distribution, median = mode = 300 minutes and skewness = kurtosis = 0.

38. The 54 time values in Table 3.6 are entered into A1:A54 in an EXCEL worksheet. The expression =1/A1 is entered into B1 and a click-and-drag is executed from B1 to B54. Finally, the expression =54/SUM(B1:B54) is entered into C1 with the result H = 4.898. This value is the *harmonic mean*.

39. The 54 time values in Table 3.6 are entered into A1:A54 in an EXCEL worksheet. The expression =A1 is entered into B1. Then =B1*A2 is entered into B2. Then a click-and-drag is performed from B2 to B54. This gives the product of the 54 values in column A in B54. This gives a tremendously large number in B54. **Do not be frightened**. Now enter =B54^(1/54) into C1. This is the 54th root of the product of the 54 numbers. We have G = 4.934. This value is the *geometric mean*.
Problems 37 and 38 once again illustrate the power of EXCEL. **These problems are extremely difficult and time consuming on a calculator**.

40. H = 4.898, G = 4.934, and M = 4.968 or H ≤ G ≤ M.

CHAPTER 4

16. The range is 23 − 0 = 23.

17. Entering the values we know, we have 27 = maximum − 7. Adding 7 to both sides of the equation, we obtain maximum = 27 + 7 = 34. The maximum is 34.

18. The range is defined as range = maximum − minimum. Entering the values we have 17 = 35 − minimum. Solving the equation for minimum we get minimum = 35 − 17 = 18. The minimum is 18.

19. Because $(\sum X)^2/10 = 40$ and $S^2 = \dfrac{\sum X^2 - \dfrac{(\sum X)^2}{n}}{(n-1)} = 0$. The standard deviation is 0.

20. $S = 7.1522 \qquad \sigma = 7.0320 \qquad ((\sigma - S)/\sigma) \times 100\% = 1.7\%$

21.

	A	B	C	D	E	F	G
1	X	X - 55	(X - 55)^2		X	X^2	
2	10	-45	2025		10	100	
3	20	-35	1225		20	400	
4	30	-25	625		30	900	
5	40	-15	225		40	1600	
6	50	-5	25		50	2500	
7	60	5	25		60	3600	
8	70	15	225		70	4900	
9	80	25	625		80	6400	
10	90	35	1225		90	8100	
11	100	45	2025		100	10000	
12			8250		550	38500	
13							
14	30.2765				30.2765		
15	SQRT(C12/9)				SQRT((F12-E12^2/10)/9)		
16							

22. Using EXCEL, the data are entered into A1:J3. =STDEV(A1:J3) gives 7.152204 and =AVEDEV(A1:J3) gives 6.275556.

6.275556/7.152204 = 0.87743 rather than 0.8.

23. Using EXCEL, the data are entered into A1:J3. =STDEV(A1:J3) gives 7.152204 and =0.5*(PERCENTILE (A1:J3, 0.75)-PERCENTILE(A1:J3, 0.25)) gives 5.75. 5.75/7.15224 = 0.8039 rather than 0.67.

24. Range = 23.

23/4 = 5.75 and 23/6 = 3.83.

The standard deviation is not between these limits. Note that Problems 22, 23, and 24 are more likely to hold if the sample data come from a normal population.

25. Semi-interquartile range = 0.5(IQR) = 0.5(25.75 − 15.25) = 5.25.

26. Semi-interquartile = 0.5(Q_3 − Q_1) or 3.5 = 0.5(27.75 − Q_1). Solving for Q_1 gives Q_1 = 20.75.

27. a.

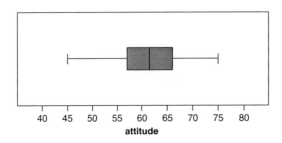

b.

Descriptive Statistics

	N	MINIMUM	MAXIMUM	MEAN	STD. DEVIATION
Attitude	100	45	75	61.21	6.829
Valid N (listwise)	100				

28. a.

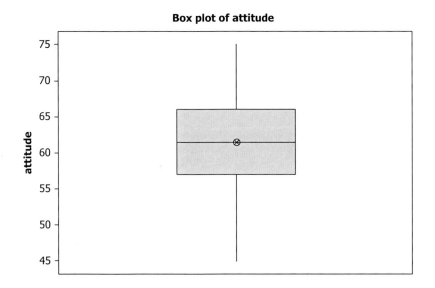

Box plot of attitude

b. **Descriptive Statistics: attitude**

```
Variable    Mean    StDev    Minimum    Maximum
attitude    61.210  6.829    45.000     75.000
```

29. a.

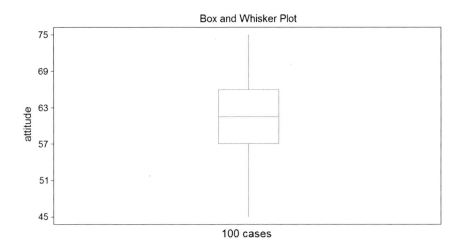

Box and Whisker Plot

b.
```
Statistix 8.1
Descriptive Statistics
Variable    Mean     SD       Minimum    Median    Maximum
attitude    61.210   6.8288   45.000     61.500    75.000
```

30. a.

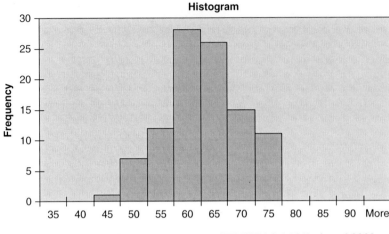

Histogram

b. =AVERAGE(A2:A101) gives 61.21   =STDEV(A2:A101) gives 6.8288

CHAPTER 5

21. $Z = \dfrac{53.7 - 48.0}{6.5} = 0.88$

22. $Z = \dfrac{60.0 - 65.5}{3.5} = -1.57$

23. A z-score for an observation tells you how many standard deviations the observation is from the mean. If the z-score is positive, the observation is to the right of the mean. If the z-score is negative, the observation is to the left of the mean.

24. Since the observation is to the right of the mean, the z-score must be positive, not negative.

25. The kurtosis for the z-scores is −0.5 and the skewness for the z-scores is 1.0.

26. Kurtosis of the data = 0.080357. Skewness of the data = 0.0

Kurtosis of the z-scores = 0.080357. Skewness of the z-scores = 0.0.

27. The distribution of the z-scores will be skewed to the right.

28. The measures will be the same.

29. 0

30. 0

31. 1

32.

	A	B	C	D	E	F
1	x	z-scores				
2	0.1	-1.4863		-1.33227E-16	mean of Z-scores	
3	0.2	-1.15601		1	SD of Z-scores	
4	0.3	-0.82572				
5	0.4	-0.49543				
6	0.5	-0.16514				
7	0.6	0.165145				
8	0.7	0.495434				
9	0.8	0.825723				
10	0.9	1.156012				
11	1	1.486301				
12						
13		0.55	mean of X			
14	0.302765	SD of X				
15						

33. $X = 25 + (0.75)(5) = 28.75$.

34. $X = \mu + \sigma$.

35. $X = \mu$.

36. False.

37. Take the first data set and convert every observation to a z-score by using the transformation z-score $= (X - a)/b$. Then take the z-scores and convert them to observations by the equation $Y = c + \text{z-score}(d)$. The set of Y values will have mean c and standard deviation d.

38. The z-score for 65 in the non-standardized system is $Z = \dfrac{65 - 70}{7.4} = -0.68$. The 65 will have a standardized score of $Y = 100 + (-0.68)(15) = 89.8$. z-score for 80 in the non-standardized system is $Z = \dfrac{80 - 70}{7.4} = 1.35$. The 80 will have a standardized score of $Y = 100 + (1.35)(15) = 120.25$.

39. The z-score for 45 in the non-standardized system is $Z = \dfrac{45 - 50}{5} = -1$. The 45 will have a standardized score of $Y = 100 + (-1)(15) = 85$. The z-score for 60 in the non-standardized system is $Z = \dfrac{60 - 50}{5} = 2$. The 60 will have a standardized score of $Y = 100 + (2)(15) = 130$.

40.

	A	B	C	D	E
1	x	Z-score		standard score	
2	40	-0.7458		88.81294433	
3	45	-0.53864		91.92045979	
4	50	-0.33147		95.02797526	
5	55	-0.1243		98.13549072	
6	100	1.740209		126.1031299	
7					
8					
9	58	mean		100	mean
10	24.13504	SD		15	SD
11					

Microsoft Excel - Book1

CHAPTER 6

29. 6X6X6 = 216 outcomes in the sample space.
A = {(5,6,6), (6,5,6), (6,6,5)}
$P(A) = 3/216 = 0.0139$

30. The sample space consists of the combination of 52 cards taken four at a time. $\dbinom{52}{4} = \dfrac{52!}{48!4!} = 270725$. The hand consisting of the four aces is one of these 270,725 hands. $P(\text{four Aces}) = 1/270725 = 0.000003694$.

31. The sample space consists of 30 outcomes. There are 10 outcomes in the event that a freshman was selected. The probability that a freshman was selected is $10/30 = 0.33$.

32. $S = \{6, \overline{6}6, \overline{6}\,\overline{6}6, \overline{6}\,\overline{6}\,\overline{6}6, \ldots\}$ where 6 means a 6 was obtained on the first roll, $\overline{6}6$, means a six was not obtained on the first roll but a 6 did occur on the second roll, $\overline{6}\,\overline{6}6$, means a six was not obtained on the first two rolls but did occur on the third, etc. The event "a 6 on or before the third roll" is the same as 6 or $\overline{6}6$ or $\overline{6}\,\overline{6}6$. $P\{6$ or $\overline{6}6$ or $\overline{6}\,\overline{6}6\} = P\{6\} + P\{\overline{6}6\} + P\{\overline{6}\,\overline{6}6\} = \dfrac{1}{6} + \dfrac{5}{6}\dfrac{1}{6} + \dfrac{5}{6}\dfrac{5}{6}\dfrac{1}{6} = \dfrac{91}{216}$.

33. A and B are mutually exclusive and exhaustive.

34. Solving $P(A \text{ or } B) = P(A) + P(B) - P(A \text{ and } B)$ for $P(A \text{ and } B)$ gives $P(A) + P(B) - P(A \text{ or } B) =$ $0.35 + 0.65 - 0.80 = 0.20$ or $P(A \text{ and } B) = 0.20$.

35. $P\{\text{anxious or depressed}\} = 0.30 + 0.50 - 0.15 = 0.65$.

36. $P\{\text{middle-aged and happy}\} = 0.40 + 0.67 - 0.85 = 0.22$.

37. $\dfrac{10}{25} \dfrac{9}{24} \dfrac{8}{23} = \dfrac{30}{14375}$

38. $P\{\text{at least one will have relatives that have done time}\} = 1 - P\{\text{none have relatives that have done time}\} =$ $1 - 0.52^{10} = 0.9986$.

39. $P\{\text{at least one would suffer from depression}\} = 1 - P\{\text{none would suffer from depression}\} = 1 - 0.95^{50} = 0.9231$.

40. $P\{\text{none have a mental health or substance abuse disorder}\} = 0.75^{10} = 0.0563$.

41. X is based upon 10 trials. Success on each trial is the person admitted has a mental health or substance abuse disorder. Failure is that the person admitted does not have a mental health or substance abuse disorder. The probability of success is 0.25 and does not change significantly when you remove the 10 in your sample from the total large group. Random sampling means independence from trial to trial. X is binomial with $n = 10$ and $p = 0.25$.

42. The number of trials n is 5, p is 1/6 on each trial and does not change from trial to trial. X must equal one of the numbers 0, 1, 2, 3, 4, or 5.

43. The number of trials n is 25, p is 0.05 on each trial and does not change from trial to trial. X must equal one of the numbers 0, 1, 2, 3, ...,25.

44. The number of trials n is 10, p is 0.25 on each trial and does not change from trial to trial. X must equal one of the numbers 0, 1, 2, ...,10.

45. =BINOMDIST(3, 10, 0.25, 1) = 0.7759

46. =BINOMDIST(1, 5, 0.166667, 0) = 0.4019

47. =BINOMDIST(2, 25, 0.05, 1) = 0.8729

48. =BINOMDIST(2, 10, 0.25, 1) = 0.5256

49. =1 – NORMDIST(27, 25, 5, 1) = 0.3446

50. =NORMDIST(130, 100, 20, 1) – NORMDIST(90, 100, 20, 1) = 0.6247

51. =NORMDIST(64, 66, 3, 1) = 0.2525

52. =1 – NORMDIST(45, 51, 5, 1) = 0.8849

53. First the normal random variable must be transformed to a standard normal random variable by the transformation, $Z = \dfrac{X - \mu}{\sigma}$. We are asked to find $P(X > 27)$ where X has $\mu = 25$ and $\sigma = 5$. This probability is equal to $P(Z > 0.4)$. Using column C of Table 6.1 and reading opposite $Z = 0.40$, our answer is 0.3446, the same as obtained in Problem 49.

54. First the normal random variable must be transformed to a standard normal random variable by the transformation, $Z = \dfrac{X - \mu}{\sigma}$. We are asked to find $P(90 < X < 130)$, where X has $\mu = 100$ and $\sigma = 20$. This probability is equal to $P(-0.5 < Z < 1.5)$. Using Table 6.1 and column D read opposite -0.5 to find $P(0 < Z < 0.5)$ which, due to symmetry, is the same as $P(-0.5 < Z < 0)$. The answer is 0.1915. Using Table 6.1 and column D read opposite 1.5 to find $P(0 < Z < 1.5)$ which is 0.4332. The answer is $0.1915 + 0.4332 = 0.6247$, the same answer obtained in Problem 50.

55. First the normal random variable must be transformed to a standard normal random variable by the transformation, $Z = \dfrac{X - \mu}{\sigma}$. We are asked to find $P(X < 64)$ where X has $\mu = 66$ and $\sigma = 3$. This probability is equal to $P(Z < -0.67)$. Using column C of Table 6.1 and reading opposite $Z = 0.67$ our answer is $P(Z > 0.67) =$

0.2514, the same as $P(Z < -0.67)$. The answer is 25.14%, the same as obtained in Problem 51, except for round-off error.

56. First the normal random variable must be transformed to a standard normal random variable by the transformation,

$Z = \dfrac{X - \mu}{\sigma}$. We must find $P(Z > -1.2)$. This is the same as $P(Z < 1.2)$. Using column B and reading opposite

$Z = 1.2$, we see that $P(Z < 1.2) = 0.8849$. This also equals $P(Z > -1.2)$. That is 88.49% score above 75.

CHAPTER 7

21.

	A	B	C	D	E	F	G
1	x	p(x)	x*p(x)		x^2*P(x)		
2	0	0.0625	0		0		
3	1	0.25	0.25		0.25		
4	2	0.375	0.75		1.5		
5	3	0.25	0.75		2.25		
6	4	0.0625	0.25		1		
7				2 mean	5	1 variance	
8						1 S.D.	
9							

22.

	x	p(x)	x*p(x)		x^2p(x)	
9	x	p(x)	x*p(x)		x^2p(x)	
10	3	0.2	0.6		1.8	
11	4	0.2	0.8		3.2	
12	5	0.2	1		5	
13	6	0.2	1.2		7.2	
14	7	0.2	1.4		9.8	
15				5 mean	27	2 variance
16					1.414 S.D.	
17						

23.

	x	p(x)	x*p(x)		x^2*p(x)	
17						
18	x	p(x)	x*p(x)		x^2*p(x)	
19	5	0.1	0.5		2.5	
20	10	0.2	2		20	
21	15	0.3	4.5		67.5	
22	20	0.3	6		120	
23	25	0.1	2.5		62.5	
24				15.5 mean	272.5	32.25 variance
25					5.679 S.D.	
26						

24.

	K	L	M	N	O
26					
27	x	p(x)	x*p(x)	x^2*p(x)	
28	20	0.2	4	80	
29	40	0.6	24	960	
30	60	0.2	12	720	
31			40 mean	1760	160 variance
32					12.65 S.D.
33					

25. This table is used to form the distribution of *M*.

J	K	L	M	N	O
	first item	second item	M	probability	
	0	0	0	0.00390625	
	0	1	0.5	0.015625	
	0	2	1	0.0234375	
	0	3	1.5	0.015625	
	0	4	2	0.00390625	
	1	0	0.5	0.015625	
	1	1	1	0.0625	
	1	2	1.5	0.09375	
	1	3	2	0.0625	
	1	4	2.5	0.015625	
	2	0	1	0.0234375	
	2	1	1.5	0.09375	
	2	2	2	0.140625	
	2	3	2.5	0.09375	
	2	4	3	0.0234375	
	3	0	1.5	0.015625	
	3	1	2	0.0625	
	3	2	2.5	0.09375	
	3	3	3	0.0625	
	3	4	3.5	0.015625	
	4	0	2	0.00390625	
	4	1	2.5	0.015625	
	4	2	3	0.0234375	
	4	3	3.5	0.015625	
	4	4	4	0.00390625	
				1	

Distribution of *M*

M	P(M)
0	0.00390625
0.5	0.03125
1.0	0.109375
1.5	0.21875
2.0	0.273438
2.5	0.21875
3.0	0.109375
3.5	0.03125
4.0	0.00390625

26. This table is used to form the distribution of *M*.

	A	B	C	D	E
1	first item	second item	M	probability	
2	3	3	3	0.04	
3	3	4	3.5	0.04	
4	3	5	4	0.04	
5	3	6	4.5	0.04	
6	3	7	5	0.04	
7	4	3	3.5	0.04	
8	4	4	4	0.04	
9	4	5	4.5	0.04	
10	4	6	5	0.04	
11	4	7	5.5	0.04	
12	5	3	4	0.04	
13	5	4	4.5	0.04	
14	5	5	5	0.04	
15	5	6	5.5	0.04	
16	5	7	6	0.04	
17	6	3	4.5	0.04	
18	6	4	5	0.04	
19	6	5	5.5	0.04	
20	6	6	6	0.04	
21	6	7	6.5	0.04	
22	7	3	5	0.04	
23	7	4	5.5	0.04	
24	7	5	6	0.04	
25	7	6	6.5	0.04	
26	7	7	7	0.04	
27					

Distribution of *M*

M	P(M)
3	0.04
3.5	0.08
4	0.12
4.5	0.16
5	0.20
5.5	0.16
6	0.12
6.5	0.08
7	0.04

27. This table is used to form the distribution of *M*.

	A	B	C	D	E
1	first item	secons item	M	probability	
2	5	5	5	0.01	
3	5	10	7.5	0.02	
4	5	15	10	0.03	
5	5	20	12.5	0.03	
6	5	25	15	0.01	
7	10	5	7.5	0.02	
8	10	10	10	0.04	
9	10	15	12.5	0.06	
10	10	20	15	0.06	
11	10	25	17.5	0.02	
12	15	5	10	0.03	
13	15	10	12.5	0.06	
14	15	15	15	0.09	
15	15	20	17.5	0.09	
16	15	25	20	0.03	
17	20	5	12.5	0.03	
18	20	10	15	0.06	
19	20	15	17.5	0.09	
20	20	20	20	0.09	
21	20	25	22.5	0.03	
22	25	5	15	0.01	
23	25	10	17.5	0.02	
24	25	15	20	0.03	
25	25	20	22.5	0.03	
26	25	25	25	0.01	
27				1	
28					

*

Distribution of *M*

M	P(M)
5	0.01
7.5	0.04
10	0.10
12.5	0.18
15.0	0.23
17.5	0.22
20.0	0.15
22.5	0.06
25.0	0.01

28. This table is used to form the distribution of *M*.

	A	B	C	D	E
1	first item	second item	M	probability	
2	20	20	20	0.04	
3	20	40	30	0.12	
4	20	60	40	0.04	
5	40	20	30	0.12	
6	40	40	40	0.36	
7	40	60	50	0.12	
8	60	20	40	0.04	
9	60	40	50	0.12	
10	60	60	60	0.04	
11				1	
12					

Distribution of *M*

M	*P(M)*
20	0.04
30	0.24
40	0.44
50	0.24
60	0.04

29.

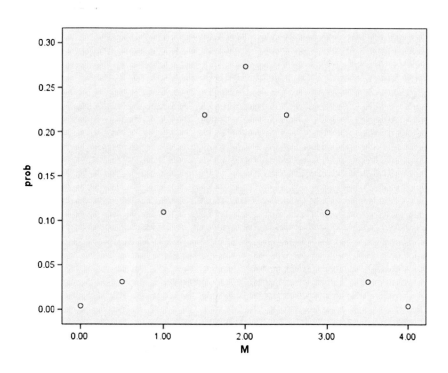

	A	B	C	D	E	F
1	M	P(M)		M*P(M)	M^2*P(M)	
2	0	0.00390625		0	0	
3	0.5	0.03125		0.015625	0.007813	
4	1	0.109375		0.109375	0.109375	
5	1.5	0.21875		0.328125	0.492188	
6	2	0.273438		0.546876	1.093752	
7	2.5	0.21875		0.546875	1.367188	
8	3	0.109375		0.328125	0.984375	
9	3.5	0.03125		0.109375	0.382813	
10	4	0.00390625		0.015625	0.0625	
11			mean	2.000001	4.500002	
12			variance		0.500002	
13	The mean is 2 and the variance is 0.5					
14						

30.

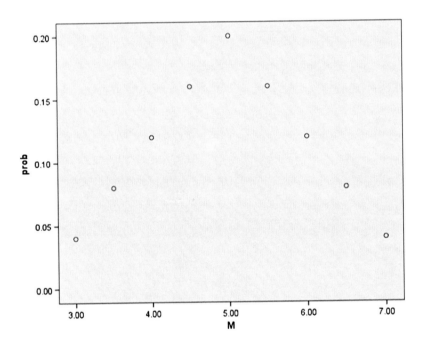

	A	B	C	D	E	F
1	M	P(M)		M*P(M)	M^2*P(M)	
2	3	0.04		0.12	0.36	
3	3.5	0.08		0.28	0.98	
4	4	0.12		0.48	1.92	
5	4.5	0.16		0.72	3.24	
6	5	0.2		1	5	
7	5.5	0.16		0.88	4.84	
8	6	0.12		0.72	4.32	
9	6.5	0.08		0.52	3.38	
10	7	0.04		0.28	1.96	
11			mean	5	26	
12			variance		1	
13						

31.

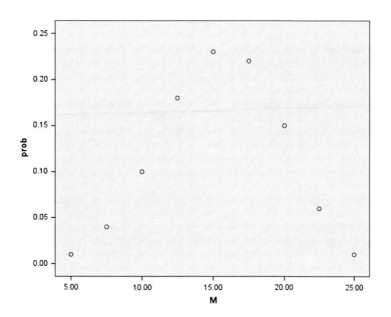

	A	B	C	D	E	F
1	M	P(M)		M*P(M)	M^2*P(M)	
2	5	0.01		0.05	0.25	
3	7.5	0.04		0.3	2.25	
4	10	0.1		1	10	
5	12.5	0.18		2.25	28.125	
6	15	0.23		3.45	51.75	
7	17.5	0.22		3.85	67.375	
8	20	0.15		3	60	
9	22.5	0.06		1.35	30.375	
10	25	0.01		0.25	6.25	
11			mean	15.5	256.375	
12			variance		16.125	
13						

32.

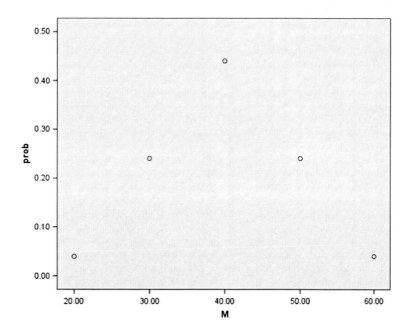

	A	B	C	D	E	F
1	M	P(M)		M*P(M)	M^2*P(M)	
2	20	0.04		0.8	16	
3	30	0.24		7.2	216	
4	40	0.44		17.6	704	
5	50	0.24		12	600	
6	60	0.04		2.4	144	
7			mean	40	1680	
8			variance		80	
9						

33. $\sigma_M = \sqrt{0.5} = 0.71$

34. $\sigma_M = \sqrt{1} = 1$

35. $\sigma_M = \sqrt{16.125} = 4.02$

36. $\sigma_M = \sqrt{80} = 8.94$

37. M has a normal distribution with mean equal to 2 and standard error equal to $\sqrt{\dfrac{1}{n}}$.

38. M has a normal distribution with mean equal to 5 and standard error equal to $\sqrt{\dfrac{2}{n}}$.

39. M has a normal distribution with mean equal to 15.5 and standard error equal to $\sqrt{\dfrac{32.25}{n}}$.

40. M has a normal distribution with mean equal to 40 and standard error equal to $\sqrt{\dfrac{160}{n}}$.

CHAPTER 8

25. This is a one-sided test.

26. This is a one-sided test.

27. This is a two-sided test.

28. This is a one-sided test.

29. Let μ represent the average weight for the infants who have increased playtime before age 2.
    $H_0: \mu = 26$　　$H_1: \mu > 26$

30. Let μ represent the average food consumption of the rats given the weight-reducing drug.
    $H_0: \mu = 12$　　$H_1: \mu < 12$

31. Let μ represent the average test score for the students who have their course taught with increased use of statistical software.
    $H_0: \mu = 70$　　$H_1: \mu \neq 70$

32. Let μ represent the average weight of the rats given the growth hormone.
    $H_0: \mu = 930$　　$H_1: \mu > 930$

33. $H_0: \mu = 26$ $H_1: \mu > 26$ $Z = \dfrac{M - 26}{\dfrac{\sigma}{\sqrt{n}}} = \dfrac{27.1 - 26}{\dfrac{3.5}{\sqrt{36}}} = 1.89$

The p-value is the area under the standard normal curve to the right of 1.89. Using EXCEL, we find $=1 - \text{NORMSDIST}(1.89)$ which equals 0.029. The p-value for this hypothesis test is 0.029, which is less than $\alpha = 0.05$, and therefore we reject the null hypothesis.

34. $H_0: \mu = 12$ $H_1: \mu < 12$ $Z = \dfrac{M - 26}{\dfrac{\sigma}{\sqrt{n}}} = \dfrac{11.2 - 12}{\dfrac{3}{\sqrt{50}}} = -1.89$

The p-value is the area under the standard normal curve to the left of −1.89. Using EXCEL, we find $=\text{NORMSDIST}(-1.89)$ which equals 0.029. The p-value for this hypothesis test is 0.029, which is less than $\alpha = 0.05$, and therefore we reject the null hypothesis.

35. $H_0: \mu = 70$ $H_1: \mu \neq 70$ $Z = \dfrac{M - 70}{\dfrac{\sigma}{\sqrt{n}}} = \dfrac{69.3 - 70}{\dfrac{5}{\sqrt{50}}} = -0.99$

The p-value is the area under the standard normal curve to the left of −0.99 plus the area to the right of 0.99, or simply double the area to the left of −0.99. Using EXCEL, we find $=2*\text{NORMSDIST}(-0.99)$, which equals 0.322. The p-value is 0.322, which is greater than $\alpha = 0.05$ and we are unable to reject the null hypothesis.

36. $H_0: \mu = 930$ $H_1: \mu > 930$ $Z = \dfrac{M - 930}{\dfrac{\sigma}{\sqrt{n}}} = \dfrac{945 - 930}{\dfrac{25}{\sqrt{50}}} = 4.24$

The p-value is the area under the standard normal curve to the right of 4.24. This area is given by $=1 - \text{NORMSDIST}(4.24) = 0.000011$. Because the p-value $< \alpha$, reject the null hypothesis.

37. A type 1 error occurs if the sample evidence leads us to conclude that $\mu > 26$ when $\mu = 26$.
A type 2 error occurs if sample evidence does not lead us to reject that $\mu = 26$ when $\mu > 26$.

38. A type 1 error occurs if the sample evidence leads us to conclude that $\mu < 12$ when $\mu = 12$.
A type 2 error occurs if sample evidence does not lead us to reject that $\mu = 12$ when $\mu < 12$.

39. A type 1 error occurs if the sample evidence leads us to conclude that $\mu \neq 70$ when $\mu = 70$.
A type 2 error occurs if sample evidence does not lead us to reject that $\mu = 70$ when $\mu \neq 70$.

40. A type 1 error occurs if the sample evidence leads us to conclude that $\mu > 930$ when $\mu = 930$.
A type 2 error occurs if sample evidence does not lead us to reject that $\mu = 930$ when $\mu > 930$.

41. 1. Let μ represent the average weight of 2-year-olds who had increased playtime as infants.

$H_0: \mu = 26$ The average weight of 2-year-olds who had increased playtime as infants is equal to 26 pounds, the same as the general population.

$H_1: \mu > 26$ The average weight of 2-year-olds who had increased playtime as infants is greater than 26 pounds, the general population mean for 2-year-olds.

2. α is set equal to 0.05.

3. Thirty-six children had increased playtime as infants and their average weight is determined (at age 2) to be 27.1 pounds.

4. The value of the test statistic is $Z = \dfrac{M - \mu_0}{\dfrac{\sigma}{\sqrt{n}}} = \dfrac{27.1 - 26}{\dfrac{3.5}{\sqrt{36}}} = 1.89$.

5. p-value = area under the standard normal curve to the right of $1.89 = 0.029$. Because the p-value is less than α, reject the null and conclude that extra playtime as an infant increases the weight at 2 years of age.

42. 1. Let μ represent the average food consumption of the rats given the appetite-reducing drug.

$H_0: \mu = 12$ The average food consumption of the rats given the appetite suppressant is the same as the general population.

$H_0: \mu < 12$ The average food consumption of the rats given the appetite suppressant is less than the food consumption of the general population.

2. α is set equal to 0.05.

3. Fifty rats are given the food suppressant and their average food consumption is 11.2 grams.

4. The value of the test statistic is $Z = \dfrac{M - \mu_0}{\frac{\sigma}{\sqrt{n}}} = \dfrac{11.2 - 12}{\frac{3.0}{\sqrt{50}}} = -1.89.$

5. p-value = area under the standard normal curve to the left of -1.89 = 0.029. Because the p-value is less than α, reject the null and conclude that the appetite suppressant drug does reduce food consumption.

43. 1. Let μ represent the average test score of the students who are taught using statistical software.

$H_0: \mu = 70$ The average test scores are the same as when the course is taught in the usual manner.
$H_0: \mu \neq 70$ The average test scores are not the same as when the course is taught in the usual manner.

2. α is set equal to 0.05.

3. Fifty students are taught the course using statistical software. The average test score for the sample is 69.3.

4. The value of the test statistic is $Z = \dfrac{M - \mu_0}{\frac{\sigma}{\sqrt{n}}} = \dfrac{69.3 - 70}{\frac{5.0}{\sqrt{50}}} = -0.99.$

5. p-value = 0.322. Because the p-value is greater than α, do not reject the null and conclude that the increased statistical software has no effect on the test score.

44. 1. Let μ represent the average weight of the rats given the growth hormone.

$H_0: \mu = 930$ The average weight of the rats given the growth hormone is the same as the general population.
$H_0: \mu > 930$ The average weight of the rats given the growth hormone is greater then the general population.

2. α is set equal to 0.05.

3. The average weight of the 50 rats given the growth hormone is 945 grams.

4. The value of the test statistic is $Z = \dfrac{M - \mu_0}{\frac{\sigma}{\sqrt{n}}} = \dfrac{945 - 930}{\frac{25}{\sqrt{50}}} = 4.24.$

5. p-value = 0.000011. Because the p-value is less than α, reject the null and conclude that the growth hormone does cause an increase in average weight.

45. The MINITAB output follows. The standard deviation is assumed to be 3.5, the value of M computed from the data is 26.194, the computed test statistic is $z = 0.33$, and the p-value is 0.369. The null hypothesis is not rejected.

One-Sample Z: Weights

```
Test of mu = 26 vs > 26
The assumed standard deviation = 3.5
                                  95% Lower
Variable    N     Mean    StDev   SE Mean   Bound    Z      P
Weights    36    26.194   3.413   0.583     25.235   0.33   0.369
```

46. The MINITAB output follows. The standard deviation is assumed to be 3, the value of M computed from the data is 11.12, the computed test statistic is $z = -2.07$, and the p-value is 0.019. The null hypothesis is rejected.

One-Sample Z: food

```
Test of mu = 12 vs < 12
The assumed standard deviation = 3
```

```
                                        95% Upper
     Variable    N     Mean    StDev   SE Mean    Bound     Z      P
     food        50    11.120  3.192   0.424     11.818  -2.07   0.019
```

47. The MINITAB output follows. The standard deviation is assumed to be 5, the value of M computed from the data is 71.96, the computed test statistic is $z = -2.77$, and the p-value is 0.006. The null hypothesis is rejected.

One-Sample Z: test scores

```
Test of mu = 70 vs not = 70
The assumed standard deviation = 5
Variable     N    Mean    StDev   SE Mean    95%      CI          Z      P
testscores   50   71.960  4.435   0.707    (70.574, 73.346)  2.77  0.006
```

48. The MINITAB output follows. The standard deviation is assumed to be 25, the value of M computed from the data is 937.04, the computed test statistic is $z = -1.99$, and the p-value is 0.023. The null hypothesis is rejected.

One-Sample Z: weight

```
Test of mu = 930 vs > 930
The assumed standard deviation = 25
                                       95% Lower
     Variable    N     Mean    StDev   SE Mean   Bound     Z      P
     weight      50    937.04  25.04   3.54     931.22   1.99   0.023
```

CHAPTER 9

21. True.

22. True.

23. =NORMSDIST(2) – NORMSDIST(–2), which gives 0.9545.

24. The standard deviation of the t-distribution with 30 df is $\sqrt{\dfrac{df}{df-2}} = \sqrt{\dfrac{30}{28}} = 1.035$. Two standard deviations is 2.070. The area within 2 standard deviations of the mean is given in MINITAB as follows.

Cumulative Distribution Function

```
Student's t distribution with 30 DF
x        P( X <= x )
2.07     0.976422
```

Cumulative Distribution Function

```
Student's t distribution with 30 DF
x        P( X <= x )
-2.07    0.0235784
```
Area = 0.9764 – 0.0236 = 0.9528.

25. From Table 9.1, the area to the right of 2.160 under the t-curve with df = 13 is 0.025. The area under the curve to the left of 2.160 is $1 - 0.025 = 0.975$.

26. From Table 9.1, the area to the right of 2.567 under the t-curve with 17 df is 0.01. By symmetry, the area to the left of –2.567 is also 0.01. Therefore the area to the right of –2.567 is $1 - 0.01 = 0.99$.

27. The 23 df line in Table 9.1 is as follows.

df	0.25	0.1	0.05	0.025	0.01	0.005
23	0.685	1.319	1.714	2.069	2.500	2.807

The area between −1.714 and 2.500 is found as follows: The area to the right of 2.500 is 0.01. The area to the left of −1.714 is 0.05, the same as the area to the right of 1.714, because of symmetry. The area between −1.714 and 2.500 is $1 - 0.01 - 0.5 = 0.94$.

28. The 27 df line in Table 9.1 is as follows.

df	0.25	0.1	0.05	0.025	0.01	0.005
27	0.684	1.314	1.703	2.052	2.473	2.771

The area between −2.771 and 2.771 is $1 - 0.005 - 0.005 = 0.99$.

29. The output from the one-sample t-test of SPSS is as follows.

One-Sample Statistics

	N	MEAN	STD. DEVIATION	STD. ERROR MEAN
mood scores	20	41.8000	3.27028	0.73126

One-Sample Test

	TEST VALUE = 45				
	t	df	SIG. (2-TAILED)	MEAN DIFFERENCE	95% CONFIDENCE INTERVAL OF THE DIFFERENCE	
					LOWER	UPPER
mood scores	−4.376	19	0.000	−3.20000	−4.7305	−1.6695

The one-sample statistics box shows that for the $n = 20$ test scores, $M = 41.8$, $S = 3.27028$, and the standard error is 0.73126. The one-sample test box shows that t = −4.376, df = 19, two-tailed p-value = 0.000, and $M - 45 = -3.2$. The null hypothesis would be rejected and it would be concluded that environment affects mood.

30. The output from the one-sample t-test of SPSS is as follows.

One-Sample Statistics

	N	MEAN	STD. DEVIATION	STD. ERROR MEAN
scores	20	73.2500	4.74480	1.06097

One-Sample Test

	TEST VALUE = 70				
	t	df	SIG. (2-TAILED)	MEAN DIFFERENCE	95% CONFIDENCE INTERVAL OF THE DIFFERENCE	
					LOWER	UPPER
scores	3.063	19	0.006	3.25000	1.0294	5.4706

The one-sample statistics box shows that for the $n = 20$ test scores, $M = 73.25$, $S = 4.7448$, and the standard error is 1.06097. The one-sample test box shows that t = 3.063, df = 19, two-tailed p-value = 0.006, and $M - 70 = 3.25$. The null hypothesis would be rejected and it would be concluded that the severely depressed score higher than individuals who are not severely depressed on the average on the test.

31. The output from the one-sample t-test of SPSS is as follows.

One-Sample Statistics

	N	MEAN	STD. DEVIATION	STD. ERROR MEAN
memory	20	88.5000	3.73462	0.83509

One-Sample Test

			TEST VALUE = 90			
	t	df	SIG. (2-TAILED)	MEAN DIFFERENCE	95% CONFIDENCE INTERVAL OF THE DIFFERENCE	
					LOWER	UPPER
memory	−1.796	19	0.088	−1.50000	−3.2479	0.2479

The one-sample statistics box shows that for the $n = 20$ test scores, $M = 88.5$, $S = 3.73462$, and the standard error is 0.83509. The one-sample test box shows that $t = −1.796$, $df = 19$, two-tailed p-value = 0.088, and $M − 90 = −1.5$. The null hypothesis would be rejected because the one-tailed p-value = 0.044 and it would be concluded that combat veterans score lower on the average on the memory test.

32. The output from the one-sample t-test of SPSS is as follows.

One-Sample Statistics

	N	MEAN	STD. DEVIATION	STD. ERROR MEAN
vocabscore	20	60.1500	2.70039	0.60383

One-Sample Test

			TEST VALUE = 60			
	t	df	SIG. (2-TAILED)	MEAN DIFFERENCE	95% CONFIDENCE INTERVAL OF THE DIFFERENCE	
					LOWER	UPPER
vocabscore	0.248	19	0.806	0.15000	−1.1138	1.4138

The one-sample statistics box shows that for the I = 20 test scores, IM = 60.15, S = 2.70039 , and the standard error is 0.60383. The one-sample test box shows that $t = 0.248$, $df = 19$, two-tailed p-value = 0.806, and IM − 60 = 0.15. The null hypothesis would not be rejected because the p-value = 0.806.

33. A 95% confidence interval for the difference is −4.7305 to −1.6695. This means that $−4.7305 < \mu − 45 < −1.6695$. If 45 is added to each part of the inequality, we obtain $40.2695 < \mu < 43.3305$, a 95% confidence interval on μ.

34. A 95% confidence interval for the difference is 1.0294 to 5.4706. This means that $1.0294 < \mu − 70 < 5.4706$. If 70 is added to each part of the inequality, we obtain $71.0294 < \mu < 75.4706$, a 95% confidence interval on μ.

35. A 95% confidence interval for the difference is −3.2479 to 0.2479. This means that $−3.2479 < \mu − 90 < 0.2479$. If 90 is added to each part of the inequality, we obtain $86.7521 < \mu < 90.2479$, a 95% confidence interval on μ.

36. A 95% confidence interval for the difference is −1.1138 to 1.4138. This means that $−1.1138 < \mu − 60 < 1.4138$. If 60 is added to each part of the inequality, we obtain $58.8862 < \mu < 61.4138$, a 95% confidence interval on μ.

37. Shapiro-Wilk Normality Test

Variable	N	W	P
mood	20	0.9801	0.9354

The null hypothesis is that the data came from a normal distribution. Because the p-value, 0.9354, is no where near 0.05 the null hypothesis would not be rejected. Hence, we assume normality.

38. Shapiro-Wilk Normality Test

Variable	N	W	P
score	20	0.9056	0.0525

The null hypothesis is that the data came from a normal distribution. Becayse the p-value, 0.0525, is not less than 0.05, the null hypothesis would not be rejected. Hence, we assume normality.

39. Shapiro-Wilk Normality Test

Variable	N	W	P
scores	20	0.9373	0.2130

The null hypothesis is that the data came from a normal distribution. Because the p-value, 0.2130, is not less than 0.05, the null hypothesis would not be rejected. Hence, we assume normality.

40. Shapiro-Wilk Normality Test

Variable	N	W	P
scores	20	0.9590	0.5245

The null hypothesis is that the data came from a normal distribution. Because the p-value, 0.5245, is not less than 0.05, the null hypothesis would not be rejected. Hence, we assume normality.

CHAPTER 10

17.

The *sum of squares*, SS, is defined to be $\sum X^2 - (\sum X)^2/n$ and the values for SS_1 and SS_2 are shown in F1 and F2. The data for drug A are in A2:A6 and the data for drug B are in B2:B8. $\sum X$ is in A9 and is given by =SUM(A2:A6). $\sum X^2$ is in C9 and is given by =SUM(C2:C6). SS_1 is found in F1 and is given by =C9–A9^2/5. SS_2 is found similarly.

18. The means are $M_1 = 328/5 = 65.6$ and $M_2 = 507/7 = 72.43$. The *pooled variance* is defined to be

$$S_p^2 = \frac{SS_1 + SS_2}{df_1 + df_2} = \frac{67.20000 + 47.7143}{4 + 6} = 11.4914.$$ The *two-sample standard error* or the *standard error of the difference* is

$$S_{(M_1-M_2)} = \sqrt{\frac{S_p^2}{n_1} + \frac{S_p^2}{n_2}} = \sqrt{\frac{11.4914}{5} + \frac{11.4914}{7}} = 1.9849$$

Finally, putting it all together, the t-statistic for testing H_0: $\mu_1-\mu_2 = 0$ is

$$T = \frac{M_1 - M_2 - 0}{S_{(M_1-M_2)}} = \frac{-6.83}{1.9849} = -3.44 \text{ with 10 df.}$$

19. $SS_1 = (n_1 - 1)S_1^2 = 4(16.8) = 67.2$ $SS_2 = (n_2 - 1)S_2^2 = 6(7.9524) = 47.7144$. These are the same values found in Problem 17.

20. Give the MINITAB pull-down **Calc → Calculator** to activate the MINITAB Calculator.

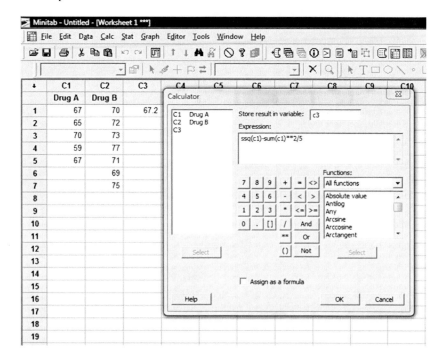

Note that expression ssq(c1) – sum(c1)**2/5 is used to compute SS_1 and that the result is stored in C3. SS_2 is calculated similarly.

21. $SS_1 = (n_1 - 1) S_1^2 = 4(16.8) = 67.2$ $SS_2 = (n_2 - 1) S_2^2 = 6(7.9524) = 47.7144$
Note that S_1^2 is given by =VAR(A2:A6) and S_2^2 is given by =VAR(B2:B8).

22.

	A	B	C	D	E
1	TV in bedroom	No TV in bedroom			
2	X	Y	X squared	Y squared	
3	2.98	3.32	8.8804	11.0224	
4	3.01	3.14	9.0601	9.8596	
5	2.25	2.89	5.0625	8.3521	
6	2.75	3.25	7.5625	10.5625	
7	2.88	2.68	8.2944	7.1824	
8	3.12	3.35	9.7344	11.2225	
9	2.89	3.56	8.3521	12.6736	
10	3.17	3.78	10.0489	14.2884	
11	2.11	2.55	4.4521	6.5025	
12	3.27	3.89	10.6929	15.1321	
13					
14	28.43	32.41	82.1403	106.7981	
15					
16	1.31381	1.75729			
17					

$\sum X$ is given in A14 as =SUM(A3:A12), $\sum Y$ is given in B14 as =SUM(B3:B12), $\sum X^2$ is given in C14 as =SUM(C3:C12), and $\sum Y^2$ is given in D14 as =SUM(D3:D12), SS_1 is given in A16 as =C14-A14^2/10, SS_2 is given in B16 as =D14-B14^2/10.

23. The means are $M_1 = 28.43/10 = 2.843$ and $M_2 = 32.41/10 = 3.241$. The *pooled variance* is defined to be

$$S_p^2 = \frac{SS_1 + SS_2}{df_1 + df_2} = \frac{1.31381 + 1.75729}{9 + 9} = 0.1706.$$ The *two-sample standard error* or the *standard error of the difference* is

$$S_{(M_1 - M_2)} = \sqrt{\frac{S_p^2}{n_1} + \frac{S_p^2}{n_2}} = \sqrt{\frac{0.1706}{10} + \frac{0.1706}{10}} = 0.1847.$$

Finally, putting it all together, the t-statistic for testing H_0: $\mu_1 - \mu_2 = 0$ is

$$T = \frac{M_1 - M_2 - 0}{S_{(M_1 - M_2)}} = \frac{-0.398}{0.1847} = -2.15 \text{ with } 18 \text{ df.}$$

24. $SS_1 = (n_1 - 1)S_1^2 = 9(0.1460) = 1.314 \qquad SS_2 = (n_2 - 1)S_2^2 = 9(0.1953) = 1.7577$

25. Give the MINITAB pull-down **Calc → Calculator** to activate the MINITAB Calculator.

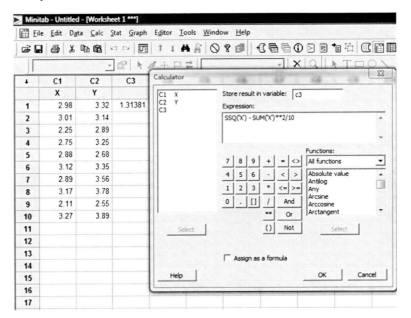

26. $SS_1 = (n_1 - 1)\ S_1^2 = 9(0.1460) = 1.314 \qquad SS_2 = (n_2 - 1)\ S_2^2 = 9(0.1953) = 1.7577.$
Note that S_1^2 is given by $=VAR(A3:A12)$ and S_2^2 is given by $=VAR(B3:B12)$.

27.

	group	score	var
1	1	67.00	
2	1	65.00	
3	1	70.00	
4	1	59.00	
5	1	67.00	
6	2	70.00	
7	2	72.00	
8	2	73.00	
9	2	77.00	
10	2	71.00	
11	2	69.00	
12	2	75.00	

28. The pull-down menu **Analyze → Compare means → Independent samples t-test** is given to perform the analysis.

Group Statistics

	GROUP	N	MEAN	STD. DEVIATION	STD. ERROR MEAN
Score	1	5	65.6000	4.09878	1.83303
	2	7	72.4286	2.82000	1.06586

The group statistics portion of the SPSS output gives the two groups as 1 = drug group sample and 2 = non-drug group sample. The two sample sizes are 5 and 7, the two means are 65.6 and 72.4286, and the two standard deviations are 4.09878 and 2.82.

The SPSS independent samples test output has not been modified below.

Independent Samples Test

		LEVENE'S TEST FOR EQUALITY OF VARIANCES		t-TEST FOR EQUALITY OF MEANS						
		F	SIG.	t	df	SIG (2-TAILED)	MEAN DIFFERENCE	STD. ERROR DIFFERENCE	95% CONFIDENCE INTERVAL OF THE DIFFERENCE	
									LOWER	UPPER
Score	Equal variance assumed	0.338	0.574	−3.440	10	0.006	−6.82857	1.98492	−11.25125	−2.40589
	Equal variances not assumed			−3.220	6.655	0.16	−6.82857	2.12039	−11.89568	−1.76147

The independent samples analysis assuming equal variances is: t-statistic = −3.44, degrees of freedom is 10, the two-tailed p-value = 0.006, the mean difference is −6.82857, and the standard error of the difference of two sample means is 1.98492.

29.

	group	gpa	var
1	1	2.98	
2	1	3.01	
3	1	2.25	
4	1	2.75	
5	1	2.88	
6	1	3.12	
7	1	2.89	
8	1	3.17	
9	1	2.11	
10	1	3.27	
11	2	3.32	
12	2	3.14	
13	2	2.89	
14	2	3.25	
15	2	2.68	
16	2	3.35	
17	2	3.56	
18	2	3.78	
19	2	2.55	
20	2	3.89	
21			

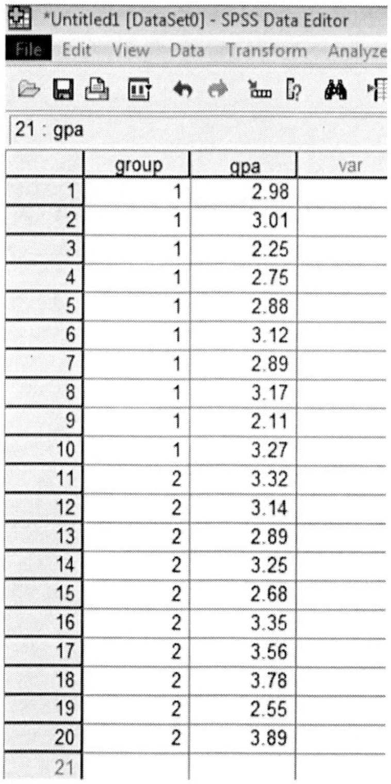

30. The pull-down menu **Analyze → Compare means → Independent samples t-test** is given to perform the analysis.

Group Statistics

	GROUP	N	MEAN	STD. DEVIATION	STD. ERROR MEAN
gpa	1	10	2.8430	0.38207	0.12082
	2	10	3.2410	0.44188	0.13973

The group statistics portion of the SPSS output gives the two groups as 1 = TV in bedroom sample and 2 = no TV in bedroom sample. The two sample sizes are 10 and 10, the two means are 2.843 and 3.2410, and the two standard deviations are 0.38207 and 0.13973.

The SPSS independent samples test output has not been modified below.

Independent Samples Test

	LEVENE'S TEST FOR EQUALITY OF VARIANCES		T-TEST FOR EQUALITY OF MEANS							
	F	SIG.	t	df	SIG (2-TAILED)	MEAN DIFFERENCE	STD. ERROR DIFFERENCE	95% CONFIDENCE INTERVAL OF THE DIFFERENCE		
								LOWER	UPPER	
gpa Equal variance assumed	0.265	0.613	−2.155	18	0.045	−0.39800	0.18473	−0.78609	−0.00991	
Equal variances not assumed			−2.155	17.632	0.045	−0.39800	0.18473	−0.78667	−0.00933	

The independent samples analysis assuming equal variances is: t-statistic = −2.155, degrees of freedom is 18, the two-tailed p-value = 0.045, the mean difference is −0.398, and the standard error of the difference of two sample means is 0.18473.

CHAPTER 11

9. The sum of the differences is $5 + 4 + 1 + 3 + 2 + 1 + 1 - 1 + 5 + 2 = 23$, and the sum of the squares is $25 + 16 + 1 + 9 + 4 + 1 + 1 + 1 + 25 + 4 = 87$.

$$M_D = 2.3$$

$$S_D = \sqrt{\frac{\sum D^2 - \frac{(\sum D)^2}{n}}{n-1}} = \sqrt{\frac{87 - 52.9}{9}} = 1.9465$$

and

$$T = \frac{M_D - \mu_D}{\frac{S_D}{\sqrt{n}}} = \frac{2.3 - 0}{\frac{1.9465}{\sqrt{10}}} = \frac{2.3}{0.6155} = 3.74.$$

10.

	A	B	C	D
1	D			
2	-5	-1.8	AVERAGE(A2:A11)	
3	-2	9.554522	STDEV(A2:A11)	
4	5	3.021405	B3/SQRT(10)	
5	-5			
6	-15	-0.59575	(B2-0)/B4	
7	-9			
8	-13			
9	2			
10	10			
11	14			
12				
13				

M_D is shown in B2, S_D in B3, the standard error of the difference in B4, and the computed t in B6. The EXCEL commands are shown in column C.

11. The data are entered into the worksheet and the pull-down **Analyze → Compare Means → Paired Samples T Test** is given. The following output is produced.

PAIRED SAMPLES STATISTICS

		MEAN	N	STD. DEVIATION	STD. ERROR MEAN
Pair	Before	15.30	10	5.851	1.850
1	After	13.00	10	5.907	1.868

PAIRED DIFFERENCES

PAIR	MEAN	S_D	$\dfrac{S_D}{\sqrt{n}}$	t	df	SIG(2-TAILED)
Before–After	2.300	1.947	0.616	3.74	9	0.005

$M_D = 2.300$, $S_D = 1.947$, and t = 3.74. The two-tailed p-value is given as Sig(2-tailed) = 0.005. These are the same values given in Problem 9.

12. The data are entered into the worksheet and the pull-down **Analyze → Compare Means → Paired Samples T Test** is given. The following output is produced.

PAIRED SAMPLES STATISTICS

		MEAN	N	STD. DEVIATION	STD. ERROR MEAN
Pair	Before	128.6000	10	11.07750	3.50301
1	After	126.8000	10	7.59825	2.40278

PAIRED DIFFERENCES

PAIR	MEAN	S_D	$\dfrac{S_D}{\sqrt{n}}$	t	df	SIG(2-TAILED)
Before–After	1.8000	9.5545	3.0214	0.596	9	0.566

$M_D = 1.8000$, $S_D = 9.5545$, and $t = 0.596$. The two-tailed p-value is given as Sig(2-tailed) = 0.566. These are the same values given in Problem 9.

13. The sum of the differences is $-15 -5 + 5 - 5 - 5 -15 - 7 - 15 - 10 -15 = -87$, and the sum of the squares is $225 + 25 + 25 + 25 + 25 + 225 + 49 + 225 + 100 + 225 = 1149$.

$$M_D = -87/10 = -8.7$$

$$S_D = \sqrt{\frac{\Sigma D^2 - \frac{(\Sigma D)^2}{n}}{n-1}} = \sqrt{\frac{1149 - 756.9}{9}} = 6.6005$$

$$T = \frac{M_D - \mu_D}{\frac{S_D}{\sqrt{n}}} = \frac{-8.7 - 0}{\frac{6.6005}{\sqrt{10}}} = \frac{-8.7}{2.0873} = 4.168.$$

14. M_D is shown in B2, S_D in B3, the standard error of the difference in B4, and the computed t in B6. The EXCEL commands are shown in column C.

	A	B	C	D
1	D			
2	2	-0.5	AVERAGE(A2:A11)	
3	-1	1.900292	STDEV(A2:A11)	
4	-3	0.600925	B3/SQRT(10)	
5	1			
6	-3	-0.83205	(B2 - 0)/B4	
7	-1			
8	1			
9	-2			
10	2			
11	-1			
12				
13				

15. The data are entered into the worksheet and the pull-down **Analyze → Compare Means → Paired Samples T Test** is given. The following output is produced.

PAIRED SAMPLES STATISTICS

		MEAN	N	STD. DEVIATION	STD. ERROR MEAN
Pair	Placebo	95.7000	10	8.84496	2.79702
1	Meditation	87.0000	10	5.86894	1.85592

PAIRED DIFFERENCES

PAIR	MEAN	S_D	$\frac{S_D}{\sqrt{n}}$	t	df	SIG(2-TAILED)
Placebo–Meditation	8.7000	6.6005	2.0873	4.168	9	0.002

$M_D = 8.7000$, $S_D = 6.6005$, and t = 4.168. The two-tailed p-value is given as Sig(2-tailed) = 0.002. These are the same values given in the solution to Problem 13.

16. The data are entered into the worksheet and the pull-down **Analyze → Compare Means → Paired Samples T Test** is given. The following output is produed.

		MEAN	N	STD. DEVIATION	STD. ERROR MEAN
	PAIRED SAMPLES STATISTICS				
Pair 1	GEODON	5.8000	10	1.75119	0.55377
	therapy	5.3000	10	2.00278	0.63333

PAIR	MEAN	S_D	$\dfrac{S_D}{\sqrt{n}}$	t	df	SIG(2-TAILED)
	PAIRED DIFFERENCES					
Placebo–Meditation	0.5000	1.9003	0.6009	0.832	9	0.427

$M_D = 0.5000$, $S_D = 1.9003$, and t = 0.832. The two-tailed p-value is given as Sig(2-tailed) = 0.427. These are the same values given in the solution to Problem 14.

Index